THE LAST
DECADE OF
CINEMA

WRITTEN BY SCOTT RYAN

SCOTT LUCK STORIES
(2014)
THIRTYSOMETHING AT THIRTY: AN ORAL HISTORY
(2017)
THE LAST DAYS OF LETTERMAN
(2019)
BUT, COULDN'T I DO THAT? ANSWERING YOUR QUESTIONS ABOUT SELF-PUBLISHING (WITH ERIN O'NEIL)
(2021)
MOONLIGHTING: AN ORAL HISTORY
(2021)
FIRE WALK WITH ME: YOUR LAURA DISAPPEARED
(2022)
LOST HIGHWAY: THE FIST OF LOVE
(2023)
MASSILLON AGAINST THE WORLD
(WITH BECCA MOORE)
(2024)

EDITED BY SCOTT RYAN

THE BLUE ROSE MAGAZINE
(2017-CURRENT)
THE WOMEN OF DAVID LYNCH
(2019)
THE WOMEN OF AMY SHERMAN-PALLADINO
(2020)
TWIN PEAKS UNWRAPPED
(WRITTEN BY BEN DURANT & BRYON KOZACZKA)
(2020)
MASSILLON TIGERS: 15 FOR 15
(WRITTEN BY DAVID LEE MORGAN, JR.)
(2020)
MYTH OR MAYOR: THE SEARCH FOR MY FAMILY'S LEGACY
(WRITTEN BY ALEX RYAN/AFTERWORD BY SCOTT RYAN)
(2021)
BARBRA STREISAND: THE ALBUMS, THE SINGLES, THE MUSIC
(WRITTEN BY MATT HOWE)
(2023)

THE LAST DECADE OF CINEMA

SCOTT RYAN

Cover design by Hannah Fortune
Cover photo by Scott Ryan
Author photo by Faye Murman
Graphs and tables by Alex Ryan
Edited by Alex Ryan, David Bushman
(All dangling modifiers are Scott's fault)
Book designed by Scott Ryan

Published in the USA by Fayetteville Mafia Press
Columbus, Ohio

Contact Information
Email: FayettevilleMafiaPress@gmail.com
Website: TuckerDSPress.com
Twitter: @Scottluckstory
Instagram: @Fayettevillemafiapress
ISBN: 9781949024708
eBook ISBN: 9781949024715
Audio Book available (It's really good)

"Something erratic,
Something dramatic,
Something for everyone—a comedy tonight!"
-Stephen Sondheim

CONTENTS

"There is a principle in philosophy and rhetoric called the principle of charity, which says that one should interpret other people's statements in their best, most reasonable form, not in the worst or most offensive way possible."
- *The Coddling of the American Mind* - Lukianoff & Haidt

Introduction

Let's start with a compromise: I won't blame you for watching superhero movies if you don't blame me for not watching them.

Superhero Saturation

In current times, movie after movie is either a superhero or franchise film. It's all Marvel, DC, Star Wars, Harry Potter, or a film where the plot points are focused around being fast and/or furious. I am probably one of the few people on the planet who has not partaken in the Marvel Universe. Every film just seems like a man in tights trying to stop a daddy-like villain in a colorful costume. It got even more insulting to this true lover of story when studios took the same plots they had used in the 2000s and just recycled them in the 2010s but now with a female superhero, or changed the race of the heroes from white to nonwhite and then pretended they offered us something new. It's all the same story. I'm not alone in my frustration. One of the best directors of all time, Martin Scorsese, who certainly made one of the best films from the nineties, just about lit the world on fire when he said in a *New York Times* op-ed piece, "Cinema is an art form that brings you the unexpected. In superhero movies, nothing is at risk." I am always glad to side with the director of *Goodfellas* on any film topic. I will freely admit I loved Tim Burton's *Batman* when it came out in 1989. I even enjoyed *Spiderman* in 2002 starring Tobey Maguire. But I sure didn't mind that in the thirteen years between those two summer blockbusters, besides three *Batman* sequels in

1992, '95, and '97, there were no superhero franchises born in the nineties. *The Rocketeer*, *Blade*, *The Shadow*, and *The Phantom* were all released, but they didn't make big splashes, and the studios didn't junk smaller pictures for costume capers. For every *Batman* sequel, a slew of other movies were released like *Sister Act*, *Shakespeare in Love*, *Crimson Tide*, *Misery*, and *The Ref.*

I discovered it truly annoys others that I will not watch superhero movies. I don't really care if the spaceman saves the city with their magic powers. I am just not that interested if the one spaceship shoots the other spaceship. I find nothing to bond with when zombies cause the end of the world. I don't mind that the majority of the world seems to love them; I just wish there was still room for a variety of stories from a spectrum of writers and directors that covered all forms of art—just like there was in the nineties (and that studios gave them the money to make them for the big screen). Give me the stories shepherded by Mike Nichols, Quentin Tarantino, Paul Thomas Anderson, Spike Lee, Rob Reiner, Barbra Streisand, or Nora Ephron. Before you tell me there are still films made that are not about superheroes, let me clarify that the films labeled as dramas today are so dour and depressing that I need to take a shot of tequila and chase it down with Prozac in order to go back to work the next day. As I will point out when this book gets into covering specific films, movies used to be funny *and* sad. They were not meditations on just one emotion. There are true belly laughs in *The Shawshank Redemption*, and there are serious moments in *Mermaids*. As a society, we were perfectly fine with holding two thoughts in our mind at once, sometimes even three or four at a time. (Scary, I know.) I have always been drawn to a movie that creates a world and a story that I haven't seen before. I want the writer and director to take a risk. Be brave. Dare to offend someone with their thoughts. But even that isn't correct, because no one considered telling a complex story a risk back then. It was art. Films were made to make you think, make you feel, and sometimes make you upset. I will discuss one of the best examples of this in the 1992 chapter when I cover the king of pushing an audience's buttons, Spike Lee, and his masterpiece *Malcolm X*. Not only are studios currently avoiding risk, they now recycle the *exact* same stories. We live in a time where movie studios make an animated movie, then take it to Broadway, add some new songs, then remake the same story as a live-action version with no songs, and then refilm the same damn story but this time with the new songs, and then top it all off with another animated version. And somehow, each version is a success. How many times can one person watch a monkey hold up a lion cub? I realize the success is because audiences have adapted to the comfort of knowing the story before they see it, but there was a time when that same audience demanded to have new stories that were full of uncertainties. The time was the nineties.

Summary of DC and Marvel Movie Trends in America (1960 – 2022)[1]			
Decades	**Superhero Box Office Revenue**	**Total Box Office Revenue**	**Percent of Total Box Office Revenue**
1960s	$34.7	-	-
1970s	$594.7	-	-
1980s	$1,260.4	$76,771.7	2%
1990s	$1,000.0	$102,910.7	1%
2000s	$6,355.7	$135,777.3	5%
2010s	$15,767.5	$133,554.7	12%
2020s[2]	$3,636.8	$14,494.7	25%

This table shows only superhero movies, but it makes the point. As the current decade begins, we are at a quarter of all revenue coming from superhero movies. In the nineties, only 1 percent of the films involved people who could fly.

Notes:
[1] Revenue presented in millions of USD 2022;
[2] 2020s decade including releases as of December 31, 2022
Data compiled by Alex Ryan

The Awakening

The genesis for this book came from a movie that had been forgotten to me. One night while looking for a movie, any movie, to stream, I scrolled upon the Penny Marshall-directed film *Awakenings* starring

Robin Williams and Robert De Niro. I hadn't seen the film in thirty years. I knew I had seen it when it first came out, but it wasn't one I ever owned. (We used to *own* copies of our favorite films on VHS or DVD and could watch them whenever we wanted without paying ten bucks a month for life. It is a crazy multiverse that my timeline originates from.) What initially shocked me about this film was that Robert De Niro doesn't show up on-screen for twenty minutes. Can you imagine a movie being made today where one of the two stars isn't in 16 percent of the movie? Not to mention a superstar like Robert De Niro. This is not a cameo role; he is one of the two major characters in the film. In fact, the first act isn't even about encephalitis lethargica, which is the disease De Niro's character awakens from. They spent the beginning of this movie, wait for it, developing the Robin Williams character. This is a characteristic I soon discovered many of the films from the nineties shared. In *Scent of a Woman*, the story of Al Pacino's last hurrah in New York City doesn't start for thirty minutes into the picture, and Kevin Costner doesn't arrive at his military camp until twenty-six minutes into *Dances with Wolves*. They earned your buy-in to the characters before their journeys started. The filmmakers didn't expect you to already care about the characters because you already read the comic book. This also happened in movies based on comic books. *Batman Returns* uses more than the first thirty minutes to develop the backstory of Catwoman and the Penguin. Michael Keaton doesn't say more than two words until thirty-seven minutes into the film. To flip things around from *Awakenings*, Robin Williams doesn't show up in *Good Will Hunting* until thirty-three minutes into the picture. In the nineties, movies were expected to develop characters and make you feel for the person. That is what made the endings so satisfying, or heartbreaking, because the filmmakers *showed* us who the characters were; they didn't just *tell* us.

Awakenings is another example of a movie that has a lot of humor in it. Yes, it is a heartbreaking topic of patients who lost so much of their lives to a disease, but the writer (Steven Zaillian) didn't beat us over the head with sadness. We experience joy as De Niro and the other patients remember what it was like to live life, and then we are saddened when they start to lose that ability. The script isn't just pure misery, which is exactly what dramatic films of current times seem to strive for. (I know you want me to give titles from movies made after the nineties as examples. Here is the thing, though: I have a rule about not being mean to art or artists. I like to lift things up, not tear them down. Plus, you know the movies I am talking about; just look at practically any drama made in the last decade and you will find the rumination-on-one-emotion-only films I am talking about.) Movies in the nineties respected their audience, developed characters, took their time to get going, while balancing that with respect for the viewer's time. The icing on the cake is that *Awakenings* came out in 1990. That got me thinking. (We know how dangerous a thing that can be.)

Video Time

I wondered what else I would learn if I started watching other films from the nineties. Over the past decade, I watched maybe one current movie a year. Television was where it was at for me. (Although lately television is falling into the franchise/superhero trap. I smell a sequel to this book.) But when I looked at all the DVDs and Blu-rays shoved into boxes in my closet, I remembered how much I used to actually love movies. I read movie magazines; I collected posters; I saw films on opening day. One of the main reasons for this love came from the fact that when I was in college I worked at Video Time, a store that rented VHS tapes. What year did I start working there? You guessed it. 1990. Hmm, a pattern appears to be forming. Video rental stores were the greatest thing to happen to college kids since the invention of the bong. We must digress here to truly remember how spectacular video stores were. The store I worked at had a very simple pricing plan. Older movies were $0.99, and new releases and porn were $1.99. (Strange side note: the owners of the store allowed us to take older movies and porn home for free, but we had to pay for new releases. My theory about this policy? They wanted us to be knowledgeable in the classics and to have the ability to have sex with multiple species.) I took full advantage of this perk. WAIT. A. MINUTE. The classics, not the porn! I worked at Video Time for three years, and in that time, I watched every new release (never paid for a one of them) and a ton of classics. This is when I first saw *The Godfather*, *Funny Girl*, *Casablanca*, *Taxi Driver*, *Chinatown*, *American Graffiti*, *Citizen Kane*, and *Eraserhead*. I mixed them in with *Do the Right Thing*, *Dangerous Liaisons*, *Reservoir Dogs*, *Bob Roberts*, *Slacker*, and what has somehow become the center of my freaking universe, *Awakenings*. When you work at a video store, you have this overriding belief that you *have* to watch every film released. I probably did see just about every movie released in the early nineties and late eighties. I watched them while I was at work, and then I would take a couple of them home to watch after work. I brought a few with me to parties. Working at the video store was like owning the keys to all the world's entertainment.

I love thinking about this era for writers and film aficionados like myself. Every movie was available to everyone in my small town of Massillon, Ohio. All anyone needed was $0.99 and their mind could be open to all of cinema. If video stores were invented today, customers would have to pay a monthly fee and a surcharge on top of that to rent each flick. Each store would not be specially run by a mom-and-pop owner like Video Time was, but by corporate-run studios. Renters would only be able to get Paramount movies from a Paramount video store. Wanna rent the latest HBO movie? You have to go to the HBO rental store. Wanna see the fifth version of *The Lion King*? You can't rent that from Video Time. You have to go to Video Disney Time. Today streaming is more split apart than a divorced- family tree. Back catalogs are only available to those who can pay month after monthly fees and to every different studio. In the early nineties, the heyday of the VHS tape, Video Time had *all* the movies in one spot. Get your Star Trek or Star Wars side by side in the science fiction section. Find your dramas from Miramax, animated movies from Disney, and slightly riskier Disney movies from Touchstone Pictures, along with comedies from Universal and horror films from New Line Cinema. Everyone was welcome. Damn, we didn't have a clue how lucky we were.

I have written several books about television and film, hosted podcasts and celebrity panels after film screenings, even written and directed small films and documentaries, but it was my three years at a video store that I feel gives me the qualification to write this book.

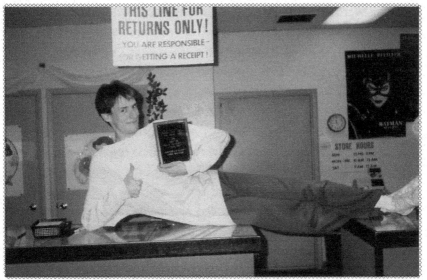

Here is a twenty-two year old Scott Ryan, mockingly holding the employee of the month award that he never won while working at Video Time in the nineties.

I would never compare myself to the master of nineties films, Mr. Quentin Tarantino, but like him, I got my film education at a video store, and I have used that education a hell of a lot more than I ever used my marketing degree from the University of Akron.

Something for Everyone

A quick trip to IMDb showed me there were 36,931 films released between January 1, 1990, and December 31, 1999. Well, I figured I should be able to watch all those in a week. No problem. One week later: Okay, new plan. Time to pare that list down. I wanted to take a look at films I might have forgotten or hadn't seen in a while. The list came out to be a little over one hundred and sixty films. That would mean I would watch 0.004 percent of all films made that decade; I was very glad no one knew how to do math anymore, so they couldn't bust me out for making my sweeping claim about the entire film industry based on such a small sample. (But let's not forget my video store experience; that at least rounds me up to a solid zero percent.) I figured I would start by picking ten to fifteen pictures a year. I wasn't trying to watch the most obscure art films from the decade, but movies that were made for everyone, played everywhere, and made some impact, small or large, on film culture. For some reason, and I feel this somehow makes my claim even more valid, 1995 had the most films that seemed worthy of my time, with twenty-six films. (My spreadsheet can be found in the back of this book.) I decided right away to jettison horror (sorry, *Scream*), documentaries (sorry, *Hoop Dreams*), foreign (sorry, *La Femme Nikita*), and animation (sorry, *Aladdin*). Those genres didn't need tending to, as they are still alive and well and were always marketed to their respective audiences. Kids movies aren't specifically made for adults, documentaries are fact based, and horror movies are really their own genre for adults and teenagers. (Plus, I never watched one again after Freddy Krueger scared me to death in the movie theater, but I did hold hands with Mindy Morrow, so it was worth it.)

I also felt there wasn't as much of a need for me to cover art house films like *My Own Private Idaho*, *Spanking the Monkey*, or any David Lynch film because those types of movies will always be made for small budgets and find limited, devoted audiences. My overall plan was to focus on movies that were geared toward mass-marketed adult audiences and made a small to moderate pop culture impact. I had a few people argue with me over whether there really is such a thing as a movie made for adults. How would that be defined? Then I read in Quentin Tarantino's *Cinema Speculation* book where he described the renaissance of film in the late sixties and early seventies, driven by a new generation of filmmakers bored by cinema of the fifties, as "an adult-oriented Hollywood." If it was a good enough term for Tarantino and his book, it was good enough for me and my book. It's adult-oriented films I miss—the kind of studio films that were replaced by franchise movies. The more I watched nineties films, the more I felt that everything I enjoy about movies had disappeared and the more I began to believe that the nineties was the last decade of cinema for adults who wanted to think, feel, and be positively impacted by stories told through light and sound.

While I am certain many will argue with that assertion, I don't think anyone will argue it was the last decade in which small pictures had a fighting chance of making money and being seen in multiplexes across the country. It truly was the last decade in which every genre of movie had a shot at success. I specifically remember seeing small pictures like *Beautiful Girls*, *Boxing Helena*, and *Chasing Amy* at my local cinemas, and I lived in Ohio, not New York or California. The movie theaters around me played small films as well as the blockbusters. I would never claim that there were no action or franchise films in the nineties; they just weren't the only meal served on our plates. You had your blockbuster action pictures, *Twister*, *Armageddon*, *The Matrix*, but you also had full-fledged dramas filling movies theaters, *Glengarry Glen Ross*, *Bridges of Madison County*, *How to Make an American Quilt*, as well as independent, small films, *The Crying Game*, *Two Girls and a Guy*, *To Die For*. There also was a healthy dose of Black cinema with *Friday*, *Boyz n the Hood*, and *Devil in a Blue Dress*, along with the beginning of queer movies crossing over to the mainstream with *Jeffrey*, *The Birdcage*, and *My Own Private Idaho*.

Anyone and everyone was welcome to make a movie. A director could be as technically gifted as Steven Spielberg (*Saving Private Ryan*) or Martin Scorsese (*Casino*) or could be known for being a verbal director like Ed Burns (*Brothers McMullen*) or Kevin Smith (*Clerks*). No doubt there was a lack of female directors in this decade, but we did have Amy Heckerling (*Clueless*), Penny Marshall (*A League of Their Own*), Jodie Foster (*Home for the Holidays*), and Jane Campion (*The Piano*) helming classic films of the time. Romantic comedies were a huge staple, as Meg Ryan (*Sleepless in Seattle*) and Julia Roberts (*Something to Talk About*) carried picture after picture. Teenagers were not supposed to go see *Six Degrees of Separation* or *The Straight Story*; they could go watch *Billy Madison* or *10 Things I Hate About You*. But guess what? Grown-ups could also get something out of a film like *Pump Up the Volume*, because no matter whom the film was intended for, it was expected to be well-made and entertaining. Let's also not forget about sex. Oh, how we loved our mainstream erotic movies back before porn was everywhere on the internet. Michael Douglas would be living in a smaller mansion today if it weren't for movies like *Basic Instinct* or *Disclosure*, and how else could we have seen all of Madonna if it weren't for her skin flick *Body of Evidence*? (I guess we would have had to buy her *Erotica* book, subscribe to *Playboy*, or watch MTV?) The point is there were so many different options for movies to watch in the nineties. It was never one size fits all. As my Sondheim quote that started this book points out, it truly was something for everyone.

So why did they stop making these films if they were successful and people like me loved them so much? While it would be so much more fun to just blame the studios, it might actually be our fault. (Gasp!) It all goes back to my beloved video store. There was such a healthy home video market that a movie had at least three chances to make money. First, at the box office. Second, during the video rental market. Third, when the VHS was rereleased at a price at which fans could actually purchase the VHS tape. Do you remember that each movie on VHS cost somewhere around 100 American dollars when it was first released? (That is around $220 in current dollars. Would you pay that much to own *Lyle, Lyle, Crocodile*?) Later on, the studios would start selling them at the sell-through price of $20, but in the beginning, owning a movie cost a pretty penny.

Matt Damon explained how the rental market truly helped smaller, adult-type movies make their money back when he guested on the YouTube program *First We Feast*. He said, "The DVD was a huge part of our revenue stream, and technology has made that obsolete. The movies we used to make, you could afford to not make all of your money when it played in the theater because you knew you had the DVD coming behind the release, and six months later you would get a whole other chunk; it would be like reopening the movie almost. When that went away, it changed the kind of movies we could make."

Technology and our reluctance to leave our homes forced studios to make only the kinds of movies guaranteed to recoup their investment at the box office. Once the masses decided they didn't want to own movies anymore, they would just stream them, studios had to make movies that could recoup their expenses in the theater. To do this, the movie had to appeal to the widest audience possible. (There goes *Slingblade*.) It had to offend no one. (There goes *Citizen Ruth*.) It had to appeal to ticket buyers with a ton of discretionary funds. (There goes *Little Man Tate*.) It had to play as many times as possible in the day. (There goes *Meet Joe Black*.) It had to play well outside of the United States. (There goes *Fargo*.) You can see how the loss of the home video market had a huge impact on which films were made.

Storytelling vs. Technology

As I began As I began to make my way through the list of films I had, and had never, seen before, I quickly discovered these movies were complex, adult, and filled with character development. They strived to be artistic and were backed up with modern technology when it came to editing, scoring, lighting, and cameras. It is this balance of storytelling and technology that is my actual claim. I am well aware that no matter how many times I proclaim otherwise in this book, reviewers and online foes are going to claim that I said the nineties was the *only* decade of good cinema. I am not saying that. My claim will never be that movies weren't good in the seventies or eighties or that no good movies have been released in the new century. What I discovered is that none of the movies I rewatched from the nineties felt as old as movies from prior decades. My contention is if you made a graph and you put storytelling on one side and technology on the other, storytelling would start high and fall steadily after. Technology would start low and keep rising. The intersection on that very nonscientific graph would be the nineties.

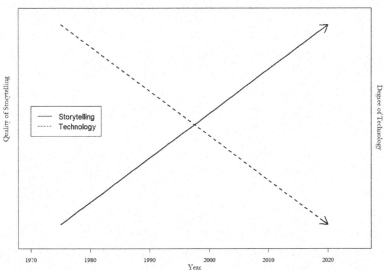

The intersection of this graph is at the end of the nineties. Storytelling ability drops and technology continues to rise. The data for this graph is nonexistent, but I saw a different graph that facts don't matter anymore. (Graph by Alex Ryan)

Of course movies in the seventies are known for being complex and the decade is hailed as the American movie industry's coming-out party for character-based cinema realism,, but man, some of those movies are really tough. They have a heavy-handed, overly dramatic "bum-bum-bum-bummmmm" feel to them. The films, while complex, move at a pace that feels old, outdated. They just aren't as technologically advanced as films from the nineties. I can already hear you saying technology and special effects got much better after the nineties, so movies now must be even better. Not so. The quality of storytelling slipped as special effects took precedence over character development. Now I know you are just dying to argue with my theory. Let me be on your side for a moment. Whenever I am asked what my all-time favorite movie is, I always answer, without a thought: *Broadcast News*. When did that film come out? 1987. I believe *Broadcast News*'s script is one of the best ever written and is so quotable. ("I am singing, while I'm reading. I can sing, while I read . . . Both!") But have you watched it recently? It looks old. It *feels* old. The pacing is just a bit off. The technology of cameras, lighting, editing, scoring, they just aren't quite there in films from the eighties. Holly Hunter is amazing, the acting is modern, but the film just isn't. It doesn't mean there aren't great scripts before 1990, or after 2000. In fact, directors like Quentin Tarantino, Alexander Payne, Paul Thomas Anderson, who made their fame in the nineties, kept making nineties-esque movies throughout their career. But most directors who came of age after are just not as brave or skilled at telling human stories. And let's not forget my entire idea is a generalization. Decades are human made. What is the best romantic comedy of all time? Easy: *When Harry Met Sally*. That came out in 1989. My second favorite film is *Wonder Boys,* and that came out in 2000. Both of those films would have fit nicely into this book, but I wanted to go with the neat and tidy use of a decade. What really is a decade but a made-up line that we drew in the endless sands of time. (I promise I wasn't high when I wrote that sentence.) Of course there are great movies before and after, but I am speaking in generalities, and I generally do believe the combination of the skill of the artists, the filmmakers' respect for the viewers, and, above all things, the heavy dose of adult themes collide so perfectly in the decade when I was in my twenties.

No doubt special effects came of age in the nineties. They were set free in *Terminator 2* and *Jurassic Park* and then filled the entire screen in 1999's *Star Wars: The Phantom Menace*. (The genesis of modern special effects truly came in 1989's *The Abyss*, and it took a decade for it to drown the rest of the movies.) When that dreadful *Star Wars* movie came out, studios went all in. Why hire all those background extras in *Evita* outside Eva Peron's balcony as she belts out "Don't Cry for Me Argentina"? They could just be computer generated, like the audience watching little Darth Vader win a go-cart race. Once I saw that I could begin this book with *Goodfellas* in 1990 and point out the decade ends with *Phantom Menace* in 1999, I was pretty damn secure in my theory that cinema ends with the invention of Jar Jar Binks. Can we please tell *Goodfellas*'s Joe Pesci's "Tommy" character that Jar Jar thinks he is funny and send him after Jar Jar?

35mm

Films in the nineties were just that: film. They were shot on glorious 35mm, and more importantly, they were SCREENED in 35mm. From the beginning of movies all the way through the nineties, when you went to see a movie what you were seeing were pictures projected on a white screen brought to life with light. It was not a computer, but a human that changed the film reels that spooled through the projector. It was a human who set up the projector, balanced the contrast, fiddled with the sound, checked the gate. There were crackles and pops in the soundtrack as the movie played. There were hairs in the gate and missing frames, and sometimes the bottom of the screen was even cut off. Sounds wonderful, doesn't it? What you see today in a movie theater is all digital projection (DCP). Every screening is exactly the same and devoid of the human element. The same thing happened with vinyl records when CDs were released. Everyone told us it was better because it was perfect. They were wrong about music, and they were wrong about movies. Perfection doesn't mean better.

I have been lucky enough to see a lot of films recently in 35mm, and it is incredible the difference of seeing a movie as it was intended to be seen: in a dark, large room, with strangers, and not from a digital master. After watching *Pulp Fiction* and *True Romance* so many times at home on DVD, I was shocked when I saw a local screening of both films in 35mm in an old movie theater. You know the type of theater I mean, where stars are painted on the ceilings and gargoyle or angel statues are sculpted along the balcony. Hell, it has a freaking balcony, for one thing. Whatever happened to balconies? They used to build movie theaters like churches, and for most of my life it was my religion. I had another opportunity to dive into the world of 35mm when I was the moderator at a weeklong David Lynch film fest in Chicago at the historic Musicbox Theatre. The theater screened all of Lynch's work in 35mm. As his 1992 *Twin Peaks: Fire Walk With Me* was screened, I sat in the back of the theater, and that is when I heard it: the ticking of the reel spinning and the film clicking as each frame took its one chance of lighting up the screen. I hadn't heard that noise in years. It was the sound of film. The sound of movies. Former projectionist and current musician and David Lynch curator Daniel Knox programmed the event. I asked Daniel why it was so important to him that the films he screens are shown in 35mm. He said, "There is something to be said for the technical nature of watching a film print. There are details you catch on 35mm that get obscured on digital. It is a different experience. Sometimes things can look too perfect, and seeing the images with the film grain makes it feel more cinematic. It is also an overall mood and atmosphere that film presents that is perfect for Lynch's films. A digital version can lose the eerie quality." In the nineties, people were just used to the high level of picture quality. Knox went on to say, "The nineties were the apex of cinematic storytelling, style, presentation and of that format. The basic technology for presenting 35mm film stayed virtually the same for nearly eighty years, and watching a 35mm film from the nineties is a demonstration of a format at its finest."

And we chucked it all for *Star Wars: Attack of the Clones* and *Revenge of the Sith*. Hold me like you did by the lake on Naboo.

How big of a deal was it that George Lucas wanted to shoot *Phantom Menace* (1999) in digital and then did shoot all of *Attack of the Clones* (2002) and *Revenge of the Sith* (2005) in digital instead of 35mm? There were articles in the *Los Angeles Times* containing quotes like "This distinction in language may seem insignificant, but these two little words—'film' and 'digital'—stand at the center of a battle in Hollywood. The vocabulary shift is affecting everything from worker paychecks and union contracts to job definitions and distribution deals." The industry wasn't even sure if these projects should count as a movie. For *Phantom Menace*, Lucas shot one or two scenes in all digital and buried them among the rest of the film, which was shot on 35mm. It was a test to see if he could do it and whether it would be noticeable to audiences. It went over just fine, and no one could tell the difference. The Rubicon had been crossed. Lucas went on a mission after *Phantom* was released on film to get two thousand screens across the country to be equipped to screen *Attack of the Clones* in digital only. So if a theater wanted to compete with another local theater, the only thing it could do was to be the first place to have a digital projector by 2002, when *Clones* would be released. So just like everyone tossed out their record player for a CD player and then tossed out their CD player for an iPod and then tossed out their iPod to stream compressed music, theaters were tossing their 35mm projectors in the dumpsters across the world and replacing them with digital projectors. Well, what good is having a digital projector without more special effects movies and digital characters? With that came more films like *Star Wars* and fewer films like *The Ice Storm*. Digital was cheaper and made the transfer to DVD easier. This meant seeing a movie in the theater would have the same look as seeing it at home. So just as we left the quality of an uncompressed vinyl record behind, we left the beautiful look and feel of film behind for the perfection of digital. This is just one of the many factors that back up my title that the nineties was truly the last decade of cinema, because no one can argue against the fact that it most definitely was the last decade where 35mm was king.

The Big Screen

There are so many wonderful experiences I can vividly remember sitting in a darkened movie theater when I had a moment I knew I would never forget. Some of them will be revealed in later chapters, and some of them happened outside of the nineties. (As a kid, I specifically remember the feelings I had upon seeing *Star Wars*, *E. T.*, and *Tootsie*, just to name a few.) Today, we just stream every movie at home because it has horrifyingly become a *possibility*, though not a probability, that going to the theater could get you shot and killed or you could contract a virus that could make you severely ill. Might as well stay at home and stream the current vanilla pudding pops they are passing off as pictures. But back in the day, there used to be a very good reason to go see a movie: the hope that you might just have a deeply personal moment while being surrounded by hundreds of strangers. You might hear others laugh at the exact same moment you laugh and discover you are not alone in your taste. You are no different from the unknown people of your shared community. The inverse could happen as well. Everyone else might react to something that means nothing to you, so you decide to take another look at it to find out why. Going to the movies propelled us forward together, as a society. It was a shared litmus test of what was funny, what was not, and how we all felt about certain subjects.

Twice in 1994 I had life-cracking moments while watching a movie in a theater. I'll save one for the 1994 chapter and share one of them now. It was the moment I first discovered I was actually part of an entire generation. The opening credits to *Reality Bites* is definitely one of the most exciting moments I have ever experienced in a movie theater. (Obviously, I have never gone to see a movie with Alanis Morissette as my companion.) I so wish I could remember why I went to see *Reality Bites* on opening weekend. I just can't remember. I didn't have the soundtrack yet, which is still one of my favorite soundtracks of all time, so it wasn't that. I was a huge Winona Ryder fan, so it might have been that, but I'm not sure. Maybe the studio's marketing plan just truly worked on me. Maybe we just went to see movies all the time back then? Either way, my stomach dropped, and I was totally embarrassed as the characters played by Winona Ryder, Ethan Hawke, Janeane Garofalo, and Steve Zahn mentioned scamming the Columbia records and tapes monthly club, knowing your social security number because of going to college, singing *Schoolhouse Rock* songs, speaking in TV commercial sound bites, fearing getting a corporate job, and being embarrassed to admit that they wanted to

Seeing *Reality Bites* and this foursome of characters in 1994 became the first moment when I clearly saw my generation depicted on the big screen.
(Photo courtesy of Jersey Films)

make a positive difference in the world. All these topics are thrown up for debate and then immediately mocked from the four friends who eat pizza and drink beer on a roof as the credits roll. And this was just the opening four minutes of the film. This was the movie, and the moment, when I learned I was part of Gen X. (Side note: the words "Gen X" are delightfully never mentioned in the film.)

Gen X

A quick Google search, right now as I write this, tells me that "psychologist Jean Twenge observed the 'birth year boundaries of Gen X are debated but settle somewhere around 1965–1980.'" I was born in 1970, so that fits. (I have to say the fact that even the dates are debated sounds just about right for Gen X. We are a generation that loves to *rassle* an idea to death.) All the references from *Reality Bites* felt like someone opened the diary I never kept and told everyone in the movie theater about my life. I couldn't believe someone (Helen Childress) wrote a film specifically for me. I have never in my life read anything published about Gen X, mostly because I am from Gen X and we never subscribed to any labels, authority, or bought into any philosophy or belief system. We mock; therefore we are. I don't take very much in life seriously. The Indigo Girls sang to me in 1989 that it was "only life after all," and who was I to disagree with them? I was from the generation that came after the one that believed "the one with the most toys wins" and came before the one that believed "meme lives matter." Gen X believed in nothing.

But how does being from Gen X matter in discussing movies from the nineties? We were the generation those movies were targeting. I was in my twenties during the entirety of the nineties. The decade started with me being single, working at a video store, living with my parents, and commuting to Akron University to get a college degree, and it ended with me being married with two kids, owning a house, and running a video editing business. So many of these movies were made with the hopes that my generation would buy tickets to them. But who were Gen Xers? Even today they are the forgotten generation. Boomers and Millennials fight each other on the internet while Gen Xers just goes about their business. We didn't destroy the world by using up all the gas and plastic like Boomers. We didn't expect anyone to care about our feelings or think we were important or that we mattered like Millennials. We weren't offended by others not liking exactly what we liked, and we loved debate. As you will see, or have seen from reading my other books, I am happy to dissect any piece of art, argue about it, but never judge it. I can discuss if I thought it was good or not, but I don't expect it to reflect only my ideas or beliefs. Gen X didn't buy into all the big ideas the Baby Boomers did. That generation had its Gordon Gekko in *Wall Street* claiming "greed is good." We were debaters, self-assured thinkers, and the last generation of American kids who were raised by parents who weren't interested in being our friends, caring about our feelings, or asking what we did after school. My teenage years weren't spent fearing the Vietnam War or being involved in a school shooting. I spent so much of my time as a child alone, without parental guidance, watching movies made for a much older audience.

Blogger Rebecca Morris wrote an article about how Gen Xers got all their sex education from reading books that were way over their head. I think this was the same with movies. I remember watching movies on HBO like *Same Time, Next Year, Chapter Two, Saturday Night Fever, The Goodbye Girl, Starting Over,* and *A Star is Born*—all movies that were made for grown-ups and were way over my preteen head. I believe it was this practice of watching movies that were above my paygrade as a child that prepared me for the complex plot points of *The Usual Suspects, Lost Highway,* or *Trainspotting.* There just weren't a ton of kids' movies coming out in the seventies. I watched what was available on HBO, and it frankly wasn't playing *Bedknobs and Broomsticks* every day. So I watched *Foul Play* or *S. O. B.,* and it made me grow to be comfortable at being uncomfortable when I was a little lost in the plot. I can't begin to tell you how many times I have had to tell my Gen Z daughter while we are watching a movie from the past, "You aren't supposed to know that yet. Just keep watching. You'll see." This generation can't be lost for a second. They have never been lost or on their own without a GPS to immediately direct them back home. Gen X was born lost and on its own. (That can't be right. I know that. But it sounded good and you know what I mean.)

My friends and I in high school and college used to debate everything. "You loved that movie? That TV show? That song? Really? Why?" And you sure as hell better have a good reason, because if anyone smelled any fear or doubt, you were sunk. This is why I have no guilty pleasures. If I am going to love an artist, I am ready to defend them, and I really don't care if anyone agrees with me. I am so thankful I came from a time when one could argue with one's best friend over which roommate was the best on *Three's Company* and still eat lunch with them in the cafeteria (answer is Terri, of course). There was no unfriending in my day.

Just Say No . . . to Taxes

Gen X was also the last generation for whom education was still seen as a communal good for which people were willing to pay. In 1981, the first year after Gen X ended, President Reagan unleashed an idea that would truly create the system Millennials and Gen Z would be educated in. He introduced, and then normalized, the idea that paying taxes to better society was a bad thing, that the government shouldn't offer services, that investing in public projects was a waste of money.

This was not a Republican or Democrat idea; it became an American idea, and it is still going strong today. Across party lines, people believe that investing in education through taxes is a waste of resources and not our problem. Reagan proudly said, "The most terrifying words in the English language are 'I'm from the government, and I'm here to help.'" So people slowly stopped helping.

It continued through the 2000s, when the policy became "No child left behind," which steered education away from freethinking, debating, creating, and focused more on teaching to the tests, banning books, and worrying about how learning made students feel. My parents never cared, or even knew, what books I read in school, and they sure as hell didn't care about my feelings about my homework. I never told them my feelings, anyway. We didn't have that kind of parent/child relationship in the seventies. I am almost certain they didn't know any of my teachers' names. They wouldn't have ever sided with me over the school when it came to my education (and shouldn't have). When the school said to read that book—you read that book. You did what you were told. So in school, I read all the classics, had a ton of homework, had to constantly write essays and reports. I am not exaggerating when I say both my daughters, who went to public school in Columbus, Ohio, in the late 2010s, NEVER had to write one report, do homework, or take any tests that required them to memorize anything. When the populace becomes less educated, fears debate, and finds freethinking scary, then popular storytelling (aka movies) is by default diminished, dumbed down. Send an uneducated viewer who doesn't know how to be lost in a movie to watch Oliver Stone's *JFK* and see what happens. They will shut that shit off and put on a *Bugman* movie right away. (I'm assuming there is a movie about a *Bugman* by now.)

Not Political

Settle down, reader. Take a breath. You are okay. All that happened in that prior paragraph was someone expressed an opinion without worrying if you agreed with them or not. Get used to it; this book is just beginning. There are about to be a lot of stories and characters who don't behave like you would have them behave. Yes, I know you are close to tossing this book in the trash can because I almost mentioned politics and that is illegal in today's culture, but you aren't in the 2020s anymore. It's the nineties around here. (You can't throw this book in the trash because you are most likely reading it on your electronic device, so that would be a huge waste of money.) But the scary part is over. That is as current or as political as I am going to get. I plan on spending no time trying to culturally correct the films of the nineties with the current cancel culture attitudes. While I will point out how the authors created sometimes shocking, sometimes maddening plot points to engage their audience, I will not be judging the stories from a 2020s perspective. This is a look at the nineties, not a look at today. Of course, it would have been nice if more of the movies covered in this book were directed by women or people of color, but let's face it, they weren't given the opportunities then because white old men had a strong hold over the world. Spoiler alert: they still do. I can't fix that. There are stereotypes in these movies because that was the way things worked back then. I am sure some of the actors who starred in some of these movies are now thought of as bad people. They were most likely bad people then too. I can't fix that either. This book is not a morality lesson. I want to look at art, storytelling, character development, and risk-taking in the medium of films. I certainly didn't pick *The Prince of Tides* to write about in the 1991 chapter just so I was sure I had a movie directed by a woman in this book. I picked it because it is as close to a perfectly made movie as any. This movie also happens to be directed by a woman named Barbra Streisand. I didn't pick *Menace II Society* so I could cover my bases and include a movie directed by someone (or two someones: Allen and Albert Hughes) who are Black. I picked it because this film is an amazing example of how much more beneficial it is to take an honest look at how horrible America has treated its Black citizens over trying to pretend it never happened. I am always annoyed when I watch a current movie or TV show that pretends that Black people and White people commingled in America in the fifties and sixties. That is offensive to all the innocent Blacks who were lynched by racist, criminal, White bigots of the past. Movies in the nineties were made with truth in mind; this book will set out to do the same.

King of the Forrest

Here is a major admission that needs to happen. There are two very, very famous movies from the nineties that I boycotted back then, and I won't break my boycott for this book. Everyone has their prejudices, and these are mine: *Titanic* and *Forrest Gump*. Neither of these films will be covered or mentioned in any real way. I suppose I could have done the journalistic thing and watched them, but I hate to break a thirty-year streak. My reason for never seeing *Titanic* is pretty flimsy. As late 1997 ended and 1998 began, I was already becoming leery of films that were carried by special effects. I was so into small pictures like *Good Will Hunting* that I just didn't care about seeing all the water and F/X tricks. Also, I just couldn't get behind watching a long movie where I knew the ending. I just wasn't interested in the story, and the more popular the movie got, the more my Gen X heels dug in. I love Kate Winslet so much in *Eternal Sunshine of the Spotless Mind* (2004) that I will watch that over *Titanic* any day. Leonardo DiCaprio has made a ton of great movies and didn't need me to support this one. It is part of who I am that if the whole world went to see *Titanic*, then I am not going to.

Forrest Gump just seems ridiculous to me. And I have a feeling it probably hasn't aged too well either. (Although it is not one of the points of this book to look at a film and judge it by today's standards. I have a strong feeling *Gump* would have landed the same to me in 1994 as it would in 2024—badly.) I, at least, have a story to go with why I have never seen this film. I was in the theater to see some movie in early 1994 when they played the trailer for *Gump*. I saw the film was directed by Robert Zemeckis, whom I liked. I saw it was Tom Hanks, whom I always loved. As the trailer went on, it sure seemed to me like the preview was giving away the entire movie. They used the catchphrases of "Life is like a box of chocolates," "Stupid is as stupid does," and "Run, Forrest, run." So I knew all those even though I never saw the film. The trailer shows him growing up, falling in love with his best girl, playing football, going to Vietnam, saving Gary Sinise, meeting the president, watching his mom die, Gump finding Robin Wright later in life. The entire story of the film is given away in two minutes and eighteen seconds. I'd like to see a hack editor try to explain the complexities of *Magnolia* in that amount of time. Then, just when you think it can't show you anymore, it has a one-minute music montage where they show clips of every small plot point they didn't ruin in the first two-thirds of the worst trailer ever made. I yelled out in the theater (remember, I was twenty-four, and people weren't getting shot so much in those days), "Well, I don't have to pay to see that movie. I just saw it." I remember people laughed. But the last laugh was on me, because just about everyone paid to see that movie. It would always anger folks (see a pattern emerging yet?) when I would say, "No, I don't need to see *Forrest Gump*, because I saw the preview." They would say, "No, you haven't seen it. There is more you don't know." I would say, "Does the girlfriend get AIDS at the end?" They would say, "How could you know that?" It was easy. It was in the preview. He says, "I could take care of you." Robin Wright is also in the same bed where his mom died. Watch the trailer on YouTube and see the genesis of dumbing down movie audiences. Don't let anything be a surprise for them and they will feel comfortable and smarter than the writer when they finally see the film in the theater because they were already told the entire journey in the preview. I could go on to discuss the overly dramatic music and the classic stereotyped voice-over voice that dominates the trailer. No need to think; we'll tell you what to think.

Well, in 1994, my mind was cracked wide open with a film that was the opposite of comfort. It was a movie that was proud to be smarter than its viewers. It was *Pulp Fiction*. While the culture was quoting, "Stupid is as stupid does," I was on the side of films that didn't "sound like the usual, mindless, boring, gettin'-to-know-you chit chat." I was always looking for a movie that actually had something to say. (Just because it is so much fun, I'll do one more.) Don't serve me Bubba Gump Shrimp; I'll take a Royale with cheese.

The Plan

The Last Decade of Cinema contains twenty-five essays about films chosen from each year of the nineties. I have tried to pick a variety of films from comedy, drama, western, action, and mystery to prove there were all kinds of films made throughout the decade. I tried to choose unique films that were also popular and made either a title wave or a ripple in the waves of pop culture. The idea here is to show the progression of the art form as we move through the decade. Brian Raftery wrote in his book *Best. Movie. Year. Ever: How 1999 Blew Up the Big Screen* that the last year of the nineties was the best year of movies ever. I have never read his book, but I am assuming he might agree with me that the decade culminated quite well. With *Magnolia, Fight Club, Eyes Wide Shut,* and *Being John Malkovich* all released in 1999, you can certainly make the case for it being the best year, but I personally believe 1994 is a stronger year, with *Pulp Fiction, Shawshank Redemption,* and *Reality Bites* all coming out that year. In 2022, the top ten grossing films of the year were ALL sequels or franchise films. In 1994, there were zero. You read that correctly— not one film among the top ticket sellers was a franchise in 1994. They were all original ideas sitting in the top ten. That is my kind of film year.

So how did I pick these twenty-five films? What scientific bases did I use? What were the factors that I entered into the HAL supercomputer that spit out these perfect specimens for this divine proclamation of hardened fact? Well, I don't have a good answer to that. I first made my big list of over 160 films, trying to have an even amount per year over the ten years this book covers. Then, from that list I picked two or three films a year, but also didn't want to lean too heavily on one genre. The point was to show diversity in plot and concept. These are not my favorite films of all time, or even that decade, and a few of them I had never seen before, and most of them I hadn't seen since the nineties. It had more to do with whether there was something in the movie that inspired me while rewatching it. This book is not a recap of films from the nineties. For the huge movies, I barely even tell you the plot. I am assuming if you are reading about it, you've seen it. If it is a lesser-known film, I try to help you along, but also, I won't give any big spoilers away. My hope is that you revisit these stories and then join in the conversation with me about how well written and directed these stories were.

Before we get started, I will circle back to my theory one last time to try to drive the point home. I am not saying the nineties are the only decade of good movies. There have been good movies made before and after. I am saying the nineties was the last complete decade when filmmakers could tell their story without fear of retribution, mixed with the fact that studios would fund risky films with small, grown-up stories. They would actually greenlight movies for just a particular slice of the ticket-buying audience, and at the same time, they would make big, tentpole action films. The movies that were released were actually shot on film and they looked beautiful. The era of digital film was still years away. There were choices at the multiplex theater. There was variety, risk, and true character development. It also is the decade in which technology allowed directors to capture their stories with high-quality lighting, sound design, camera equipment, editing, scoring, and, yes, special effects. It is the perfect intersection of brave storytelling and modern technology. No one knew that fear would soon take over all artistic and corporate decisions. It is a look at the last time where we just went to the movies to be entertained, to dream, to feel, to cry, to laugh, to escape, to reflect. If you were a wannabe writer from Ohio like me, it was also a time where I learned how to create from artists who had experiences different from my own.

Enough of all these previews; let's just watch the films.

Chapter 1
1990

A: *Goodfellas*

"Everything was for the taking. And now it's all over."

If you are ever in a position where you have to defend a ridiculous claim about an entire industry, such as something as highfalutin as "the nineties were the end of complex movies," I sure hope you get to start off with a mic drop example like Martin Scorsese's *Goodfellas*. Not only do I believe this is the best movie of 1990, it really should be in any argument for one of the best movies ever made. I love that this is where I get to start my argument. It feels more like where it should end.

The film was released eighteen years after *The Godfather* and three months before *The Godfather, Part III*. I often wonder if Francis Ford Coppola's stomach ached when he saw what his friend had accomplished with *Goodfellas*. There was nothing Coppola could change about *Part III*. It was filmed. It was done. The third *Godfather* picture is much maligned and rightfully so. It is clunky, sluggish, and is a great example of a movie that just *feels* old. That is from rewatching it today, but I wonder how the film would have been received in December 1990 if it didn't have to be compared with the superior *Goodfellas,* which blew open the genre of Mafia movies with its plot and pacing. Based on the book *Wiseguys* by Nicholas Pileggi, the script, written by Scorsese and Pileggi, took the real-life story of Henry Hill and melted it down into a rocket ship of a movie—destroying everything, including its characters' lives, in its path. But that comes later; at first it is all fun in the sun.

Rags to Riches

Goodfellas begins in New York 1970 where we are introduced to Jimmy Conway (Robert De Niro), Henry Hill (Ray Liotta), and Tommy DeVito (Joe Pesci). They have a dead body in the trunk that isn't as dead as they thought. As they finish the job with knives and guns, the camera zooms in on Liotta's face. We hear the voice-over "As far back as I can remember, I always wanted to be a gangster," the title card of *Goodfellas* appears on-screen, and the music soundtrack kicks in with Tony Bennett's version of "Rags to Riches." Pop songs from the fifties will play for the next fourteen straight minutes of the film, one after another; they play quietly, and most times in their entirety. This is only layer number one of the soundscape for this film. One can imagine these songs playing as 45s on a jukebox or coming out of a transistor radio in any of the establishments the young Henry Hill runs between doing odd jobs for the mob. Pop music was the language everyone spoke in the fifties and for the next few decades. Everyone wasn't blocking out the world with their own music on their own headphones.

The second layer of sound, also quieted, is the dialogue spoken between the characters we watch on-screen—Paulie (Paul Sorvino) giving orders to the mobsters busting each other's balls as they hang out on the street. Characters are talking to each other nonstop as a young Henry performs mundane tasks for all of them. These pointless conversations happen while the music plays, but neither track is turned up to a normal volume. The third and main sound is adult Henry's voice-over. Liotta is explaining to us what is going on. All three of these soundscapes are coming at us while the pictures are moving fast. These opening fourteen minutes takes us through Henry's teenage years, and it is virtually impossible not to long to be him. We can totally see why being a part of this world is enviable.

Scorsese says in the DVD commentary that the film's concept is "nostalgia of a world filled with gods." This is a perfect description of what the opening sets up. Paulie runs the neighborhood with his eyes. A look from him can make the baddest bad buy quiver. Even the middle- to lower-level men in the organization are seen as gods through young Henry's eyes. The entire film revolves around the idea of a world filled with gods, but I would add one change to Scorsese's description, and say *Goodfellas* is a film filled with nostalgia for a time when this country was *competent*. There is no doubt all of these men are evil. They commit heinous crimes—they murder, steal, and terrorize—but they also provide a service for the neighborhoods. The reason the Mafia existed in the first place is because the country banned alcohol, and the Mafia just supplied citizens with that service. It was a group of people who got things done. In a time when we have to wait twenty minutes in a Starbucks drive-through for a cup of coffee, it is a joyous experience to watch an organization that is competent. But there is a price to be paid for this service, but we don't have to pay it for the first fifty-two minutes of the film.

Music plays for so much of the front part of the film. There are only a few scenes that play without a song scoring the film. Each of those scenes is key to the story. The first time the music stops is when Jimmy comes to bail out Henry, who is arrested as a teenager for the first time. There is nothing to distract us when De Niro tells the teenager the most important thing is to never rat on his friends and to always keep his mouth shut. These are the two rules Henry will eventually break. Scorsese wants us to pay attention, but only for a moment; the music kicks back in as they walk out of the courtroom and everyone, including Paulie, is there to congratulate Henry on "getting his cherry popped." Billy Ward and His Dominoes start singing their up-tempo version of "Stardust," and we are back on the good-times train.

Be My Baby

Consequences are not a part of this story at this point. The concept that sets this film apart from other movies is that it isn't told like a movie, it is told like a story. Henry Hill and, later on, Karen Hill (Lorraine Bracco) are sitting down to tell you the story of their life. Many films use voice-over to help the audience keep up with the plot, but this is the opposite; the voice-over *is* the plot, and what we witness on the screen is the backstory. It's all just a goodfella spinning a yarn for the ages. One of the first scenes to prove this point is the first of three oners I want to cover. A oner, for those of you who weren't film nerds in the nineties and didn't discuss these kinds of things over and over at Video Time, is a sequence in a film that has no edits. The actors complete all the action in one take. There is no coverage or second chances. The DP (director of photography) for the TV show *thirtysomething* Ken Zunder explained a oner to me as, "A oner doesn't mean the camera just sits there in a wide shot. It moves in and moves out. The camera moves with, around, through, and behind the actors." The more complex the shot, the better for film geeks like myself. But Scorsese wouldn't just do a oner without a reason. From 16:45 to 17:51, we are introduced to all the gangsters in Henry Hill's world as he enters a bar. This is not the famous oner with Lorraine Bracco and Ray Liotta, which we will get to in a moment. This is a shorter one, but it has a ton of actors saying hello to Liotta while he voices over their names. Scorsese explained why he had them talk directly to the camera: "Introducing a character was not as important to do it conventionally. It would take up too much time conventionally. We had other things to talk about." The film is an exercise in storytelling, not moviemaking. So to follow moviemaking rules would be pointless. Therefore, it isn't really breaking the fourth wall by having these characters introduce themselves to the audience any more than it is when Liotta, at the end of the film in court, jumps off the witness stand and delivers his voice-over directly to the audience as he walks out of the courtroom. Scorsese is moving the story along. The story, not the plot. The actions of every character comes from the idea that someone is telling you a story.

The next oner is the famous one. It lasts for over three minutes, from 31:33 to 34:38. This is a shot referenced in several other 90s films covered in this book—the shot is just that famous. I have seen this scene, which contains my all-time favorite sixties tune, "Be My Baby" by the Ronettes, about a million times. It is so much fun to watch what the background players are doing and to watch all the action that occurs. Liotta takes Bracco on a date to the Copacabana, one of the most famous nightclubs during that time. There have been directors who certainly have had longer shots and some directors have tried to make it look like their entire movie is just one or two takes. Hitchcock did it in *Rope*, Alejandro Gonzàlez Iñárritu did it *Birdman*, and I suppose those are cool, but after a while an entire film in one take can get tedious to watch. The point of a oner is to keep tension going for the audience. In life, there are no cuts—you experience that moment uninterrupted. Another nineties movie, *The Player* by Robert Altman, opens the film with a long oner and even mentions other films that do them, but I still pick this oner as my favorite because it services the plot and where the characters are at this point in the story. We have been moving through the world of the Mafia for the first thirty minutes, barely stopping for anything, so this shot isn't trying to show off; it just fits the moment. I am sure there are a ton of viewers who watch this scene and don't even notice there are no edits, because they don't care. They care about how Karen is being sucked into a world of danger. Who could possibly blame her for being impressed with this evening?

The shot begins outside of the Copa on a tight shot of Liotta giving his car keys to the valet. Then we follow them across the entire street, downstairs into the kitchen, around corners, with people working at each spot. Bracco is gladly going deeper and deeper into the world with each twist and turn of the building, but it is the world of the Mafia she is truly being whisked into. They come out into the restaurant, where they talk with the host, and then a waiter brings out a table. They are not seated at a table; a table is seated with them. Waiters quickly set the table; Bracco and Liotta sit down right in front of the stage. Then the camera spins around to show Henny Youngman on stage performing his comedy before the film cuts to Liotta and Pesci on a job. The sound of the comedy routine continues over the picture, so in a way the oner continues to the next shot. I tried to do a quick count of the extras involved in this shot; it was easily over one hundred people without counting every person in the Copa lounge. All of those people had to do their job correctly or they would have to reshoot the entire scene. There's your nostalgia for competence. I can't imagine being the actor who messed up a line or a movement and made all those hundred people go back to one and have to do the entire scene again. DP Michael Ballhaus said, "We shot the scene only eight times, and it wasn't even a full day." And yes, according to Ballhaus, comedian Henny Youngman, who ends the long shot with his routine, did forget his lines a few times, and they had to redo it all over again.

The reason this is my favorite oner of all-time is because, while being impressive with the amount of action occurring during the shot, the main purpose of not cutting is that it advances the plot. Scorsese explained, "The reason why that scene had to be done in one take is through the underground labyrinth of this world and then to emerge in the spotlight like a king and queen. This was the highest he could aspire to." The film is halfway through the good-old-days section of the story. The upswing sections of these films are always the most enjoyable parts to watch. Paul Thomas Anderson does a similar thing with his 1997 film, *Boogie Nights*. The front part of the film is the fun part of being a porn star celebrity, and the back part of the film is the consequences. Facing consequences for a character's actions is a major part of making a movie for a grown-up. We enjoy the spoils and face the repercussions of every decision we make in our real life; when a movie does the same, it feels real. To cut during any moment of that long tunnel into the Copa would mean Karen had a chance to think and get out, but there was no stopping her descent into that world.

The final oner I want to point out is after Bracco is manhandled by the neighbor next-door and Liotta crosses the street and punches the guy with his gun, then comes back and gives her the gun to hide. This is another scene that wouldn't be as good with a cut in it. The tension builds inside Liotta, as well as the audience, as he walks across the street seething with anger for what this punk did to his girl. The camera spins around as he reaches halfway, and when Liotta hits him in the face with the gun, blood appears on this poor unfortunate hooligan's face within the shot. I am always a big fan of in-camera tricks. Scorsese does this a few times in the movie. I know everyone loves those postcomputer special effects, but it sure feels like it actually happened when an actor uses a sleight of hand to do the trick during the shot. What is more fun than seeing it happen in real time? Where did the blood come from? Which actor had the blood? Or was the blood on the gun? I don't know, and I don't wanna know. I want to believe the blood comes out of the nose of the guy who thought he could touch Henry Hill's girl. Later in the film, Joe Pesci blows the head off the truck driver from one of their heists, and the blood splats on the white sheet of his bed in real time. No cuts. It's all an in-camera effect. That truck driver, by the way, is none other than Samuel L. Jackson, who begins his lifelong goal of appearing in just about every movie ever made.

In 1990, MTV was still huge, and music videos were playing twenty-four hours a day. MTV is always blamed for quick cuts and never allowing viewers to get bored with any shots. *Goodfellas* doesn't fall into the trap of overcutting anything. The film is full of oners that make us feel like the story we are being told is unfolding right before our eyes with each colorful story that Henry shares. But like all roller coasters, you can only go up for so long.

My Way

At fifty-two minutes into the film, we circle back to that day in 1970 where the film started. We are given the backstory of how the body in the trunk ended up that way, and we are at the same moment at which we started with the push in on Ray Liotta's face. Once *Pulp Fiction* premiered in 1994, it almost became an unwritten law that every film had to be told out of order if it wanted to be cool. This is a trope that is still overused today. But what writers and studio executives don't understand is there has to be a reason for a story to be told out of order. I will cover the reason for *Pulp Fiction's* structure in Chapter 5, but for *Goodfellas*, we are coming back to this moment because this is the tipping point in Henry's life. It was all backdoor entrances, girlfriends on Fridays and wives on Saturdays, and poker games with the boys until Tommy kills Billy Batts (Frank Vincent) in 1970.

The last hour of the picture is Henry's slow slide into drugs, deception, and disgrace. But there was one hint in the first hour to tell us what could easily happen, and it is probably the most famous scene in the picture. Twenty minutes in, Pesci is telling a story and everyone is laughing, and Liotta so innocently says, "You're really funny." This sequence is the first major scene in the movie that is carried with dialogue between two characters. There are no pop songs playing, no voice-over. There are no external layers to protect the audience from the danger of this moment. All we have is two great actors sharing the screen. And they do share the screen. There are no tight shots in this entire sequence as Pesci asks over and over, "How am I funny?" The reason there are no close-ups of each actor is because we need to see how the rest of the background extras (the other mobsters) are processing this conversation. The more scared they get, the more unsettled the audience gets. This is our first look at the actual world Henry travels in. There is danger at every turn. Up to this point in the script, the audience has no reason not to assume Pesci's character isn't just as fun and nice as Liotta's character. Then the truth starts to shake out: they aren't nice at all. Henry plays the only card he can and says it's just a joke, and lucky for him, Tommy agrees, but there is still anger and danger in the air. So when the manager picks the worst time in the history of delivering a check to a table and asks Tommy to settle up his four-figure tab, Pesci releases the pressure that has been building up inside of him by smashing a bottle over the manager's head. He attacks another waiter and even draws his gun. He doesn't shoot him. This scene will get a reprise later in the film when Spider (Michael Imperioli) forgets to bring Pesci a drink and after a back-and-forth, Pesci shoots and kills Imperioli over nothing. The Spider shooting is brutal and made the distributor of the film very nervous. The film's producer Irwin Winkler said, "Warner Bros. desperately wanted us to take it out. We had to very, very forcefully explain to them that that scene really changes the audience's attitude towards our friends." It becomes harder for us to be on any of the main character's side as they turn on each other and start killing weaker people.

Henry is a criminal, and these men are violent and dishonorable. It is one thing to get shot in a robbery or get picked off by the cops. It's easy for a layperson to imagine that kind of danger, but by setting the main character in a situation where just for laughing at someone's story, they could, in fact, get killed, it brings the point home that his entire life is dangerous. The "How am I funny" scene shows us that any and every moment is dangerous. Never in the film does Liotta get put in any real danger while committing a crime. The danger comes when he interacts with the people he surrounds himself with. He is aware that any second could be his last. Up to this point, the film has only shown us one side of the world, and even in this moment, we aren't truly seeing a downside; it is just enough to bring the viewer back to Earth to say, "It's not all fun. It's scary as hell."

But once our main guys murder Billy Batts and Liotta lies to Paul Sorvino, who has been introduced to us as not just a god but God himself, about the murder, Liotta is basically thrown out of Eden. He starts selling drugs, starts using drugs, and starts lying to everyone. If you can lie to God, you can certainly lie to your wife about the girl in the apartment across town. Even when Henry serves some time in prison, he still hides from Paulie that he is selling drugs and running scams inside. Gangsters have no honor, and they follow no code, despite all the razzle-dazzle of the first hour of the film, where they all try to pretend they do.

After Pesci is whacked for killing Billy Batts and De Niro hoards the money from the shared caper where they pulled off the biggest heist in history, there is nothing left for Liotta but paranoia and trouble. All the fun is gone. It's consequence time. Scorsese explains, "For the last twenty minutes of the picture, there is no music. It's very quiet. They have to pay now." Not only do the characters have to pay, the audience does too. Scorsese sets up a paranoia parable for the last act of the film. Liotta is trying to bring in a shipment of drugs, sell a few guns to De Niro, and most importantly, make his homemade red sauce for dinner. All the while, a helicopter hovers over everywhere he goes. I have never done cocaine, but after watching this sequence, I sure feel like I know what it would be like. By taking a hard, honest, no preachy look at the world of the Mafia, Martin Scorsese and Nicholas Pileggi gave audiences an amazing film that feels as fresh today as it did at the beginning of the nineties. Scorsese jokes in the commentary that the climax of the movie is really just watching someone stir sauce and look for a helicopter, but it is surely no joke. It is the smallest of worries on his last day as a gangster that brings the realities of what that life is to the audience. Any momentary feelings of envy or wish fulfillment the first fifty minutes brings to the viewer, the final twenty takes it away, and then some.

B: *Pretty Woman*

"You're Late.
You're Stunning.
You're Forgiven."

As the picture fades in on Garry Marshall's *Pretty Woman*, the first line of dialogue could very well be an echo of the motto the eighties lived and died by: "No matter what they say, it's all about money." An unseen magician says this as he performs a magic trick with a coin. The more impressive sleight of hand is what Marshall achieved with this movie. The film ends by asking the viewer a simple question: "Welcome to Hollywood. What's your dream?" The two hours in between supply the movie watcher with examples of characters who live life for money or for dreams. After a decade of amassing wealth, this film kicked off the nineties by showing what happened to all those people who just went after money and got it. They forgot how to feel the grass beneath their feet, the joy of taking a day off, and, of course, the bliss of singing Prince off-key at the top of their lungs. If you haven't seen *Pretty Woman* since 1990, you probably just think of the film as a silly romantic comedy about a rich guy and a sex worker. Or as the film that made Julia Roberts a superstar. It's so much more.

The film wastes no time getting started. The elegant world of Edward Lewis (Richard Gere) is shown at a party where wealthy folk schmooze and make pointless conversation. When the audience first meets Gere, he is being dumped by his off-camera girlfriend, who says she feels like his "beck-and-call girl." Moments later, we see a real call girl, or at least a Hollywood version of one, when we meet

Vivian Ward (Julia Roberts) getting ready for a night of street walking on Hollywood Boulevard. It is quickly revealed that she is from the opposite world of Gere, as she uses a magic marker to color in the scuffs on her knee-high-faux-leather boots. The intro to her world shows us a murdered prostitute, a landlord who threatens to evict Vivian, and a roommate who spent that money on drugs. Vivian's roommate, Kit, played by Laura San Giacomo, who uses every moment of screen time to maximum use, even introduces our heroine to a pimp who is happy to have her work off the money. But no, our gal says, "When," she says, "Who," and she takes care of herself.

With both worlds set up, the two leads meet eleven minutes into the film, and our fish-out-of-water story is off and running. He has it all; she has nothing. It has all the makings of a really bad movie that should be long forgotten after all these years, but *Pretty Woman* bucks the trends of the same-old-same-old romance tropes that this picture spawned a plethora of. But how did it get its start, and where did this script come from? That story mirrors this very film. It's a Hollywood story with an improbable happy ending.

Real Wild Child

Jason Alexander, who might just have had the most amazing July of any actor in 1989 as he went from filming the pilot and first season of *Seinfeld* to being cast as Philip Stuckey, Gere's lawyer—no way was he expecting either project, let alone both, to become ingrained into the pantheon of American pop culture—said, "When we wrapped *Pretty Woman*, we all had a great time, but we all thought this will never see the light of day. There's no story. There's nothing here. But Garry had it all. We just couldn't see the forest for the trees."

So why did he feel that way? Mostly because the script they were shooting from wasn't the movie they ended up making. So much of what was filmed was improvised on set. Proving again this movie was born out of the events of the decade before it, screenwriter J. F. Lawton was thinking about the eighties hero, Gordon Gekko. He told *Vanity Fair*, "*Wall Street (1987)* had either come out or was coming out. I had heard about it and the whole issue about the financiers who were destroying companies. I kind of thought about the idea that one of these people would meet somebody who was affected by what they were doing." Lawton started a script called *3,000*, the amount of money a rich man pays a drug-addicted sex worker to stay with him for a week while he closes a business deal to buy a company with the express intent of selling it off for parts. The script discussed the underbelly of what happens when someone who has everything lets someone who has nothing into the world of excess. It was a meditation on giving someone the keys to the castle and then changing the locks after one brief week. Lawton described his original script as "a dark fable about a financially destroyed America and the perils of showing the good life to people who had never experienced it before."

In *3,000*, Vivian offers her services for $2,000 for the week but asks if she can go back home to get her drugs to keep her going. Edward informs her she will not be able to do drugs while she is with him. For that she asks for another grand, and we arrive at the $3,000 price tag. Vivian is more crass about the sexual acts in the script, and while she does go shopping and they do head to the opera, they really don't leave the hotel room for very much of the story. The script is basically a small-budget film that settles for discussion over filming locations. When they do take the plane ride to the opera, Edward tries to work on the plane, and Vivian stands up, lets her dress fall to the floor, and convinces Edward there are better things to do on a plane ride than read. The script says she is completely naked as she watches the sunset from the plane window. Along with the nudity, the language is also coarser, making it hard to imagine Julia Roberts playing this version of Vivian. *Pretty Woman* only drops one f-bomb, and it might be one of the best comic uses of it ever. When Laura San Giacomo is asked to name someone who things worked out for and she responds, "Cinder-fuckin'-rella." There is still a Cinderella mention in *3,000*, but not that classic line. When Edward takes her to the opera, he asks her if she feels like Cinderella, but this isn't a story where things work out.

At the end of the week, when Stuckey (who in this script is named William) smacks Vivian and Edward saves her, Edward doesn't throw him out; he invites him back in, but William declines. It is these changes that let you know Edward doesn't fall in love with Vivian, and it is much more of a transactional relationship. He doesn't really care if William beats up his employee. The next morning, he takes Vivian back to her life, and she can't stop crying. She totally loses control. Edward has a plane to catch, so he drags Vivian out of the car, drops her on the sidewalk, leaves the envelope of cash on the ground and it starts to blow away. Vivian literally picks the money out of the gutter. (Hey, now I get how trickle-down economics works.) He doesn't rescue her, and she doesn't rescue him right back. Credits roll.

Lawton's script was a popular script that was making some noise in the industry and was making the rounds in 1989. Patricia Arquette even auditioned for the part, and it is a lot easier to see her as that version of Vivian than it is to see Julia Roberts. Despite that, Roberts did win the part for *3,000*. Roberts admitted her own misgivings about being able to play the *3,000* version of Vivian when she said, "I couldn't do it then. I couldn't do it now. Thank God, it all fell apart." The studio that owned the script went under, and it ended up with Disney, who gave it to director Garry Marshall, who had recently been brought in to lighten up *Beaches* (1988) and did a successful job. He was then tasked with doing the same thing with *3,000*. He met with Julia Roberts and decided she still had the role, but it should be changed to reflect Roberts's strengths.

Wild Women Do

Vivian became kind, folksy, personable, and likable. Garry Marshall said, "My vision was a combination of fairy tales. Julia was Rapunzel, Richard was Prince Charming, and Héctor [Elizondo] was the fairy godmother. It didn't seem like a vision everybody would have, but I did." I believe it was Marshall's stint as a sitcom writer that truly prepared him for this assignment. On *Happy Days*, *Laverne & Shirley*, and *The Odd Couple*, it was his job to be sure that each and every scene, and certainly right before the commercial breaks, had a killer line that would make viewers stay with the show. He attacked *Pretty Woman* with that same energy. It isn't *just* about having a great closing line, but it is also about staying true to the characters and momentum of the story. Here are just a few of the classic killer closing lines from scenes in *Pretty Woman*:

- **Vivian:** "He's not my uncle." **Saleswoman:** "They never are, dear."
- **Vivian:** "You work on commission, right? Big mistake. Big. Huge. I have to go shopping now."
- **Wife:** "Close your mouth, dear."
- **Vivian:** "I'm just using him for sex."
- **Kit:** "Cinder-fuckin'-rella."
- **Vivian:** "She saves him right back."
- **Vivian:** "It was so good I almost peed my pants." **Edward:** "She said she liked it better than *Pirates of Penzance*."

That last closer is a double whammy. According to an interview that Marshall gave to the American Film Institute, Richard Gere loved the "peed my pants" line and said that no line could top it. Marshall told Gere he could always top any line. So on the next take, he gave Gere the *Pirates of Penzance* line. When they premiered the movie, the *Pirates* line got the bigger laugh, and Gere gave Marshall a big hug. He topped the closer with a bigger closer.

Successful sitcoms become classics because they develop a character and then create comedy around what the actor brings to that character. This can certainly be felt in Héctor Elizondo's hotel manager, Barney Thompson. Shades of *My Fair Lady* are seen when Elizondo teaches Roberts when she should use each of the dinner forks. He instructs her how to sit and speak. The fact that when she finally buys a new dress, but won't wear the new dress while she walks around the lobby, makes her frugal, makes her sensitive, and shows she is respectful. But by not wearing the new clothing and continuing to wear the skimpy dress, she drives Barney crazy. Garry Marshall employs a classic comedy formula that always works: understand the positions of both characters + have them be on opposite sides of the position for good reason = comedy gold.

If you can watch this section of the film and not smile, then you better check yourself for a pulse. The film spends ten minutes having Roberts try to get that first dress so she doesn't have to walk around in her midriff-exposing, white-and-blue skimpy mini-skirt/tank top outfit. How popular is this film after all these years? Her dress was rereleased for sale by the designer Hunza G in 2021. *Harper's Bazaar* said this dress is one of the "few dresses so famous that almost every woman in the world can immediately picture it when it is mentioned." Part of the reason for the lifelong recognition is the interactions between Elizondo and Roberts. All he wants is her to not walk around his lobby, his world, in that provocative dress. All she wants is to take care of her newfound, prized possession. We understand both perspectives. The viewer knows exactly why he wants her to stop wearing her provocative getup, but it makes us love Vivian even more because of the deference she is displaying toward the outfit Edward paid for. There is little doubt this is the most expensive item she has ever owned. Later in the film, this will become even more evident when Edward questions why she didn't buy multiple outfits. A selfish, greedy, entitled person would have tried to buy as many items as they possibly could. This is the first glimpse of letting the eighties go and welcoming in the nineties. We learn so much about her character in these moments. Think of all the sex workers the hotel manager has had to deal with at the hotel. He is coming at her with the same condescension everyone else in Hollywood gives all women at her level. No one is going to give someone like her the respect all humans deserve. She responds to this situation with kindness, and kindness always breeds more kindness. The most impressive thing about *Pretty Woman* isn't that it made Julia Roberts a star. She was already on that path from the moment everyone saw her in *Mystic Pizza*—not to mention people seem to forget she was in *Steel Magnolia*s the year before, and held her own against a cast of female icons. No, the truly impressive part of *Pretty Woman* is that virtually every moment and every line of dialogue serves two masters at once.

Examples of how Marshall used each moment for comedy or drama, and also propelled the story to the next beat, can be seen throughout the movie. Besides what I have pointed out from the dress buying plot, there is the through line of Richard Gere's fear of heights. When Julia Roberts first comes to his room, she goes out to the balcony only to find out that Gere never steps out there because of his fear of heights. When asked why he would get a room on the top floor, he responds,

"It's the best." That certainly lets us know a lot about his character. He is collecting everything that is given to him as a future one percenter (before that was even a term). But while he is damn sure he will collect these things, he doesn't appreciate them and even worse, doesn't even want them and can't enjoy them. It tells the audience how closed off from joy he is. But the second use of this character trait of being afraid of heights sets up the last scene in the movie. He will eventually have to face his fear (of heights and of love) by climbing high up her fire escape to "rescue" her. In that scene, it will be her who explains to him with another wonderful callback, as to why she is up on the top floor: "It's the best."

They use this same plot device with the car. Gere borrows Jason Alexander's 1990 Lotus Esprit SE, which was deemed at the time as one of the best cars, but he has no idea how to drive it. He orders champagne and strawberries but doesn't drink any of it because he doesn't drink. He gets box seats at the opera but doesn't get too close to the edge. He does say he loves the opera, but it is Roberts who cries and is moved by the story and music. One wonders if he truly does love the opera. I wouldn't be surprised if he didn't.

Another example of the writer using a scene to serve two purposes is when Gere tells Alexander who Roberts actually is. Alexander is pestering him about how she just shows up in his life and is now talking to their competitor at the polo match. Gere tries to convince Alexander there is nothing to worry about, but he persists. Gere finally tells him she is a hooker and he picked her up in his car. We are glad he tells him this because Gere is making the bad guy squirm with the thought that a street walker was sitting in his expensive car. We don't feel this is going to hurt her. He is showing us for the first time he actually cares about her. Alexander is put in his place. The audience laughs when Gere explains the truth. But moments later, Alexander propositions Roberts and strokes his finger across her bare arm. We are suddenly feeling unsafe, and the comic moment, which, as always, contained a button line of "in your car" is now making it seem like she can't trust Gere. This carries over to their first fight back at the hotel and is picked up again when Alexander shows up in the last act, smacks her, and attempts to rape her. This film is a fairy tale, and just like any good fairy tale, the evil that our heroine has to overcome is credible and scary. Because the movie started with a dead sex worker in a dumpster, and Laura San Giacomo's life is very much set in the world of pimps, drugs, and murder, we are unsure for a moment. Very few films even try to walk the thin line between comedy and fear, but several movies in the nineties will balance between these two worlds with no issues. It can be done if the writing is at a high level.

It Must Have Been Love

Romantic comedies became a staple of nineties films, and the most successful rom-coms have a strong subplot beyond romance (*You've Got Mail, The Cutting Edge, Boys on the Side*). In *Pretty Woman,* the B plot involves buying and destroying a company. Not just any old company, but one that helped save the country in World War II. Despite that fact, a US senator helps this rich man destroy the company that bailed out America. This is the secondary story that plays out while they fall in love. It isn't very cheery. Part of the reason this B story is in the film at all is because the original script was a dark look at that world. It was inspired by the greed and corruption of Oliver Stone's *Wall Street,* and flecks of Lawton's original script pop up every now and again. These dark themes (which were a part of the original script) aren't thrown in your face, because they don't need to be. Having the issues take a backseat to the love story allows the viewer to make the connection as a secondary thought and makes it more digestible to an average crowd. The film still confronts the idea that money and position determine your social status. It still shows the difference between being poor and being rich, but now the story is much more character based. There is Jason Alexander's Stuckey, a yuppie who just wants money. Héctor Elizondo's Barney, a servant who is trying to run a hotel with dignity and grace, while he is treated no differently by his guests than Roberts is treated by the Rodeo Drive salespeople. Who really is happy with their place in life? Who loves their jobs? There is no doubt Vivian is not pleased to be a sex worker; she has dreams of being more. She won't be defined by her job. Edward and Stuckey regularly put the common man out of work and send jobs overseas. They, and people like them, will do that throughout the nineties and those effects will set up the world we live in today. A pretty heavy topic to cover in a rom-com. But, the higher the stakes, the higher the rewards.

A trait that Lawton and Marshall gave Robert's character that is remarkable in any film is that she is kind. Her kindness spills out of her every moment. Certainly in current times, every character has to be dark, troubled, or, my least favorite description of any character, an antihero. Kind characters and how kindness can infect others is much more difficult to write, and when it is done correctly, audiences respond favorably. One of the first things viewers see Vivian confront is the fact that San Giacomo has taken their rent money and used it to buy drugs. Roberts is upset, but she doesn't attack her. She handles it better than most of us would. Later, she is kind to the Bellhop, she is friendly with Elizondo, and she approaches each new situation with wonder. No one in the film ever says, "Wow, Vivian, you sure are nice." Exposition dialogue like that makes me want to turn off any movie from any decade. Instead she says, "There's a band" upon seeing the orchestra at the opera. Her excitement is childlike and endearing. And just so I can beat this point to death, this opera, while being very romantic and a wish fulfillment scene for everyone who wants to be swept off their feet on a magical date, also serves another purpose. It is introducing the song that will play when Gere climbs her fire escape at the end of the film. Every scene in this movie is moving the action forward and connects together like a maze. This is the opposite of a choose-your-own-adventure book; everything is laid out and chosen for you. The ending is surprising and inevitable, just like an ending should be.

A line of dialogue that always evokes emotion in me, even while taking notes for this essay, comes when they get in the elevator and she says, "If I forget to tell you later, I had a really nice time tonight." A classic moment, but also a wonderful display of kindness, appreciation, and gratitude from a character whom we all think we are like, but we aren't. Remembering to say thank you is something we were supposed to have learned in kindergarten but it is rarely heard. During this scene, as they head to the opera, the song "Fallen," sung by Lauren Wood, plays. In 1990, this was my favorite song from the movie. I used to listen to this CD all the time. But I could never figure out if Lauren Wood was a boy or a girl. There was no internet for me to quickly find out the answer. The song wasn't a single, so there was no music video for it. The single from this album was Roxette's "It Must Have Been Love." It had a music video that played on MTV and VH1 nonstop, but no on-screen performances of "Fallen" were around in 1990 for me to learn who the singer was. All these years later, I have never Googled to find out if Lauren is a boy or a girl. It really doesn't matter anyway. So if you know, please don't tell me, because I like not knowing some things. It's a chance to wonder.

In all my research on this film everyone is quick to point out the film works due to Julia Roberts's personality and her smile. It is like watching a star be born live on celluloid, but the person who truly impressed me in this film was Richard Gere. It reminds me of Robert Redford's performance in *The Way We Were* (1973). That film is known for Barbra Streisand being the star, and her character is the quirky one viewers identify with. Katie is the one who is entering the well-to-do world of Hubble, just like Vivian is with Edward. Katie might not be an actually working girl, but she is the girl with a job that services Hubble and his friends. Both Redford and Gere play their characters much quieter than their female costars, who are loud and do most of the talking. Some actors would have passed on playing second fiddle to an actress (and in both films, many males did pass, and both actors had to be convinced to finally sign on), but in taking the risk, and trusting the scripts, both men got to create quiet characters who come alive on-screen. There are several times when Gere delivers his lines in a whisper. None is more evident than in the piano scene. Gere retreats to a banquet room in the middle of the night to play the piano while workers tear down the tables and chairs. Roberts shows up in a bathrobe. He decides there are better things to do with his hands and starts to undo her robe. He simply whispers to the room full of workers, "Gentlemen, would you mind leaving us, please?" You can barely hear the line. Volume is not what makes people move; it's power. So few actors utilize restraint when delivering lines of dialogue. In the elevator after she taunts an older couple, she says to him, "Sorry, I couldn't help it." He softly replies, "Try." Gere does so much with either one word, or just a look. His performance shouldn't be discounted. I'm not saying Julia Roberts isn't the star or that she doesn't deliver a performance for the ages; I'm just pointing out that unfortunately, back in the day, if there wasn't an actor with the confidence of a Richard Gere or a Robert Redford, we wouldn't have been gifted with seeing these female stars shine so brightly.

In the end, the reason this film stands the test of time is the script. The double meaning of scenes, the killer closing lines, and the perfect use of side characters. Each salesperson, hotel employee, and snooty person we encounter is memorable and used to perfection. But it is the lyrical writing of the dialogue I feel is the most important part. The quote I picked from the film that began this essay could totally be set to music. "You're late. You're stunning. You're forgiven" uses the rhyme of repetition. The same could be said of "I would have stayed for $2,000." "I would have paid $4,000." They just feel like song lyrics. I believe this is the reason that so many of the lines of this movie have become famous movie quotes. It is more than the fact that fans of this movie watched it over and over. It is a very lyrical script.

A sort of Easter egg for fans of romantic comedies is the appearance of actor Ralph Bellamy, who plays Mr. Morse, who owns the company Edward tries to purchase. He is a bit of a rom-com legend. He starred in what might be considered the original well-written romance movie: *His Girl Friday* (1940). At the end of the film, when he tells Gere he is proud of him, it's a nice passing-of-the baton moment. While Bellamy didn't end up with the girl in his movie, Gere does. Although I don't see how anyone could blame Bellamy; his competition was Cary Grant. Richard Gere's was just Hollywood Boulevard. But hey, as we learn as the movie ends: "Some dreams come true; some don't. But keep on dreaming."

Chapter 2
1991

A: *Terminator 2: Judgment Day*

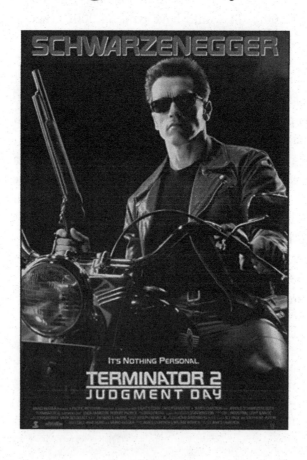

"IT'S IN YOUR NATURE TO DESTROY YOURSELVES."

In the summer of 1991, I was still happily employed at Video Time. I was the assistant manager, although since *Star Trek: The Next Generation* was the biggest show at the time, I insisted I be referred to as "Number One." (It's hard to believe I ever went on a date in my life.) That summer, the owners of the Video Time franchise had a contest to see which store could sell the most copies of *Home Alone* on VHS. My store won, and the entire staff was treated to dinner and a movie. (Hey, maybe that's how I went on dates.) The employees of the store got to vote for which movie we would go see in the theater. *Terminator 2* won. I voted for *City Slickers*. I wasn't a fan of the first Arnold Schwarzenegger film *Terminator*, or any film he had made up to that point. I had no choice but to go, as attendance was mandatory. Plus, this was my big chance to rub elbows with the owners and maybe move up to the Captain's chair. My expectations were seriously low for *T2*. I figured it would be a nothing action film. This wasn't the first time I let expectations almost keep me from seeing a great movie.

Terminator Revives

When you consider my earlier complaints about current action/ superhero movies in my introduction, *T2* might seem like a strange pick for one of the two movies to focus on from 1991. I didn't spend any time struggling over picking this film as an example of how even the action films of the nineties had strong plot and character development. This was the summer of 1991, and summers were always when action films were released. My issue is now these types of films come out year-round. But in 1991, summer was for blockbusters. But even within that summer, it wasn't all special effects-driven films; there were options. Some of the films that were granted a wide release were *Robin Hood: Prince of Thieves* (action), *What About Bob?* (comedy), *Backdraft* (mystery), *City Slickers* (comedy), *Naked Gun 2 ½: The Smell of Fear* (spoof), and *Boyz n the Hood* (drama). The champion of all of them was *T2*. The film dominated and "Hasta la vista, baby" was the catchphrase of the moment. The special effect of the liquid T-1000 morphing from character to character was something we had never seen to this extent. That effect would make its way through pop culture, ending up in Michael Jackson's music video "Black or White" that fall. If your effects ended up on MTV, you reached the pinnacle of that era.

The first sign that this film is more than just a trite action picture can be found in the first line of the movie. Linda Hamilton voices over, "Three billion human lives ended on August 29, 1997." How's that for a fun summer beginning? Do you feel up for a BBQ and some fireworks now? All who sat in the movie theater were just informed they only had six years left to live. Director James Cameron begins the film by showing a traffic jam on the freeway, then fades to children swinging on a swing set, and then to a burnt car with a skeleton behind the wheel. Sitting here in 2024, is there a more apt visual for our future than the sight of us all dying while we clutch our steering wheel before we would ever give up our cars? Our addiction to oil is only surpassed by our addiction to shooting each other. *T2* doesn't shy away from the realities of the modern world and where everything was headed. In the nineties, the stock market thrived as tech stocks soared on Wall Street. This growth would create the one percent who would rule the world and begin to shrink the middle class. With these heavy political topics at its core, one cannot be surprised that what *T2* is remembered for is the special effect of morphing one character to another. If Americans can't focus on the dangers of global destruction today, they sure weren't going to back then, when things weren't as dire. This film is an action flick. No doubt. But within its plot, Cameron released two ideas into the film industry that would last for quite a while.

Trust Me

T2 was the first action movie that felt bad about killing the indiscriminate extra. (To be sure that no *Star Trek* reference is left unturned, let's refer to these murdered extras as "Red Shirt" ensigns.) In early James Bond movies, Bond never cared how many Red Shirts he killed. He would blast his way into any building shooting people left and right. Luke Skywalker was fine to strike down as many Stormtroopers as the special effects team could afford. Killing bad guys was all in good fun. All the way back to John Wayne or Clint Eastwood picking off everyone in the Old West who was standing on top of saloons. We didn't know who those Red Shirts were anyway. Captain Kirk would send any ensign to his death on an away mission, and we were fine with it. Killing characters who had no name meant they never counted to the movie-going audience. But *T2* changed that with a simple request from a little boy.

The Terminator (Arnold Schwarzenegger) is sent back in time to protect ten-year-old John Connor (Edward Furlong) when he is a kid. The T-1000 (Robert Patrick) is also sent back in time, but he is there to kill the young John Connor so he can't defeat the machines as an adult in the future. All of this plot was set up in 1984's *The Terminator*. Schwarzenegger still plays the Terminator, as he did in the first movie, but in this movie, Schwarzenegger is the good guy. He isn't there to kill Sarah Connor (Linda Hamilton), he is there to protect her son. The Terminator is programmed to do anything to protect young John. When two bullies try to cause trouble for John and the Terminator, who looks like a regular human (did I just imply Arnold looks like a regular human?), the Terminator breaks the one bully's arm and then pulls out a gun and gets ready to kill the other. John pushes the gun aside and tells the bullies to run. He tells the Terminator he "can't just go around killing people." It took a child to stop the senseless body count in action movies. Later in the film, when Connor is trying to escape a building surrounded by police, Schwarzenegger just shoots all the cops in their legs or arms to knock them down, but not kill them. This scene of him shooting cops in the knees plays as comedy, and I specifically remember the huge laugh this got in the theater. The very idea of not killing everyone on-screen was funny to early-nineties audiences. A "kinder and gentler" action movie may not have lasted forever, but it did last a while. If you notice in movies after that, anyone who is killed in a movie always has to kick a dog or push a little kid, or say something sexual to an undeserving female, and *then* they can be killed by the hero or bad guy. Because now "Red Shirts" only die if we are able to judge them for one action before they are shot in a really "cool" way.

Exactly halfway through the film, in one of the quieter moments, is a spectacular scene that makes *T2* a nineties classic. As the Terminator, Sarah, and John regroup at a gas station between attacks from the T-1000, they fill the tank with gas and grab a bite to eat. As the Terminator works on the engine, we see two kids about eight years old running around, each with a very real looking toy gun in their hands. They shoot each other and push each other, screaming, "I shot you." "No you didn't." John, who isn't that much older in years but is so much more mature due to his being raised by a mother who believed he would have to save the world as a grown-up, looks at the two kids fighting and says, "We're not gonna make it, are we? People, I mean." The kids play in slow motion. This scene hits even harder today, when there isn't a day that goes by when a child isn't killed by a bullet. The Columbine school shooting wouldn't occur until 1999, so the idea of children killing children wasn't a thought in pop culture yet. This moment was written to show the idea that war is in our DNA. Since the Terminator is a machine, there is no sugarcoating his answer. He responds, "It's in your nature to destroy yourselves." Whether it is our obsession for plastic, our desire for oil, or our need to invent a bigger and better weapon, as Skynet does, causing humanity's demise, we are forced at this midpoint of the film to recognize the nature of humanity. The final line of dialogue in this short interaction is my favorite. It couldn't be more nineties. John Connor responds, "Yeah. Major drag, huh?" No tears, no stress, no emotion. Society's communal brain was just not "feeling our pain" yet. All that was to come. This scene lasts a mere twenty-four seconds. Three short lines of dialogue. That's it. Just think what a writer can do with two hours when you can do so much with twenty-four seconds. The opportunities in film are endless.

This scene played and replayed in my head on the morning of

September 11, 2001. A friend of mine called and told me to turn on the television. I turned it on to see the World Trade Center smoking. The buildings hadn't fallen yet. My friend told me people were jumping from the building and a plane had crashed into it. At the time, I was a stay-at-home dad with twins. They were four years old. I looked down, and they were fighting over a car that each of them wanted to play with. The one that won the car was soon greeted with a whap upside the head with the lesser car. *We're not gonna make it, are we?* I turned the TV off and have never turned the news on again. The twins didn't know of the violence that had just been unleashed in their world. They had no idea the world that they would grow up in would be totally mandated by that moment. All they knew was they wanted that toy car and they would shove and push to get it. *Major drag, huh?*

Sarah On the Run

In the first *Terminator* film, Linda Hamilton was targeted by Schwarzenegger to be killed and had to be saved and protected by Kyle Reese (Michael Biehn). The first film has limited special effects by today's standards but was seen as a major step forward during its time. Where it was also a relic of its time was in the fact that Sarah Connor needed to be protected by a man. In 1991, *T2* takes a wonderful leap forward for actresses in this genre by allowing Linda Hamilton to be self-sufficient and an action star in her own right. Audiences loved what Hamilton brought to the screen. She worked out, got buff, and was just as much of a badass as Bruce Willis, Sylvester Stallone, or Arnold Schwarzenegger. Anyone who tries to baby Sarah Connor is likely to get their face pummeled.

It isn't just as an action star that Hamilton gets to change things for female roles. It is also in the plot of the film. It is the female Connor who comes up with the idea of stopping Skynet from developing the computer chip that creates the cyborgs. She decides to go after and kill Miles Bennett Dyson (Joe Morton) so that if he dies now, he can't invent the chip. James Cameron said, "In a very real way, she becomes the Terminator of the second film, at least in a kind of physiological level." Female roles in action films were not very integral to plot points besides screaming or having to be saved. If you look at how helpless the female leads are in films like *Die Hard* or *Indiana Jones and the Temple of Doom*, it is refreshing to see Hamilton given the meatiest scenes in the film. She is the one who has been living with the knowledge that the world will end on August 29, 1997. This fact weighs on her every moment of the film. Her scenes with the doctors who try to convince her it is all in her head are heartbreaking. The most disturbing scene in the film is her watching children play on a swing set and then she imagines them being destroyed by a nuclear bomb. All the death and destruction the men of this film cause are carried by Linda Hamilton. She said about the character, "She's a great warrior, but so what? She doesn't have anything that makes it worthwhile."

What Hamilton did with her Sarah Connor character has been more than worthwhile. Women started to not be relegated to just playing victims in these types of films. I am not saying it changed overnight; sexism can't be squashed by one film. But films that didn't create a strong female role were seen as out of step, or more importantly to the studios, noncommercial. *Speed* (Sandra Bullock), *Courage Under Fire* (Meg Ryan), *A Perfect World* (Laura Dern), *Out of Sight* (Jennifer Lopez) and *Jackie Brown* (Pam Grier) all had female characters who were crucial to the plot. The actresses didn't have to play just the girlfriend or wife, but they affected the plot and the outcome of the story. All of them owe a debt to what Linda Hamilton did in *T2*.

Sarah is the one who wants to end the war before it starts. She is relentless in her pursuit of this goal. She has raised her son to believe he must spend every moment preparing to be a warrior. There aren't too many films that have a woman set aside her motherly tendencies without being the villain of the story. The fact that Hamilton is so convincing, and that audiences made *T2* a success, allowed other filmmakers to evolve their female characters into the plot and develop them as women and as characters that we can relate to. No one could watch *T2* and think they just created the character of Sarah as a male and cast it to a woman to appease the concept of diversity. Sarah Connor is by far the most developed character in the entire film because the story demands it. Action pictures are a fun summer night out, but just like any story, it is so much better with a relatable character who behaves in a logical way that advances the story and makes the action worthwhile.

Bad To The Bone

When watching *T2* in current times, it is easy to watch the building blow up, the truck flip over, the war between the cyborgs and the humans, or all the bullets bouncing off Arnold's face and just think, "Eh, so what? It's computer graphics." The liquid T-1000, who can morph from one character to another or just walk through steel bars, can make you think all the effects were done digitally, but the majority of the effects were done in camera. Stan Winston, who created the cyborgs and makeup effects for the first film, was back for *T2*. He balanced these action sequences between optical and digital effects.

While the morphing effect is all computer generated, they actually did shoot in the flood-control channels of Los Angeles; they actually did blow up a four-story building. The cop cars are actually exploded. For me, as a viewer, there is something exciting about that. I find my mind wanders when a filmmaker is just drawing everything we see on a computer. When the Terminator jumps on a truck that is sliding across the ground, that truck actually slid across the ground and was pulled by another truck with chains, and a stuntman is actually surfing on top of it. They had to actually create a safe way to make these moments. They don't look fake, because they did it. This was something that made me enjoy action pictures. Today, a computer can make anything happen. And yes, we don't see the strings that suspend the Good Witch anymore, but I also don't believe in the fairy tale anymore. I like knowing Harrison Ford was actually running as the big rock chased him in *Raiders of the Lost Ark*. Yes, I know it wasn't a real rock, but it was *something* he was running from. Now a computer chases Harrison Ford and de-ages him so he can act like he is younger.

T2 was shot on 35mm, and it is beautifully shot. The action sequences, while going a little overboard in the last thirty minutes, are wonderfully staged, and are backed up with a film that is trying to warn us about the dangers of turning humanity over to computers. Just like the characters in the movie, the film industry would ignore the warnings and go all digital, all machine. Rewatching this film,

I felt a little like Sarah Connor, knowing the date when this kind of film will take over all of cinema, but the new films won't even give us twenty-four seconds of a reality check that violence is our Achilles' heel. There is no superhero in *T2* who can save us, because the enemy is humanity, and no one can save us from ourselves, our greed, our desire to consume, and our propensity to hate what we don't understand. Luckily, this book is only in 1991, and we have a lot of wonderful small stories to cover before we get to that fateful date.

But just like Sarah Connor—I know it's coming.

B: *The Prince of Tides*

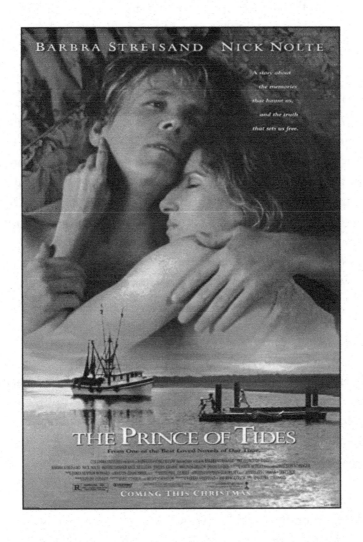

"WHO TAUGHT YOU TO BE SO CRUEL? YOU DID, MAMA."

In 1987, author Pat Conroy released a best-selling novel called *The Prince of Tides*. A male-centric novel about a football coach whose marriage is falling part, his twin sister has attempted suicide, and his mother is a divisive figure in the family. All the women in the main character's life, including his three daughters, are fodder for his inappropriate comedy, his reluctance to speak the truth, and are reeling from his closed-down persona. The main character of Tom Wingo was perfectly cast in the 1991 film with eighties macho actor Nick Nolte. The novel covered four generations of the Wingo family saga, with Tom Wingo being the center that holds all the stories together. When director and costar Barbra Streisand finally won the option to turn the novel into a film, she rightly hacked the story down to a summer of Tom's adult life. A novel is best told from all sides, but a film works best when it is less sprawling and more focused.

Turning books into films has always been a staple of cinema. Many times they transform well, and many times they don't. One factor that seems to help the success rate is to have the original author of the book play a part in the script. Pat Conroy was highly involved in creating the script, which is credited to Becky Johnston and Pat Conroy. Director Barbra Streisand also had a hand in the script. Pat Conroy even moved into her New York apartment to work with her on the final draft. This film has a little bit of everything in it. It is one of the most perfect examples of how a film doesn't need to have just one trait, which is one of my major complaints of modern films. This film has comedy, drama, violence, football, romance, heartbreak, parenting issues, beautiful scenery, flashbacks, plot twists, mystery, children, and even a wonderful dog scene. Just like real life, this movie takes viewers on an amazing journey through twists and turns and ups and downs, and it all happens in only two hours and twelve minutes. This is a film that doesn't waste a second of time. Every moment is meticulously used to move the story forward and keep the audience, who didn't read the book, wondering what secret Tom Wingo has been holding on to since his childhood.

Sweet Forgiveness

"It's a film about forgiveness," says Streisand, "about saying, 'I need to love my mother and father in all their flawed outrageous humanity.' I chose to put that line at the end, because I felt this is the lesson of the movie." One of the main reasons I wanted to focus on this film is that forgiveness is the theme of the picture. I suspect that many film buffs might have skipped this movie because they had preconceived notions about Streisand as a singer or personality. In full disclosure, Barbra Streisand is my all-time favorite singer and I am a huge fan of hers, but that is not why I think this is a movie that needs to be remembered. It is the directing and construction of the film and the fact that the themes and stories are extremely grown-up that makes me want everyone to remember it, with the hope that maybe movies like this could exist again.

One by one, we meet characters who are connected to each other through family bonds, but they are holding on to something from the past and refusing to move forward. Nick Nolte needs to forgive his parents for his childhood, but he also needs forgiveness from his wife for how he has treated her over the past years. Dr. Lowenstein (Barbra Streisand) and her son (Jason Gould) need to forgive each other as well. The film tackles these issues one by one and shows the struggle involved in forgiving someone who has truly hurt you, sometimes in small ways, sometimes in devastating ways, but how forgiveness, as an act, is always a better choice than holding on to bitterness. The idea of forgiveness is slipping away from our culture, as we easily unfriend anyone who doesn't vote for our candidate, doesn't like the same song we do, or maybe drinks Pepsi instead of Coke. (Okay, that last one might actually be a valid reason to not like someone.) There is no reason too insignificant not to unfriend or unfollow someone. It is a delight to have a story like *The Prince of Tides* that contains huge reasons to never forgive someone but allows the characters to work through their feelings through therapy and talking out their issues rather than jettisoning the person from their life. A film where people talk to each other instead of killing each other will always be something I want to check out. Tom also doesn't try to change his mother and father; he learns to accept them. It remains to be seen if Tom's children will be able to forgive him, but isn't that always the question? Will the next generation be able to forgive the one that came before it?

Memory

I have tried to approach writing about each of these films, as if the reader has seen the film so I have not worried too much about spoilers. I mean, it's been thirty years, so I feel pretty safe talking about the plots of these films. But this is a film that by my count has two twists in it, and I will not be giving away either of those twists. Part of the joy of watching *The Prince of Tides* is wondering what secret Tom is keeping. If you have never seen the film, or it has been a while, I don't want to take that joy away. I will never understand why people like to ruin movies. I have been watching a lot of Siskel and Ebert reviews while doing research for this book, and the number of times they give away the ending is comical to me. So Tom's secret is safe with me. Here is what I will tell you about the film: Tom's twin sister Savannah (Melinda Dillon) has attempted suicide, and he is asked by his sister's psychiatrist to help her piece together her memories from their childhood to try to figure out why she is suicidal. Dr. Lowenstein is not Tom's doctor and has no doctor/patient relationship so it's all fine as they slowly fall in love throughout the film. The stories from Tom's childhood have been hidden and unspoken aloud by Tom for many years.

The handling of these flashback memories are a wonderful display of how to craft a film. Thankfully, director Streisand constructs a more complex way of showing us flashbacks than other movies do. Tom doesn't just go to Dr. Lowenstein's office, sit down, and then the camera pushes in for a *Wayne's World* blur effect. That isn't how memories come back to us in real life, so why would they happen that way in film? At first, Tom is rightfully reluctant to share any memories from his traumatic childhood. But as Lowenstein gets him talking, these memories come over Nolte, and the audience, by surprise. They are so swift and surprising that sometimes we don't even know we have started one. This is about respecting the audience. Streisand expects her audience to be able to keep up, and they can, because she leads the viewer with signposts along the way. Streisand explained these flashbacks, "The human mind makes those cuts. Some sense memory happens, whether it's the smell of something, the color of something, the place."

There are several great examples of these flashbacks throughout the film, but I want to focus on the memory that happens at an hour and eighteen minutes. This scene is a nice lesson in editing and directing. Tom is dropped off at his mother's house. He is wearing a sports jacket that is white with vertical, thin blue stripes. He approaches the picket fence gate that leads to steps that take visitors to the front porch. As he opens the gate, the camera changes positions to the front porch, where we now see teenage Tom Wingo and his younger mother (Kate Nelligan) opening the gate and walking up the stairs. The cars in the background went from modern cars to cars from the sixties. His mother is excited to get to go to the richest man in the town's house. Young Tom got in a fight with Mr. Newbury's son, and his mother wants him to apologize. His mother fidgets with her armpits, spits on his hair, and calls him a cracker, saying they are not "white trash," while behaving like someone from a lower class. She knocks on the door. When the door opens, a suddenly older Mr. Newbury welcomes an older Tom into his home. We have another time jump in the scene. As older Tom enters, the camera changes positions to inside the house, where young Tom and his mother are back on-screen and a younger Mr. Newbury welcomes them in. The scene continues to flip between the past and the present. Young Mr. Newbury is wearing the exact blue-and-white-striped jacket that older Tom is wearing. At this point in the film, we don't know how this could happen. How could a lowly Wingo end up going to the Newburys' house? Tom was supposed to visit his mother. Why would his mother live there? The film, as it does many times throughout the feature, leaves viewers wondering how these things are happening. Streisand leaves us momentarily wondering and then answers the question and immediately poses a new one. It is a joyful experience for someone who likes to think at a movie and not have it spoon-fed to them. I now want to discover how his mother in the present could be at the house of the richest man in town. Is this Tom's secret? Is this what haunts the Wingo children? We don't know yet. But it's okay, dare I say it, it is actually *fun*—to not know everything at once; the journey is the reward. I don't want to be smarter than the film I am watching, I want it to purposefully lose me, and then for me to catch up.

Back in the past, Lila and Mr. Newbury flirt, and then he asks her to sit down in the hallway while he and Tom have a discussion in his study. The next ten seconds of the film are a moment I would teach in directing school. (And when is someone going to ask me to teach that class?) Back in the past, Mr. Newbury enters the study and young Tom slowly walks down the hall, his mother sits on the bench and whispers, "Tom," pointing overly dramatic to the floor, "It's an Oriental carpet!" The fifteen-year-old son of a fisherman shrugs this information off. Lila exaggerating her whisper says, "FROM THE ORIENT." Tom rolls his eyes and walks to the study as Lila sniffs the roses and looks around. I saw this film in the theater three times back in 1991. I have also screened it with friends many times. This moment always gets a laugh. To see this lower-class woman overreact to a rug and think she is fitting in says so much about her character. Director Streisand plants this laugh in order to catch her audience off guard. She even allows time for the audience to laugh while Lila smells the roses to leave a space, because back in 1991, movies were edited to play in front of hundreds of people and spaces for laughs were actually a thing editors had to worry about. Suddenly, there is a jump cut to young Tom in the study getting hard slapped across the face by Mr. Newbury. We fell for Streisand's trap. She put the laugh in to trick us into letting our guard down, so the slap lands even harder. Young Tom is informed that he better never touch Mr. Newbury's son again and better tell no one that he hit him or he will run his family out of town.

Tom's memory is inner cut with the present (left side) as he returns to the
place of a traumatic moment from his childhood (right side).
(Photos courtesy of Columbia Pictures)

Tom takes the slap, and then the study door opens, but we are back in
the present and older Lila enters and kisses Mr. Newbury as Tom and
him have pleasant words. Through this flashback, we learn his mother
married the man who slapped Tom as a child, and she ended up going
from a fisherman's wife to the wife of the man who ran their town.
No one in the film ever says, "You married Mr. Newbury after he was
so mean to us when we were kids." There is no reason for that line of
dialogue; we experienced it. This is how film is supposed to work.

We know these are the stories that Tom is telling Dr. Lowenstein,
but to have them come alive while he is living his life makes them feel
more real. Who among us hasn't relived a moment from our childhood
when we return to the scene of the crime? Because the film teeters
from comedy to drama, from silly comments to painful memories, we
are left as uncertain as Tom Wingo is. This is something that a one-
emotion film can never achieve because they are only keeping us down
and expecting the worst thing that can happen at every moment.
Having comedy mixed in with drama makes us wonder where we
will go during each and every scene. When Tom finally speaks to his

mother alone, he tells her he must tell their family secret to Savannah's doctor in order to save her. We have been witness to so many horrific memories up to now. Streisand as a director has set us on a path where we are begging to know what happened, but also we don't want to find out because we just know it is going to be rougher than the memories we have already seen.

The following scene in the film, between Nick Nolte and Barbra Streisand, is a masterclass in writing, directing, and acting. Both actors convey the nervousness we feel about hearing the secret. Lowenstein senses that Tom is ready to talk. Nick Nolte delivers a pitch-perfect performance as he bears his soul and shares his secret. Director Streisand uses sound so well during his story. They keep cutting from the silence of the doctor's office to the noise of the family Wingo secret. Silence is a technique that can be so jarring in a film. Again, going back to my time of seeing this film in the theater on opening weekend, I remember that during this scene, the theater was as quiet as any movie I have ever been in, and the place was packed full of ticket buyers. By this part of the film, the audience was so invested in these characters that people could barely breathe. There might have been a few sniffles after the reveal, but during the reveal, nothing but eerie silence. Only great filmmaking can create a moment like that, and it can *only* happen in a theater. For those who think there is no reason to see a drama in the theater, this film is a perfect example of how having this emotional experience surrounded by strangers, hopefully strangers who respect film and are respectful of their neighbors, can't be overstated. Not every film can have a story that backs up what *The Prince of Tides* has to tell. Pat Conroy is an accomplished storyteller. His books always have a plot to back up his wonderful writing, but when that can be transferred to film, something truly magical happens.

You Are Woman, I Am Man

With its complex plot and many characters who are changed over the course of the film, *The Prince of Tides* could have easily become a mess. The movie needed a director who could manage the story and tell it with respect while not giving away the twist too early. Barbra Streisand accomplished this. She was able to because she is a great director and someone who had been starring in films since 1968. In the way that Clint Eastwood or Kevin Costner went from actor to director, she did the same. But of course this was 1991; it wasn't the same, was it? They were men. She was a woman. Shockingly, that still mattered then. In 1983, Barbra Streisand became the first female to write, star, produce, direct, and sing in a major motion picture. The film was *Yentl*. It was also her directorial debut. The movie was filmed in London, and Streisand has said many times the crew was wonderful, respectful, and there were no issues. The film was released to positive reviews, but Streisand said most of the negativity came from women. "I get attacked a lot for who I am rather than what the work is about. I thought women were very cruel about *Yentl*. Not the men, the men were very perceptive." She speculates the fact that she had no pushback from her *Yentl* crew could be a British mentality since they are used to having a queen.

When *The Prince of Tides* was filmed seven years later in America, it wasn't quite the same. Being a professional and knowing that speaking out in 1991 would not have gone over well, Streisand never publicly discussed how the American cast and crew behaved taking orders from a female director. Although for a great example of how differently the press treats a male versus a female director, one only has to watch the embarrassing behavior of CBS reporter Mike Wallace when he interviewed Streisand on *60 Minutes*. He attacks her over and over until he literally makes her cry. This isn't an interview for someone running for office. This is a director promoting a big budget Hollywood film. Memories are never long in American culture, so now, only a few years after the Me Too movement it is easy to forget how men were allowed to treat women on television. He literally says to her, "You have the reputation for bitchery." Besides making up a word, it is incredible that someone on a major network could get away with calling a female director that word because she strives for perfection. You know, just like Tarantino, Spielberg, Coppola, and every other director who actually makes classic films. He goes on to say he doesn't like her and never did, mocks her for getting therapy, and complains about how she behaved as a guest on his show thirty years ago. This was just the tip of the iceberg of what women had to go through to create art and have it be seen.

I asked Matt Howe, author of *Barbra Streisand: The Music, the Albums, the Singles* and curator of the Barbra Streisand Archive to put this interview in context. He said, "*60 Minutes* was a ratings hit in the nineties, so Wallace could afford to punch down during the interview, and he did. 'Why are you so accusatory?' Streisand asked at one point. But he kept needling her until he found her breaking point: her stepfather. Streisand broke down in tears and waved at the camera to stop filming. Wallace agitated and got an honest reaction from Streisand, but it was unfair, especially since Streisand had committed years of her life producing and directing *The Prince of Tides*, a film about healing the rifts with mothers and fathers."

Streisand battled this same misogyny on the set. She never mentioned it during interviews in the nineties because that would have been a terrible time to do that, as proven by the *60 Minutes* interview. However, years after, when the culture was more attuned to the way females were treated in the industry, Streisand chose to discuss it with fellow director Robert Rodriguez in 2017 at the Tribeca Film Festival. Streisand said, "When we did *The Prince of Tides*, on that movie, it was very interesting because the AD was kind of a chauvinist and the cameraman and his crew were not helpful." She went on to explain how she had to convince the crew to get the shots she wanted. When she wanted Henry Wingo (Brad Sullivan) to push a plate away and the camera to follow the plate across the table and up to Lila Wingo's face, the cameraman said it wasn't possible. Readers can look back at what was achieved in *Goodfellas* to know there are much more complex shots than this two second shot. Rodriguez, who directed major action flicks like *From Dusk Till Dawn* and *Sin City*, is totally shocked by this statement. It is evident that no crew member ever told him that a shot can't be done. When I interviewed cameraman Scott Ressler, who worked with David Lynch on *Lost Highway*, he stated over and over how he would do anything to try to get the shot that Lynch wanted, and sometimes Lynch wanted some impossible shots.

Streisand continued, saying in one shot where she was in the scene, they were filming her side of the scene and Nick Nolte wasn't delivering the same lines for her to react to. She stopped the take and told Nolte his lips wouldn't match the dialogue, and the cameraman said you couldn't see his lips in the shot anyway. Streisand, who had a monitor at her feet, could clearly see his lips were in the shot. When she confronted the man as to why he had just lied to Nolte, he shrugged and said, "Boys' club." Rodriguez is clearly amazed by this story and asks, "Why didn't you fire him?" It would never occur to him that a crew member would get in the way of him achieving his vision, and if one did, they would be fired. Streisand correctly pointed out that she would have been crucified in the press and with the rest of the crew if she had done that. Women were, and still are, held to a different standard.

Streisand clearly helped to crack the glass ceiling for female directors like Jane Campion, Jodie Foster, and Kathryn Bigelow. But she also opened the door for actresses who wanted to produce films. In the seventies, Streisand was one of the first to develop her own films. Julia Roberts singled out Streisand as one her mentors. She said, "Particularly someone like Barbra Streisand, I think of that, I'm just walking in the path that she has hacked out with a machete." That path was hacked over the seventies and eighties, and we all were able to leave the woods and have a wonderful film like *The Prince of Tides* waiting for us like an oasis. Don't let this one slip past you.

Chapter 3
1992

A: *Unforgiven*

"It's a hell of a thing, killing a man. You take away everything he's got and everything he's ever gonna have."

In 1992, Clint Eastwood's legacy was not the same as it is today. Depending on your political persuasion, he might be most known today for talking to an empty chair or he might be known as a quiet, thoughtful director. For some, it might be a splash of both. But in 1992, he was still known as Dirty Harry or the man with no name, basically an old-timey action hero of the sixties and seventies. Sure, he had directed plenty of films before *Unforgiven*, but it was this western that changed his legacy and started him on a streak of directing thoughtful, provocative, grown-up films—each one different from the one before it. The film changed his reputation to more than just an action star. He became known as a masterful director, and he did it all at the young age of sixty-two. Watching this film, as well as *The Bridges of Madison County,* which he made three years later, he seemed "young" even though he was in his midsixties. It stood out as another way how filmmaking has changed so much in the past thirty years. In today's era, it is unlikely that a sixty-five-year-old actor would get to headline a major studio release of a love story, not to mention a western revenge saga. Eastwood did produce and direct the films, so we know how he got cast in both parts, but it's incredible to watch these films today with the knowledge that he wasn't winding down his career. I am sure there were people who viewed *Unforgiven* as a swan song film. Nope. He was just getting started. He has crafted at least twenty-four more films over the past thirty years. That is more films than he had directed before *Unforgiven*—from 1971-1992, he directed sixteen pictures.

Villainous Friends

Westerns and musicals were out of style throughout the eighties. Eastwood only made one western in the eighties, *Pale Rider*. Westerns made a bit of a comeback after *Dances with Wolves* and *Unforgiven*, but musicals would have to wait for the next decade to have its comeback with *Chicago*. According to IMDb, twenty westerns were made in the eighties and twenty-four in the nineties, but it lists over two hundred in the last twenty years. This shows how the nineties really weren't into genre pictures. Films were more focused on creative, unique, smaller scripts over blanket genre movies like westerns, superheroes, or musicals. All three genre just weren't huge in the nineties. But while there is no doubt that *Unforgiven* is a western, I mean it even has a bar saloon shootout, the script has a lot to say about murder, guns, revenge, alcoholism, parenting, sexism, justice, the law, and even marriage. It just hides those topics among the horses, the skyline, and classic actors from decades past. Richard Harris and Gene Hackman make you remember what supporting actors, character actors were truly like when actors were cast for parts and not magazine covers. Richard Harris plays English Bob and he likes to poke the newly minted American citizens about having a president instead of a monarchy. The film is set in the weeks following the assassination of President Garfield by the man who might have invented the concept of being thirsty for likes on Instagram: Charles Guiteau. This minor subplot of the assassination of President Garfield, which is mercilessly mocked by English Bob, is another analogy in the brilliant script by David Peoples about the heritage of violence and murder in American history. The film is packed with so much morality that Fox News would ban it for being antipatriotic if it were made today. But in the nineties, these were just plot points to shape the past of the murderous but now reformed William Munny (Clint Eastwood), who just wants to live out his life in Wyoming in 1880.

According to Clint Eastwood, on one of my favorite nineties TV series, *Inside the Actors Studio* hosted by James Lipton, Peoples's script was submitted to Eastwood's production company in 1980, and the script reader hated it. She put a note on it that it was too violent. The script was given to Eastwood as reference for a different film he was prepping, but he read it and liked it. At that time, it was called *The William Munny Murders,* and Francis Ford Coppola was attached to direct it. Eastwood called and was told that Coppola's contract expired the day before. Eastwood was able to option it. He waited eleven years until he felt he aged into the part of Munny. Eastwood told Lipton that what attracted him to the script was that "there were so many oddities to it." These oddities are the things that turn bland movies into forever classics.

Reload This

Why do we want to watch the same movie more than once? A pretty darn good answer to that question could very well be "the oddities" of the film. The first time through a film like *Fargo,* we wonder if the William H. Macy character is going to get away with the kidnapping of his wife. But the second time, we can't stop wondering why Frances McDormand meets her friend from high school for an awkward lunch. I watch *Home for the Holidays* just about every Thanksgiving. Maybe the first time I watched it I wondered if the dinner was going to go well. But now I know for certain the turkey is going to end up on Cynthia Stevenson's lap, but I don't watch for that anymore. I am watching how Robert Downey Jr. immediately takes a photo when the turkey flies in her lap and the way he makes a face before he takes the picture, and how Charles Durning worries about the spot on his tie. When a movie is watched and rewatched, it is the little moments we study. (One more just for fun.) I know I am not the only person who watches *True Romance* over and over. We aren't rewatching it because we want to see if they sell the drugs to the movie producer. We want to hear the crazy monologue Dennis Hopper delivers moments before Christopher Walken breaks his streak of not shooting people. With all the oddities—Eastwood's word; I might use the word unique—in the script, it is not surprising the first draft of *Unforgiven* sat in a drawer for years. It takes years for audiences to catch up to new art. Just take a look at any David Lynch film and you can see a film go from hated to classic in about twenty years' time.

I saw *Unforgiven* when it came out in 1992, but I never watched it again until I started working on this book. I couldn't remember if Eastwood lived or died in the end. I didn't remember that Gene Hackman was—and please forgive me for the embarrassingly simplistic description of the wonderful character he created—the bad guy. But I did remember Eastwood didn't want to kill the person he was sent after to kill. I remembered the bravada of the young punk who thought he wanted to murder someone that it would be supercool to get to kill another human being. I remembered Eastwood couldn't mount the horse and that they gave him a cold which lasted for quite a while in the movie. I had never seen a hero have the sniffles in a western. So basically, what did I remember from the movie? I remembered the *oddities*. All the things studio executives want to remove from any script or any good idea. It takes an established filmmaker, even in the fertile nineties, to put something new on the screen. Whenever it happens, even in one of the oldest genres in film, the western, it makes everything old new again. There is no doubt that this story could have been told as a pure revenge story. We know it could because a ton of other westerns already did it. The point of a good genre flick is to take what we know and turn it. This film does that expertly. What I can't remember is why I waited thirty years to watch this film again.

He Oughta' Get Shot

Gene Hackman plays the sheriff, who doesn't allow guns within the city limit but has no trouble with johns cutting up the local saloon "whores." With Hackman's likable persona, he comes off as the good guy for the first half of the film, but we see the violence that is deep within him when he interacts with English Bob and anyone else who doesn't obey his no gun ordinance. Gene Hackman didn't want to make the film, because he didn't want to make violent pictures anymore. Eastwood was able to convince him that the film, while having several violent scenes, is actually a story about justice and the effects of taking another human's life. Clint Eastwood said, "[Little Bill] didn't wear the usual costume of the bad guy. He was a sheriff who had noble ideas. He had this small town and ran it with a lot of strength. He felt that guns shouldn't be allowed in town." There has never been a time in America when violence wasn't an issue. It's true that now mass shootings are a daily event, and as a culture we have looked the other way, but even in the nineties, gun ownership was a major issue. The Second Amendment was a controversial issue, but here is a film helmed by a lifelong, vocal Republican who created a town where the government (aka the sheriff) takes the guns away from the citizens. It's not a cut-and-dried plot point. One can certainly see why the sheriff thinks this will make the town safer; however, it didn't protect the working women at the saloon. It gives audiences a reason to debate the issue. No one accused Eastwood of pushing an agenda. I could find no articles from 1992 where a Democrat accused him of trying to say that taking away guns is a good or bad thing. Nor was there a Republican blaming Eastwood for being antigun by showing a town without guns. Eastwood had a matter-of-fact description of the plot point, "You believe in gun control, especially if you are controlling it." Isn't that the truth? It doesn't matter which side of the issue you are on; you always agree with it when you have total control over the decision about it. The movies of the nineties were a protected bubble where an artist could wonder about an idea and make us think about that idea. Sometimes it was an idea that we might just have never stumbled upon without seeing it played out by the characters in the story.

Unforgiven was released the same year as Quentin Tarantino's directorial debut of *Reservoir Dogs*. The way that each film handle violence is pretty stark. The inhumane way Mr. Blonde (Michael Madsen) disfigures the police officer to the tune of "Stuck in the Middle with You" is pretty much night and day from the way Eastwood kills the lawman in his movie. While Mr. Blonde sings and dances and loves the game, William Munny only has one response to the sheriff when Gene Hackman begs for his life by saying, "I don't deserve this." In classic Eastwood acting style of a squint and a guttural growl, he just speaks the truth and says, "Deserve's got nothing to do with this." BOOM. Both films deal with crime, criminals, and the law. One from a brand new director playing in a genre film, the other from a seasoned director who practically represents the western genre.

So much of *Unforgiven* is quiet and unseen. There is darkness everywhere. The beginning of the story takes place in a saloon where a cowboy starts slashing the face of the woman he purchased. The entire scene is lit with only one small lamp. It's nighttime, and the sound creates most of the violence. Besides one shot of her face being slashed, the majority of the screen is in darkness. This is the same way the end shootout takes place. There is a thunderstorm outside, and the saloon is dark. We see parts of their faces, but most of the violence takes place in the dark with only our imagination to light the way. Eastwood wanted this look because he respected his audience. "Audiences are very smart. They don't have to see everything," he said. Trusting that the audience will get there and putting the violence in the dark makes it all the worse because we fill in what is our own personal worst idea. Does the john punch her in the gut? Does he smash her jaw or poke her eyes? I don't know what you think he did to her. Later, in a scene where she offers herself to Munny, we can see the scars of the slash we were shown, but the horrors this character experienced are only known in our imagination. It is this trust from an old-time Hollywood filmmaker that makes this picture a classic nineties film. It trusts you to draw your own conclusions. It offers up the best way to tell a morality play, it leaves the preaching and the morals to you and your friend while you debate the film on the ride home from the theater. Its characters have their own issues to contend with. They aren't going to help put the pieces together for you.

"Give [the audience] the chance to imagine with you. Give them a chance to participate in the film—not just voyeur it. That is something that will make the film a little deeper for them." - Clint Eastwood.

B: *Malcolm X*

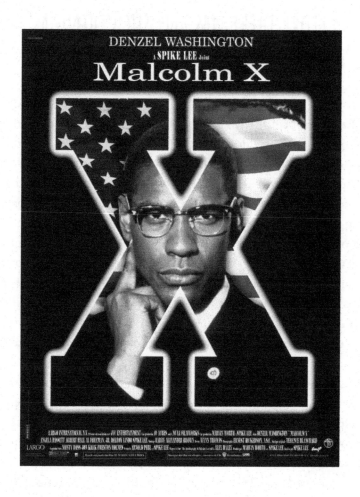

"Before there was any such thing as a Republican or a Democrat, we were Black."

Malcolm X begins with an American flag that fills the screen from side to shining side. Denzel Washington as Malcolm X delivers a voice-over in the same cadence as the real X, "Brothers and sisters, I am here to tell you that I charge the White man with being the greatest murderer on Earth." Director Spike Lee intercuts between the flag and the real-life footage of Rodney King being beaten by LA police officers. As X goes on to charge the White man with murder, destruction, kidnapping, we watch as a man is beaten to a pulp by agents representing our government. This footage was only a few months old when Lee used it to start his biopic of the Black civil rights legend Malcolm X. The flag starts to burn as we watch the violence against one Black man committed by men who pledged to protect and to serve. The flag eventually burns the stars and stripes into a charred X. Lee said he wanted to start the film with the then-current atrocity because "By doing this, we showed that the conditions Malcolm X talked about are still with us today. It's not a history lesson, it's not a museum piece, it's not a dinosaur, and these are not fossils. This stuff is still with us."

That was said in 1992, but as I write this very sentence in 2023, footage was just released of the police murder of Tyre Nichols in Memphis. If I would have written this sentence a month ago, there would have been a different murder to discuss. There will be a different one in a month from now. Whether it is the 1960s or the 1990s or the 2020s, this is a problem that won't go away until police officers are held accountable for acts of murder. The film is barely two minutes old, and all of American history, all White people, and every police officer who ever turned a blue-blindfolded eye to abuse has been called out. This must be a Spike Lee film.

Revolution

Spike Lee has been my second favorite filmmaker, after Quentin Tarantino, since the nineties. I am not saying I love all of Lee's films, but every one of them is worth watching. He commands the camera with such confidence that he must always be in the conversation with the greatest directors of all time. His use of the primary color palette in his work mixed with the layering of music, placed upon a story worth watching, is why films like *Mo' Better Blues, Da 5 Bloods, Do the Right Thing*, and *The 25th Hour* are movies I have watched over and over. (Notice only one of those films is from the nineties; see, I watch films from other decades.) But those aren't the reasons I love a Spike Lee film. I love them because he pushes our goddamn buttons like a cranky toddler who missed his nap at a theme park. The ending of *Do the Right Thing*, when they destroy Danny Aiello's pizza parlor, always burns my crust. When Bleek plays his bad solo at the end of *Mo' Better Blues*, I am so mad that his career has been taken from him.

Malcolm X has a scene, we will get to it soon, that might just be the most ultimate button-pushing scene in his career, and I couldn't be happier. Spike Lee isn't making nice films for you to watch from a comfortable distance. He gets in your face and tries his best to shake the complacency out of every White person in the audience. And every Black person. In *Mo' Better Blues*, he admonished his own community for not supporting jazz music which is a creation of his culture. Characters say over and over throughout *Malcolm X* that Black people need to stop taking the White man's poison. Lee knows he has been given a chance to open eyes to the issues of the day. He might be more interested in opening the eyes of his Black patrons, but he certainly opened mine to the racism that my country unleashed upon his people. Songwriter Amy Ray wrote a song called "Didn't Know a Damn Thing" where she talks about growing up in the seventies and eighties and not being taught anything about Black history. Her lyric that resonates with me is:

In the back of the school bus I was reading my history
but it didn't say nothing about the kid sitting next to me.

The education system in the eighties spent no time on African American history in my small Ohio town. I learned about forty acres and a mule from Spike Lee's production company. I didn't really know anything about Malcolm X's life until I saw this film. The education system is under attack today by Florida governor Ron DeSantis, who wants to remove what little ground was gained from when I was in school. But our education system was always controlled by the ruling class. The scene where Malcolm X attends an all-White school is heartbreaking. His White teacher, played by David Patrick Kelly, calls him the N word and tries to take away his dream of becoming a lawyer. When the character of Baines (Albert Hall) tells Malcolm that ALL White people are devils, it rings true to Malcolm because every White person he came in contact with was evil. It was 1946, and there was no one worried about Black lives mattering in any real way. They weren't getting loans to amass wealth, they weren't being hired for jobs with upward mobility, they weren't being educated the same as White kids. I got my Black history education from movies like *Boyz n the Hood, Menace II Society*, and Lee's films. What I learned from him, I should have learned in my education. I didn't know a damn thing.

Lee could have just made simpler films. With his talent as a director, he could have made easier-to-digest fluff pictures, but instead he made ones that inspired discussion. He said, "I'm one of the couple people that slipped through this crack, and the Black underclass is now larger than it's ever been. The anger is still there. It's evident in what happened in Los Angeles and that really is just the tip of the iceberg." Didn't he know it. This was happening almost thirty years away from Black Lives Matter. Film didn't change the world, but it did educate me and bring a way of life to my White middle class existence that just never would have happened if it weren't for films that were daring and controversial and had the opportunity to play everywhere and then be available for rent for a dollar at every local video store.

The scene that truly is the button pusher in *Malcolm X* is when he is walking across a campus and a young White girl approaches him and asks what a White person who believes in his cause can do to help the movement, and X replies, "Nothing." He walks on, and she walks away heartbroken. This is based on an actual incident that occurred which X discussed in *The Autobiography of Malcolm X* by Alex Haley and Malcolm X which the movie is based on. X said later in his life that he regretted what he said to the girl. What Spike Lee does as a director is to let this moment sit there and not sugarcoat it. He does have Denzel Washington, in a voice-over later on in the film, say that he regrets some of what he said, but Lee doesn't wipe away the power of the scene. Of course X is wrong when he says White people can do nothing to help. But at that moment, White people weren't doing anything to help. It remains to be seen if the murder of George Floyd in 2020, which seemed to wake up some Americans to the issue, will make White people demand changes for their Black brothers and sisters. With the aforementioned death of Tyre Nichols, it seems like nothing has changed, or the changes aren't enough to save Black men from dying for no good reason. Scenes like this are so important in film because they make people disagree with what they are seeing.

When a young White girl asks Malcolm X on a campus what she can do, he replied, "Nothing." Does that motivate viewers or anger them?
(Photo courtesy of 40 Acres & A Mule Filmworks)

In that moment a White person who isn't racist and wants to see the world be better can say to themselves that they can do something, and in that moment, they might also realize they have actually been doing what Malcolm X was asking them to do, "Nothing." Let's hope the scene makes people *want* to do something.

A Change Is Gonna Come

Provocative filmmaking shouldn't be canceled. It shouldn't be feared; it should be celebrated. Malcolm X is wrong about a ton of things in the film. One of the periods of his life Lee spends the most time on is his devotion to the *honorable* Elijah Muhammad (Al Freeman Jr.). X says over and over what a great and moral man Elijah is. But he wasn't. He was a womanizer who was impregnating young girls and having the temple support them, which is money laundering. This doesn't make Malcolm X a bad person for being wrong; it makes him human. His intentions were always to help his fellow Black man, but he was never perfect. Denzel Washington saw this when he was creating the man on-screen. He said, "One of the things I loved about him was the fact that he was willing to change his way of thinking. 'Maybe I was wrong about that,' and then, 'I'll try this.' He was constantly evolving, getting better, and growing in many ways. And it's something we can all learn from." It truly is something we can all learn from. We shouldn't be held accountable for life on the words we use in the moment. Even when microphones and cameras are pointed at us, we have to be allowed to grow and change. Malcolm X did, and the script by Lee and Arnold Perl allows us to see why, how, and when he changed.

There is no way to discuss this movie and not discuss Denzel Washington's performance. What can really be said about watching an actor fill a role so perfectly that doesn't sound trite and redundant? I have no idea who the second choice for playing Malcolm was, but it also should have been Denzel Washington, because he's just that perfect. The growth throughout the film is impressive. He doesn't play young Malcolm Little with any hint of the powerful man he will grow to be. He smiles wide and enjoys every moment of his renegade youth. Another side of the character is revealed in the Russian roulette scene.

Malcolm and Shorty (Spike Lee) are planning a heist with Rudy (Roger Guenveur Smith), who brought the idea to them and wants to be in charge. Washington creates such a menacing person as he sucks on a bullet and then puts just one bullet in the gun and starts pulling the trigger twice on himself before moving to Rudy. The fact that this can be the same actor who plays the comic scenes of getting his hair straightened, or swing dancing, or losing his mind in solitary confinement in prison, or giving complex and inspiring speeches is just incredible what Washington did with this part.

Malcolm X was complex and more than just one thing. It truly takes three and a half hours to try to do justice to his life that had so many different chapters in it. One can make the argument that this scene or that scene should be cut, but it was all the little moments that added up to paint a complex figure. If we want films with complex stories and characters, it will take time. Humans are more than one thing. Spike Lee has always done a great job of displaying these complexities of the human experience, filtered through his culture. He summed up his work at this point in 1992: "My six films I've done so far, for me, really show the variety of the African-American experience, that Black people are not one monolithic group." Lucky for us, neither are his films.

Chapter 4
1993

A: *Short Cuts*

"ISN'T IT WONDERFUL, MARIAN, HOW WE CAN SKATE AROUND AN ISSUE?"

Short Cuts's opening credits is a barrage of famous names of the actors who star in director Robert Altman's mishmash of Raymond Carver short stories in a script written by Altman and Frank Barhydt. Before you can say, "Hey, she's in this film?" another famous actor's name appears on-screen. Just to let you know that Altman is fine with you stargazing, he has two characters do the same thing in the second scene of the movie, where someone recognizes former *Jeopardy!* host Alex Trebek at a concert. The characters point and gawk until one of the husbands ask, "Who's Alex Trebek?" Isn't this just what we love most about fame? Someone will recognize you, and someone won't know who the hell you are. Well, as a film buff, I sure hope you know who Robert Altman is. He is one of those one-of-a-kind directors whom people think there are a million of. There was only one Robert Altman. He was famous for overlapping dialogue and for not being all that concerned with plot. *Short Cuts* has plenty of both.

His movies seemed to pop into pop culture once a decade. In the seventies, he had *M*A*S*H*; in the eighties, *Popeye*; the nineties, *The Player*; and in the aughts, *Gosford Park*, which would bear the fruit of that TV obsession *Downton Abbey*. *The Player* was the talk of 1992 and seriously has the best ending of any film ever. (Here's looking at you, *Casablanca*. Sorry, I got on the plane with *The Player*.) In fact, the end of the *The Player* is so good, I refuse to spoil it for you, because you probably haven't seen it, or you have forgotten how it ends. *The Player* was such a big hit that it afforded Altman the chance to make any movie he wanted, and he chose *Short Cuts,* which is why I am covering that film instead of *The Player* because the only way *Short Cuts* could ever have been made was by the sheer Hollywood force of someone who had momentary clout. I will always be a big fan of Robert Altman, because he took that cache and didn't make a big action picture, he made this gloriously wandering film that is about everything and nothing at the same time. Even by nineties standards, this movie is a hard sell. It is three hours and eight minutes long, has no plot, and no easy way to describe it, but hot damn, do I love it.

Prisoner of Life

So what is it about? Good question. My simple answer is marriage. No. Relationships. No. The struggles of work. No. How mankind pointlessly tries to battle nature. No. It's a look at how parenting is a no-win job. No. It's the very issue that one must face head on when one knows that we are only animals hurling on a spinning rock on the way to death. No. Maybe it's these collections of stories about:

1. A jazz singer (Annie Ross) and her cellist daughter (Lori Singer) who are trying to get over being left by their husband/father.
2. A cheating motorcycle cop (Tim Robbins) and his wife (Madeleine Stowe) and kids and a dog that the cop hates.
3. A waitress (Lily Tomlin) at a coffee shop and her husband (Tom Waits) who is a limo driver.
4. A couple (Robert Downey Jr. and Lili Taylor) who house-sit for some neighbors and can't stop snooping in the house.
5. A newscaster (Bruce Davison) and his wife (Andie MacDowell) whose son is turning nine and gets hit by a car and then they are harassed by a baker (Lyle Lovett) and reunited with the newscaster's father (Jack Lemmon).
6. A group of fishing buddies (Buck Henry, Huey Lewis, Fred Ward) who find a dead body drowned in the river.
7. Two couples who meet at the cellist concert and meet up for dinner. One couple contains a clown (Anne Archer) and one of the fishermen (Fred Ward); the other couple is a doctor (Matthew Modine) and an artist (Julianne Moore).
8. A phone sex worker (Jennifer Jason Leigh) and her pool

cleaning husband (Chris Penn).

9. A pilot (Peter Gallagher) who is spraying bug poison over LA and can't accept that his ex-wife (Frances McDormand) has moved on.

Are you riveted yet? Wait, there's more. They are all kind of connected. The jazz singer is the mother of the cellist and they live next to the newscaster, who broadcasts the news report about the spraying of the medflies that are killed by the pilot, whose ex-wife is having an affair with the motorcycle cop, who is married to the sister of the couple who is having dinner with the clown, who buys a cake at the same place where the newscaster's wife cancels her cake after the waitress hits the newscaster's kid with her car, who then tells the house-sitting wife because she is the waitress's daughter. Go ahead and try to fact-check that sentence. The film is wisely scored with jazz music, because this film is like a jazz piece that improvises on a theme and then returns to a familiar melody for a moment, and then goes off on a tangent and back around again.

The script is certainly impressive how seamlessly it bounces around through over twenty characters, never allowing us to forget where each character's emotion is within the story, but it is the directing of the film that is truly staggering. Altman is in such command of the emotional crests of the story. This is a really good example to show someone what a director does in a film. The cuts from story to story are not just done without thought. They are done with planned connections, just like the interweaving of the stories. A few examples are when the two couples meet up for a BBQ, the fish on the grill starts to smoke, and Altman cuts to a car running in a garage filled with smoke. He cuts from one person making a peanut butter sandwich to someone eating peanut butter out of the jar. After the kid is hit by the car, he cuts to the limo driver, who is watching TV, and the voice-over on the commercial says, "Accidents happen." These are all things that had to be planned before shooting. They don't just happen. There was planning and work done to keep the story rolling. The point of the film is that we are all connected, but not directly. Other films have tried this idea of multiple stories happening in the same film. Examples are *Playing by Heart*, *Go*, or *200 Cigarettes*. What makes *Short Cuts* stand out is the idea that these connections are not pointed out to the characters. They happen by accident and are not overly glorified. From here on I will address the characters by the actors' name so you can keep them straight. At Lyle Lovett's bakery, Peter Gallagher, Andie MacDowell, and Anne Archer all show up at the same time to order cakes for their own personal stories, but none of them interact with each other. We know they are all in the film, but they don't. Most of the connections are meaningful but not dramatic. By doing this, it makes the movie less gimmicky and also is such an important way to demonstrate the importance of community. That person you watch sing in a jazz club just might be the neighbor of the mother of the kid your mom hits with a car. It shows how community and society matter to us, even when we are not aware of the connections. To put it in today's parlance, it's like when you get a Facebook request from a new friend and find that you have one friend in common, and it's that old friend from high school who you haven't talked to in years. You didn't even know they knew each other.

To Hell with Love

One of the provocative recurring images in the film is the naked female body. What makes it more provocative than most film's use of nudity is that none of the scenes involve sexual intercourse. It is the image of the female body, usually distorted in some way, that we see over and over. Lori Singer strips and jumps completely naked into the pool and then floats as if she is dead. This is shown through the slats of a wooden fence as Chris Penn spies on her. In the next scene, the fishermen finds a completely naked female body floating underwater along the shoreline. Later, Madeleine Stowe poses naked for Julianne Moore, sitting twisted to the side. Moore already has several paintings of fully nude women hanging on her wall who look sort of distorted as if they are underwater. These connections had to be a nightmare to pepper through the script. But Altman juggles all these moments and cuts back and forth at the right time.

Probably the most famous scene in this movie involves a half naked Julianne Moore in one of the best scenes in film history that displays the demystification of marriage nudity. Moore and Matthew Modine have a heated argument about an affair that happened three years ago. He begs her for the truth about whether she had an affair at a party they attended. She explains what happened with a monologue about going out to buy alcohol with a stranger, while she is totally exposed from the waist down after she spills wine on her skirt and effortlessly takes off her skirt revealing she wasn't wearing any underwear. As she uses a blow-dryer on the wine spill, she admits she had sex with a drunk stranger at this party. The fact that she is naked from the waist down, and is fully on display, means absolutely nothing to her husband—the fact that she had an affair only means slightly more than nothing to him. Nudity in films is almost always glamorized, but this is just a scene between two people who have seen each other's private parts for years and just don't give a shit about them any more.

Earlier in the film, when Moore and Stowe talk about sex with their respective husbands, we get the feeling that Moore is unsatisfied and that passion is no longer alive in her marriage. The fact that her sexual anatomy is on perfect display with a top that is longer on each side which basically creates an arrow pointing to where she wants attention, is totally lost on her husband. Modine is full of anger and hurt as he learns, for the first time, about the truth of something he only suspected up to this point. We can tell it has been weighing on him for three years—and no one says any of this to us. Altman trusts his actors and his audience to read the subtext. I am sure many people weren't watching the scene like they should have. They were distracted by Moore's body. That's on them. It isn't on Altman, nor what Moore did as an actress with this scene. At the end of the scene when Modine walks away, she says, "He didn't cum in me. I swear." This unasked admission is a line of dialogue you just don't hear when people talk about affairs in films. She is trying to allow him to save face and have a completely open conversation. This nude scene caused lots of controversy at the time, but if you want to have an honest look at married life, you don't have to look further than this scene. Fred Ward and Anne Archer arrive right after the fight, and Modine and Moore put on a happy face, not showing any bruises from this suspected admission of adultery. Altman then jump-cuts to Lili Taylor's face, beat up and bloodied, but that is because her husband, Robert Downey Jr., is a makeup artist and he painted her up for fun to take pictures that look like he stabbed and killed her. Every couple puts on a face, and we don't alway see what is real. The beating one takes from a spouse can be nothing more than movie makeup and easily seen, but it is fake. Or the beating can be totally hidden from view, but it is real. I passionately love this grown-up movie. Not surprising, later on in the evening, Archer, Ward, Moore, and Modine paint their faces in clown makeup, their true faces hidden from each other.

The film allows both sexes to have affairs. Tim Robbins is having an affair with Frances McDormand, but she is having an affair with someone else. Robbins' wife, Stowe, admits she had an affair before the kids were born. Chris Penn struggles with whether Jennifer Jason Leigh is technically faithful, since she is a phone sex worker. But, there is something that makes her phone calls seem dirtier than Moore's or Stowe's nude scenes because she talks dirty to her customers while doing her daily chores, like feeding her toddler or getting ready for dinner. Her husband watches her from a distance. He wonders if she is sexually gratified by talking dirty all day while men masterbate to her words. She doesn't physically touch them, despite getting them off. In fact, just like Julianne Moore, she could use the excuse of "He didn't cum in me. I swear." This matters little to Chris Penn. But is he faithful? Earlier he watched Lori Singer through the fence strip and get in the pool, and he hits on some young girl towards the end of the film. Everything is delightfully murky and blurred in this movie.

Jack Lemmon arrives halfway through the film with a monologue that lasts five and a half minutes. Most of the film is cut together with shorter scenes and very few extended monologues. So this long story, set in the middle, feels different from the rest of the picture. It gives the viewer a break from all the jumping around. Lemmon tries to explain to Bruce Davison why he wasn't around when Davison was young and tells a story of an affair. He delivers the monologue with such grace and humanity. Jack Lemmon isn't in the film very much outside of this scene. Unlike the rest of the cast, he doesn't interact with the other characters—outside of a brief moment of bumping into Anne Archer when he first gets to the hospital to see his grandson. The film is filled with characters whom we see over and over again throughout the story. Jack Lemmon's character hasn't even met his grandson or Andie MacDowell before this tragic moment at the hospital. He hasn't been a part of Davison's life, but Lemmon sells this monologue filled with regret, like the pro that he is. The fact that this minor character tells this widespread story shows us that even the people that don't effect our lives on a daily basis still have their battle scars that they carry with them. Altman leaves no story stone left unturned. We need to pay attention to everyone around us and understand that we don't understand everything about them. It truly is a pleasure to watch Jack Lemmon in this film. He really had such a fruitful decade in the nineties, with the *Grumpy Old Men* movies and even more so as the down-in-the-dumps salesmen in *Glengarry Glen Ross*. He was blessed to be able to cap his distinguished career with such wonderful films. I am so glad I never had to see him play Aquaman's uncle, King Starfish.

Conversation on a Barstool

To give us a break from all the talking, Altman has enlisted true-life jazz singer Annie Ross to perform songs in a nightclub act. The character announces these songs are from her act from years ago, and while the songs seem to be standards from the fifties or sixties, they are actually new compositions written by nineties pop stars. The songs are quality, and I am actually kind of shocked that current jazz artists like John Pizzarelli, Hailey Tuck, or Madeleine Peyroux have never covered "Conversation on a Barstool," written by Bono and the Edge; "Punishing Kiss," written by Elvis Costello and Cait O'Riordan; or "To Hell With Love", written by Doc Pomus and Dr. John. Annie Ross broke into the music scene in the late fifties and had wonderful jazz albums like *New Sounds from France* and *Annie by Candlelight*, but my personal favorite is her jazz interpretations of the score from *Gypsy*. She has a gravelling well-traveled voice that lets the listener feel the pain in the lyrics of her songs. In the film, her music punctuates the emotions of the characters in the moment. The classical songs played by Lori Singer on the cello are also truly played by Singer, who even wrote one of the songs. Having real musicians perform the music gives the film, which already feels like a look into real people's lives, even more realism, which was always Altman's strength as a filmmaker.

With fifteen minutes left in *Short Cuts*, fisherman Buck Henry shows up at a Fotomat to pick up his one-hour photos of the dead girl floating in the river and is mistakenly given the pictures of Lili Taylor, who is there to pick up her pictures of her looking beaten and stabbed by Robert Downey Jr. Even these two characters from completely different storylines are connected for the briefest moment; both of them thinking the other is a true sicko. The point of *Short Cuts* becomes evident as they give each other the side-eye. We are all connected. We are all part of each other's story. The kid in the hospital bed next to you, the waitress at the diner, the newsman on TV, the cop on the beat, the baker, all of them. Each moment of being out of our homes affects someone else. We are so used to only focusing on the main characters in the films we watch and the people in our close circles of our life that we can forget every stranger has a backstory as well. There are no main characters, there aren't even supporting characters, in our lives. We are all just equal humans. Some people will help us in our low moments, like the baker who eventually comforts the distraught parents, and some will let the dead just float in the water while they fish, but none of it happens without it rolling over to someone else's life.

B: *Menace II Society*

"DO YOU CARE WHETHER YOU LIVE OR YOU DIE? I DON'T KNOW."

It's really hard for a movie to do something that no movie has ever done before. I am going to go out on a limb and say *Menace II Society* is the only film that uses the P word and the N word over a film company's logo. In fact, I counted thirteen swear words that are said as the New Line Cinema logo is displayed. (Wait, maybe *Teenage Ninja Mutant Turtles* also did that. I'll double-check.) Now why does this matter? Because it's worth pausing a moment to think about the fact that in 1993, a corporation allowed filmmakers to set the tone for their movie by using the vernacular of the characters from their world over top of the corporate logo. For a moment, a company allowed art to trump pretend social blowback. Today, there would be disclaimers saying the opinions expressed over New Line Cinema's logo are solely those of the filmmakers and do not represent the views of the studio. The brazenness of the first ten seconds of the film, followed by the shocking first four minutes, should ignite pleasure in any serious lover of film and art. *Menace* was my favorite film that I watched for this book that I had never seen before. I am not sure why I never saw this one, but I hadn't. I'm glad I didn't watch it back in 1993, because it landed so much harder in 2023.

The film begins with two teenagers from South Central LA going into a Korean convenience store to buy some beer. The proprietors give them the eye and keep a close watch on them. The boys complain about being followed but stay cool, buy the beer, and start to leave. That is when the male Korean worker says, under his breath, "I feel sorry for your mother." That is all it takes to set O-Dog (Larenz Tate) off. Tate isn't built like most actors who get cast in a role described as "America's worst nightmare—young, black, and didn't give a fuck." Tate was a sitcom actor, with a slight built, and was very cute. Tate said, "I had this sort of Disney look. This really fresh, young kind of look, but I'm originally from Chicago, so my interpretation of the guy was based on some guys that I had seen in Chicago." His acting and understanding of the character won over the Hughes brothers, who cowrote and codirected the film. They were looking for that "type" of character who immediately scares an audience, but by finding someone who was as nice looking as Tate, they created a truer picture of what was going on in LA. It wasn't just a certain type of kid; it could be *any* type of kid. They were all left behind. Allen Hughes summed it by saying, "This is even scarier. This charming-looking kid oozing all this evil."

The opening murder of the Korean store owners introduces us to the heavy in the film, O-Dog, as well as his accomplice, and our narrator, Caine (Tyrin Turner), who just stands there, frozen, as the murder is committed. Caine begins his voice-over which takes us through the entire film, with "It was funny like that in the hood." The title of *Menace II Society* fills the screen, and we head back to the past when Caine was a little kid as he watches crimes be committed right outside his bedroom door. While watching the film, I realized that what we are really watching here is a Black version of *Goodfellas*. The Caine character is Ray Liotta, who is our narrator/criminal—but one we root for—and O-Dog is the Joe Pesci type—the guy who just takes it a step too far and lets the audience know exactly how dangerous a world we are entering. Don't say one of them is funny; don't talk about the other one's mother. Either way, if you push them too far, they're going to kill you.

I was happy to see in interviews that the Hughes brothers pointed directly to *Goodfellas* as well as *Scarface* as their major influences. Albert Hughes said, "*Goodfellas* is what really got us into the gangster movies. We used that movie as an example of how to do something right." Twin brothers Allen and Albert Hughes were just twenty years old when they directed this no-holds-barred tale of what it was like to live in the Watts area of LA in the early nineties. This was their directorial debut. They had directed music videos for several rap artists back when MTV was still playing videos. For their first film, they wanted to pay tribute to the movies they loved from directors like Martin Scorsese and Brian De Palma. They cowrote the script with Tyger Williams and got the green light from New Line Cinema to helm a story that would focus on Black teens trying to survive life in the gun-riddled area of Watts, which had never really recovered from the 1965 riots.

Stay Strapped in South Central

The story of what it was like to grow up Black in South Central LA had been done two years before in John Singleton's *Boyz n the Hood*. But *Menace* strays far from the feel of *Boyz*, which has a more hopeful, after-school-special feel. *Menace* has a more dangerous vibe that displays what the Watts area was going through. There were gun and economic problems for the Black citizens left behind by the American dream which was only ever available to White people. This is a problem that has no easy fix and, quite honestly, might just have no solution at all. It certainly is a problem that no one bothered to solve in the nineties (or in any decade since). The violence and destruction of Black people in this area of California just bubbles up every now and again and then is ignored once more. In watching *Boyz* and *Menace* back-to-back, there was such a feeling of truth to *Menace* that made it still soar today. It isn't that *Boyz* is a bad film; it just feels like it's an easy answer. If these kids just had a dad, they would be fine. (Circling back to where we started, *Boyz* also uses the N word over the company logo of the film but not the P word, so again *Menace* tops it, but it does show how corporations weren't so scared in the nineties.)

Menace tries and succeeds to show how Caine honestly wants to do the right thing; he just truly doesn't know what the right thing to do is. White politicians who spout platitudes about education or parenting have no idea what it would be like to grow up where violence appears to be the only solution. "*Menace* came about because we were frustrated and tired of White people saying, 'They deserve what they get.'" said Allen Hughes. I don't see how anyone could watch *Menace* and not be moved by the circumstances that these kids are growing up with and empathize immediately with them. When a film doesn't judge its characters, doesn't shy away from the truth, and doesn't force a fake positive outlook onto its story, that story can be as relevant thirty years later as it was the moment it was written. One of the best examples of following the truth of a story is that there are virtually no White people in the entire film. From my count, I think there were three. One guy who hired someone to steal a car and two cops who beat Caine up for no reason. There shouldn't be White people in this film. There sure weren't any White people trying to help this situation. This isn't a movie about Black people hating White people; it's about Black people trying to stay alive in a war zone. Not every film should be a representative rainbow. Later in this book, I will point out why *Pleasantville* had to be an all-White cast. Be sure to remember that it was the exact right decision for *Menace* to be an all-Black cast and the opposite can be just as true for *Pleasantville*. This type of casting can't be done anymore, but in the nineties, truth was the guiding light, not fearing reactions to the truth.

None of these characters even mention White people. These kids are not blaming America for their lot in life; they don't even know it was America that left them behind. When Caine has the chance to move to Atlanta, he says, "Ain't nothing gonna change in Atlanta. I mean, I'm still gonna be Black." The reason I love this script is that Caine is right and wrong at the exact same time. That is the beauty of this film. Just about everyone is both. Yes, Caine will still be Black in Atlanta. Cops could still put him in a chokehold for rolling a stop sign and kill him, but the everyday violence of where he is wouldn't be the same. He would be better off with going away with Jada Pinkett and not being influenced by O-Dog, but he doesn't have a glimpse outside of his upbringing to know that. Caine may have grandparents who are shown as understanding, proud Christians, but they have not been able to counteract what Caine has learned from watching his father just shoot a man point-blank at a poker game for not paying a small debt.

Caine's grandfather delivers two moments that are subtle and doesn't stop the entire film to let the viewer know something important is happening. Caine and his grandparents are watching *It's a Wonderful*

Life on television. As Jimmy Stewart smiles and hugs his children at the climatic ending, so happy to be alive, Caine's grandfather glances at Caine and nods to the TV as if to say, "See?" Caine looks at the TV and shakes his head as if to say, "What the fuck am I watching?" The grandfather thinks the film is teaching a lesson of what is important in life, and the grandson is looking at this black-and-white old film as if it is in another language—because it basically is. It's a great way to show how these pop culture touchstones of morality that older generations grew up with are like science fiction movies to these kids. O-Dog arrives and the grandfather asks the boys to sit down. O-Dog and Caine endure a lecture from Caine's grandfather about how they are not living a good life. The speech has plenty of scripture mixed in for good measure. Neither boy responds to the word of God, despite both wearing crosses. But those crosses are fashion accessories, not a way of life. Grandfather's words are as relevant to them as Frank Capra's. As they leave the house, the grandfather stands in the doorway and asks Caine, "Do you care whether you live or die?" I thought that would be the end of the scene. If my grandfather asked me that question, it would be rhetorical. But Caine stops and actually thinks about the question. He answers sincerely, "I don't know." The answer shocked me because I didn't expect any answer at all. When Caine's answer was totally ambivalent, it truly struck a chord. Very few White kids had to wonder about the answer to that question in the early nineties. But for Black kids, it was something they had to decide. Caine isn't being snarky; he truly doesn't know the answer to the question. In a film with a lot of violence to show the way that this area of people have been left behind, this simple exchange displays the hopelessness of the situation so well.

You Been Played

The film, outside of the narration, has a *Goodfellas* connection in the fact that both films are directed by people who love movies. The Hughes brothers even do the *Goodfellas* long shot. Just as Ray Liotta and Lorraine Bracco enter the nightclub winding through the cellars of the clubs, the Hughes brothers have a two-minute shot as Caine enters a party. The camera goes from the car, through the house, outside to the backyard, to a garage. Just like *Goodfellas, Menace* has the same excitement, use of music, and confident filmmakers who use lighting, directing, and sets to tell the story. I submit that *Goodfellas* is to *Godfather III* as *Menace* is to *Boyz n the Hood*. *Boyz* and *III* try to teach us lessons and have the air of importance. *Goodfellas* and *Menace* are alive and are not trying to teach us anything. They are trying to tell a story about a confined group of people. Neither are stories of an entire culture, just a group of criminals, in a film that respects film audiences, and wants to be something new. When these comparative films are watched back-to-back, the films that rise to the top are the ones that were tightly told, had dangerous characters with motives that we understood, and felt real.

I asked the editor of *Cracking the Wire During the Era of Black Lives Matter*, Ronda Racha Penrice, who has covered Black pop culture for years, to put *Boyz* and *Menace* in its proper context during the nineties and now. This is what she had to say:

When John Singleton's *Boyz n the Hood* hit theaters in 1991, mere months after *New Jack City*, a floodgate of hood films followed. Most of those did not truly stand out until one did. That one was the Hughes brothers' *Menace II Society* just two years later. But it's almost unfair to compare *Menace* and *Boyz* because they are different films. They aren't, however, completely different realities. Because the Hollywood ecosystem has traditionally revolved around proven success, there really couldn't be a *Menace* without *Boyz*. Making *Boyz* was a risk that paid off. Since it did work, scoring huge at the box office, *Menace* got made. I just don't think we could have gotten it otherwise. So while some folks, myself included, might prefer *Menace* for its rawness, the truth is they are just two sides of the same coin. Singleton's primary message in *Boyz* is that Tre (Cuba Gooding Jr.) can survive the hood because he has a father (Laurence Fishburne). *Menace* shows the impact of not having a Black father or anyone else really present. Not in question in either is that Black boys are under attack and at risk of not surviving their young adult years in their urban neighborhoods. While that is the main thesis in both films, they play out differently based on the perspective of those telling the stories.

Boyz is more hopeful because it shows an LA where a Black community can be found. That more intact Black community is essentially nonexistent in *Menace's* LA, forcing young Black people to basically raise themselves. Because I lived in LA, I know both Singleton's and the Hughes brothers' portraits are valid. Like most cities, it just depends on where you go. Over thirty years later, what both these films most represent is how viable the creative freedom many Black filmmakers still advocate for today truly is. Instead of delivering the *Boyz* clone *Menace* studio execs probably expected, the Hughes brothers proved that Black filmmakers and Black stories are not monolithic, that they are also layered and multifaceted. So it's not a question of which film is better than the other, but rather which dose of reality the viewer can handle.

The main reason I selected to write about *Menace* was because of how refreshing it was to watch a movie that just didn't worry about if the audience was going to be offended about what they put on the screen. The Hughes brothers weren't trying to make any statements about all Black people in this film. They wanted to tell a truthful, cautionary tale, and they did it. In interviews from the time, they could see what was coming in film, how artists would be censored and held accountable in ways that are ridiculous for artists. This quote by Albert Hughes sums it up: "[Filmmakers] aren't even considered artists anymore because you have to have this social responsibility. Art shouldn't be considered a social responsibility. You shouldn't have to be socially responsible in art. You should be able to do what you want to do. If your vision is crooked, if your vision is racist, it is still your art . . . that's you. That is what you are doing, that's your personality. You shouldn't be imposed by outside people going, 'Don't do this.'" His brother Allen went on to say that not all Italians are the Italians in *Goodfellas*; it is just a story of that underclass. The same goes with their film. This is not the experience of all Black people. This is the experience of gangsters in Watts in LA in 1993, not even a specific gang. They went out of their way to not associate Caine or O-Dog with a larger gang. It is so refreshing to hear artists speak freely and explain so perfectly the difference between creating a society and reflecting one. I have never understood why directors, writers, and actors are held to standards that no politician, president, congressperson, or governor is ever held to. Politicians make the laws that directly influence people's lives. Artists make up a world that doesn't exist to open our eyes and teach us empathy. This film didn't kill anyone, didn't arrest anyone who was innocent, didn't put any guns on the street, didn't deny a loan to any person, didn't zone any neighborhood to keep a race of people out. It just made us think, feel, and hopefully inspire us to fight for change. That is what every movie could do.

C: Tyger Williams Interview

(*Menace II Society* Screenwriter)

"WE HAD A LOT TO SAY AND WE TRIED NOT TO SAY IT WITH A MEGAPHONE."

Scott Ryan: Thanks for taking the time to speak with me. This book is all about films from the nineties, and *Menace* is certainly one of the best. What do you think about nineties films?

Tyger Williams: It was when I came of age. I was in my early twenties. Nineties film, nineties culture, the coming of age of gangsta rap, the G-funk era, the birth of grunge—that was like Gen X in our prime. Then the revival of indie cinema which came out of the big spectacle films: the *Top Gun*s, the *Raiders of the Lost Ark*s. No one had ever seen a film like *Boyz n the Hood*, *Reservoir Dogs*, or *Hard Eight*—the things that P. T. Anderson was doing. People were taking risks, taking chances, doing different things, butting up against the studio system. Sequalitization and IP hadn't taken over the town yet. There was still a bit of Wild West.

Ryan: I miss that Wild West. How did *Menace II Society* come into your life?

Williams: My brother went to high school with the Hughes brothers and were really good friends. I'm like four years older than all of them. I was studying film at Long Beach State. Albert was at LACC [Los Angeles City College]. My brother said, "He's learning to direct. You're learning to write. You guys should hook up." We started hanging out, playing video games, and they were directing music videos at the time. Allen read two of my scripts. I managed to have an agent. I started to write music videos for them. They were trying to get these jobs but had to submit proposals. They couldn't get what was in their head on paper. I started doing that for them. It was a really good way to begin a relationship. We learned to have a conversation about how they see the video, and I could write what they saw. By the time we started to make a movie, we had that language.

Thematically, we all loved *Boyz n the Hood*. It was a very specific movie about a kid who makes it out of the ghetto, and coming out of the crack era in the eighties, most kids didn't make it out like that. Instead of the one kid who does makes it out, we were interested in the story of the masses and why don't they make it out. With that kind of thesis, we started talking about what is that movie. They always knew the main character would die. They always had that in their head.

Ryan: I think one of the things that got me was that the voice-over isn't there to just move the story along; it is actually the entire movie, because he is dying and this happens in that moment. How did you stumble upon that idea?

Williams: It was always baked into the idea. Not being filmmakers, but loving films, we knew the character was gonna die, we knew we wanted voice-over, and then we were like, "How do we make that work?" This was only the third screenplay I had ever written. Now that I teach screenwriting, I say, "Don't do voice-over. Don't make it more difficult for yourself." But to do that, I watched *Apocalypse Now*, *Taxi Driver*, and *Goodfellas* for the rhythms of voice-over. Those were the three films that we all considered good voice-over. It was telling you something about character. Like in *Apocalypse Now*, he is talking about one thing, but what was on the screen is completely different. In *Taxi Driver*, it was so internal. It was completely in the mind of a psychopath. *Goodfellas* had that familiar "I'm hanging out with my friends" thing. There is a shot in *Menace* where we track through a party and you meet all of his friends. That is a direct rip from *Goodfellas* when Ray Liotta is walking through the club and meets everybody.

Ryan: It's one thing for Martin Scorsese to do it; he has a bunch of pictures under his belt. But here are these new directors and a new screenwriter. Are you pitching this long take to New Line?

Williams: I am pretty sure they told New Line exactly how it was gonna get done. The magic of youth—you take it for granted when you are in the moment. We were all smart enough to understand the business. I was twenty-three; they were twenty. They treated us like children, so we could ask for things that maybe we shouldn't have asked for. We really didn't know we weren't supposed to be making a movie. New Line was looking at two twenty-year-old directors who shot a couple of videos, and they are in the room, and they are wowing them. The twins are big personalities. They had a script they really liked, and I am sure they felt like they could market this. With all that, we still wanted to make something good. I think it helped with their knowledge of cinema that they could break down Scorsese, that they could pull from Truffaut. Their knowledge was deep enough for the shots that they wanted.

Ryan: The line of dialogue that slays me is "Do you care whether you live or die?" I thought this was a rhetorical question, but he sincerely says, "I don't know." To me, that is the heart. How did you feel about that scene?

Williams: I believe it is what ends the first act of the film. The way I was structuring it was plot and then subtext right under it. He had just come back from the hospital. The effect that we were going for is that this is the premise of the film, the dramatic question of the film which speaks to the culture, to the community: Do you care whether you live or die? I always knew I would answer that question. The voice-over was structured so within the script. I knew what scenes it would go in. The voice-over had its own arc just like the story. You couldn't remove it, believe me, the studio tried in editing—but you couldn't change it because it was so baked into the script. Eventually we were trying to answer that question through the rest of the movie.

Ryan: I also love the scene before it, when the grandfather is watching *It's a Wonderful Life* and it's like it is a sci-fi movie to Caine. No one points it out.

Williams: Thanks. We talked a lot about those things. We were like, "What are we talking about?" We spent a lot of time being young Black Americans. What does the image of *It's a Wonderful Life* and a happy suburban White life mean? It is the antithesis of where we are. We had a lot to say, and we tried not to say it with a megaphone. Sometimes it worked; sometimes it didn't.

Ryan: The difference between *Boyz* and *Menace* is that *Boyz* has lessons. Your script feels like you said, "We aren't here to teach any lessons. We are telling a truthful, character-based story."

Williams: There wouldn't be a *Menace* without *Boyz*. *Menace* couldn't have been the first grand film in the "hood" genre because of what it is. It's like, "Can we get an appetizer before this entrée? This entrée is kinda rough." [Laughs.] Not to say that we are the entrée.

Ryan: You are the entrée. You don't have to say it. I'll say it.

Williams: There is no chaser. It is a whiskey, neat. I sort of see the legacy, and I was having this conversation with Barry Jenkins not long ago, and Barry said, "There could have been no *Moonlight* without *Menace* and *Boyz*," which I thought was fascinating in terms of the different views on Black masculinity in an urban environment written with drugs and violence over the span of years. There could have been no *Menace* without *Boyz* and no *Moonlight* without either of them. I think they are intricately connected, and *Menace* is a cousin to *Goodfellas*. It is much closer to *Goodfellas* than to *Boyz*.

Ryan: There was a prison riot scene, but it got cut. The script is so perfectly tied together; were you upset that that scene got cut?

Williams: I missed it at the time, but I understood why it was cut. We didn't have the budget, the days, or the time, and it was written much bigger than that. The script that New Line bought maybe cost six million to make and then said, "Go home and chop three million out of the movie," without telling us what to cut. "Just make it cheaper." So there were things that got cut. The two female characters in the script had whole other arcs, where those two and Caine were off committing other hustles and crimes. We sent Caine to prison. There was a whole sequence after the interrogation with Bill Dukes. We had a funeral scene, a scene in a church; we had big scenes that required a lot of characters.

Ryan: What was the social responsibility expected for *Menace* in 1993? You must have received some pushback on the film?

Williams: Yeah, there was pushback. There had been some movie theater violence. There was violence at *New Jack City* or a shooting at *House Party*. Whenever there was a Black movie, there might be some incidents. The media would always be like, "It's Black movies." You have to remember, we were at the tail end of the crack epidemic. It wasn't the movies. You've got gangsters and drug dealers going to see a movie. It could just as easily have been at a Stallone movie. When Spike made *She's Gotta Have It*, I don't think a Black man or woman had directed a major Hollywood film in ten years. Everyone was sensitive about the depictions of African-Americans in the media. While *Boyz* might have been an authentic type of picture, there was still hope and light. *Boyz* was like, "Don't talk about the bad part of it." And that was ALL we wanted to talk about. I had an agent, my very first agent. I will spare him his dignity, although I should really blast him. He wouldn't send the script for *Menace* out. [Stops and thinks.] I had an agent named Jon Klane. I'll say it. He was my first agent. He agreed to represent me, and he'd send my other scripts out, but he would refuse to send *Menace* out. He said it was socially irresponsible and it would create violence. I took it as an offense to have a White man tell me what was socially irresponsible. Then we got another agent, Jeff Robinov, who went on to run Warner Brothers, said, "Just let me see the script." He had it for a weekend and then called us on Tuesday and things were happening immediately. But that was what we were up against. My agent didn't want to send it out. Then there were people who liked it but were scared to make it.

Ryan: Were there any scares along the way in making it?

Williams: After New Line did buy it, we were shut down just two weeks away from starting to shoot by Bob Shaye, who ran New Line, because of two African American producers, who I will *not* name, but they were big at the time. They went to New Line and protested and said, "This movie is socially irresponsible. You'll have black bodies in the street on opening day shooting each other. You cannot make this movie as it is." It freaked New Line out. And so they said I had to do a rewrite. I said, "Fine. What's the note?" The note was: the script needs more heart. "Okay, where? What?" That was it. Off I go. I am twenty-four with my career, my life, and my future and everything hinges on whether we make this movie or not. But in the happiest of accidents, I actually think it was a great note. Someone actually made me realize it that way recently. I had never thought of it that way. I went home and I wrote the scene where Caine and Ronnie (Jada Pinkett) go to visit Pernell (Glenn Plummer) in jail, and he hadn't seen him since he was a kid, and he is gonna go to Atlanta. They do the fist bump, and the tears, and Pernell says, "Teach my son to be a better man." In hindsight, where the thesis of the film was: do you care whether you live or die? When Caine and Pernell meet and he says, "Teach my son to be a better man and to break the generational chains," that is *really* what the movie is about. That scene came out of duress.

Ryan: Wow. So you added that two weeks before filming?

Williams: Yes. That was just a "Where's the heart?" and me rereading the script and trying to find a place. Of course it made sense to try to tie up that relationship. It turned out to be a blessing, and I didn't really write the scene, the characters wrote the scene, and I was transcribing it. I am sitting there, I'm typing, I'm crying, and I'm just listening in my head and transcribing their scene. It was a happy accident.

Ryan: There are also no gangs or colors tying them to any group of people. That did show social responsibility.

Williams: That was calculated. We didn't want to offend Crips. We didn't want to offend Bloods. *Colors* came out in 1988. We were not making a gang movie. It isn't about gang culture. They were just hustlers. We were also shooting on location, and if we had an affiliation with one gang, there were real, legit gangs at that location. We figured, "Just put everybody in black and tan." We didn't want that smoke.

Ryan: How was the casting process? Were you surprised by the casting of O-Dog with Larenz Tate, who wasn't the typical kind of actor hired for a role like that?

Williams: Larenz was a child actor and looked like a child actor when he came in. Everyone was great. The twins went after Tyrin Turner [Caine]. They had seen him in the Janet Jackson "Rhythm Nation" video. They had a feeling, and that worked out well for us. The chemistry between Jada and Tyrin was incredible. Larenz came in, and his audition was great. The twins had him ad-lib. The scene when they are on the way to pull a drive-by, Larenz did all his lines and then he sat back in his chair and smoked and smiled and said, "I love this shit." And we all looked at each other and were like, "Yeah. That guy!" Same with Jada. She brought the character I had in my head to life. It was like magic. Someone appeared out of my head. It was amazing. We also cast my younger brother [Ryan Williams, as Stacy.] He had to audition. I told him, "We aren't going to just give you the role, but you should get it because you've seen the script for six months longer than anyone else." He was good and did his thing. There was a scene when Caine got shot; my brother wasted all his tears in the master shot. He didn't have any for the close-ups. But he was so caught up that other actors started crying. At this point, everyone was calling everyone by their stage name. Jullian [Roy Doster - Ronnie's child] came up and patted him on the back and said, "Stacy, are you okay? It's just work." It was the most emotional moment. I think our producer Darin Scott was twenty-eight, and he was the oldest person on the set. It was a bunch of kids making a movie. It was emotional. We weren't fifty-year-olds looking back; we were still connected to these characters, and they were contemporaries of ours.

Ryan: What sets this movie apart from others is that these characters are not mad at America. There is a lack of blaming anyone, because these characters wouldn't know that they should be angry at the rest of the country. That is a great piece of writing to remove the crutch of having characters that are political. They are just trying to stay alive. It is for the audience to realize how these characters have been left behind. It never becomes an after-school special.

Williams: We talked a lot about not judging our characters. We didn't want to condone them. We didn't want to condemn them. I do recall the twins talking a lot about how they used the words "after-school special" in regards of *Boyz n the Hood*. But they'd say, "It's cool. We like after-school specials." But if *Boyz* is an after-school special, then we had to go to the completely opposite side. We always knew we weren't going to pull any punches. The original poster tagline is: This is the truth. This is what's real.

Chapter 5

1994

A: *The Shawshank Redemption*

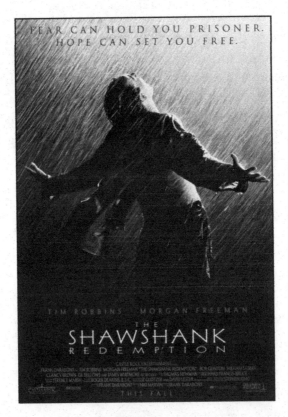

"Get busy living or Get busy dying"

It would be silly to say that a particular movie is the best movie ever made because what does that even mean? What would the qualifications be? So I won't say that. Instead, I will say Frank Darabont's *The Shawshank Redemption* has to be as close to a perfect movie as one can get. I have seen this film many, many times, and I was actually most nervous to write about it because what can be said about perfection? It isn't too long before you slip into Chris Farley interviewing Paul McCartney, but when I did my rewatch of *Shawshank* with the purpose of writing this essay, it became pretty obvious that there are a few specific tools Darabont uses in his writing and directing within the prison movie genre to accomplish his task. This film isn't about scaring us with the prospect of being locked up. Instead, it scares us with the prospect that we aren't taking advantage of the vastness of our freedom.

When Andy Dufresne (Tim Robbins) intersects with Red (Morgan Freeman) and the rest of the gang at Shawshank State Prison, he introduces something to the prison population that has never been witnessed in the high-security penitentiary before—hope. The film, which lulls the viewer into a comforting sense of repetition, isn't trying to display what a prisoner's life is like. Frank Darabont wanted to make us aware of how easy it is for each one of us to imprison ourselves by allowing the walls that hold us in to become our friends instead of our enemies. The film's true agenda is to remind us of how beautiful music is (the opera scene), how important a project is to the human spirit (creating the library), and how the power of the mind is stronger than the power of the cage (the smile on Robbins's face on the prison rooftop). Yes, this prison movie has the genre film troupes of the prison guard who beats a prisoner just because, the uncomfortable shower scenes, the mean-old warden, but that isn't what the film is about. Those are just there because that is what prison movies do. The script is based on one of the short stories contained in Stephen King's 1982 book *Different Seasons*. This is the same novel in which two other well made Stephen King movies came from, *Stand by Me* and *Apt Pupil*. The short story called "Rita Hayworth and the Shawshank Redemption" is just the tiniest blueprint of what the film became. Darabont was able to flesh out the characters, create an entire world, and lead a first-time viewer down a path that doesn't give away the ending in the title. (I will be giving away the ending of this movie, so read only if you have seen the film. If you haven't seen the film, why are you reading a book about the nineties?)

And That Right Soon

The two main writing techniques Darabont uses to convey the themes in his film are repetition and deception. From a dialogue and directing standpoint, he uses repetition throughout the film. This is an expert way of bringing viewers into the world of prison life, where today is a repeat of yesterday. Three times throughout the film, we get a hard cut to black, then prison bars slide open revealing a long hallway which opens up to a parole board. Each time, the directing is the same, the dialogue is the same, the prisoner is the same, but the parole board members change. We find comfort in this repetition. This concept is also shown through the character of Brooks (James Whitmore), who is finally released on parole at a very old age, but when he gets out of prison, he is scared and ends up killing himself. Red tells his fellow prisoners, "These walls are funny. First you hate 'em; then you get used to them. Enough time passes, you get so you depend on them. That is institutionalized." We get this feeling of comfort and institutionalization by hearing multiple times "I understand that you are a man who knows how to get things" or "I doubt they will kick up any fuss, not for an old crook like me" or "Lawyer fucked me." This isn't just about having well-written, clever dialogue in the film; this is how Darabont shows the viewer the world that our characters live in is the same thing over and over. No one in the film says, "Boy, everyday here is exactly the same. Even the things people say are the same." Most entertainment created today doesn't want to take the time to set up things like this; they just have a character declare it. Now *that* should be a jailable offense.

But is it believable, with all the horror shown in the prison, that the characters wouldn't want to be free? Of course our characters want to be free, in practice, but the truth is, if you do something day after day, decade after decade, that becomes your life. We, as the viewers, start to feel the comfort of the walls. We want to see Andy and Red interact in that friendly way because it is comforting to us. As the film goes on, we are so accustomed to the repetition that we fear for Red when he is released from prison, gets the same job as Brooks, the same room where Brooks kills himself, and when Red stands up to carve his name in the wood frame of the wall, we fear Red will take his life as well. We fear this because of the use of repetition in the way it is filmed. We expect to see it all again, including the suicide. Red finally breaks the repetition and gets busy living. When the film drops out of its repetition, it shocks us and gives our brains a little bit of serotonin that brings us joy. We have been tricked. It is moments like this that gives us the feeling the film itself is alive and creative. It becomes hard to judge Brooks or Red for being afraid of being released when we ourselves are sad for Red that Andy breaks out and is gone. We want them to stay together, even though they are not free. This is just a human condition where we love patterns and schedules even when they are detrimental to us.

If I Didn't Care

The movie from the nineties that is *supposed* to be the classic film about working in corporate America is *Office Space*. But in the ten years I worked at two major corporations, it was *The Shawshank Redemption* that people mentioned more than *Office Space*. The truth is when you are working in a cubicle, answering phones, completing menial tasks that are beneath your ability while you are micromanaged by midlevel bosses who make maybe fifty cents an hour more than you do but have complete power over when you are allowed to relieve yourself, it is *Shawshank* that comes to mind. *Office Space* is too on the nose, too painful to even consider. I never viewed *Office Space* as a comedy. It only plays like a stone-cold drama to me. It practically should be considered a horror movie. At Corporation A, we were given two minutes to aux our phone, walk across the large office building, go to the bathroom, walk back, and aux back in before our managers would come over to our desk to yell at us. I used to turn to the person sitting next to me and say, "Forty years I've been asking permission to piss." She would respond, "Lawyer fucked me." I didn't last there for forty years, but I have friends who still work there, and they are still asking for permission to pee.

At Corporation B, where I also only lasted five years, it was the tunnel of shit we talked about almost every week. The number of times we compared our five-day workweek to crawling through "five hundred yards of shit smelling foulness" is more than you would ever believe. Corporate drones like us only had a few seconds to say whatever we wanted to say as we passed someone's desk before we were yelled at for talking to our neighbor. So what else could we do but say something we had said before to make our point? Just like the repetitive dialogue that the prisoners use, we spoke in metaphors. You can walk by someone's desk while a middle manager is glaring at you and just say, "Welcome to Shawshank," and keep going before they can bust you for being human. There is very little difference between Clancy Brown's prison guard and an assistant manager at a production-based corporation. Every time any of us had a vacation scheduled, you can bet we would get a screenshot on our Facebook page of Tim Robbins standing, arms wide in the rain, washing the shit smell off. That is what would await you on your first day of vacation. The day you returned to work, you were bound to email your friends the screenshot of Tim Robbins cowering in the corner of his solitary cage, scraggly beard, dirty shirt, and blinded from the light. We were back in the hole. Each of us got two weeks of vacation, there were four of us who had this running joke. No one would take both weeks at once or you'd cut your throat halfway through the year. So that meant each of us sent that meme twice a year and four of us were in on the bit. So that is eight times a year. If you don't think repetition and comfort are how you get through a life experience you hate, or a prison sentence, then you have never hated your lot in life and you should hug your parents today. Anyone can send the destroying-the-fax-machine meme from *Office Space*; only people who truly hate their job use Andy and Red to survive.

On the Breeze

Darabont uses our thoughts and natural fears against us throughout the film. His script is such a marvelous example of how a writer can use the art of deception to allow the audience to get ahead of the film and assume the wrong path the script is taking. Very much like I pointed out in the *Pretty Woman* script, this film is laying bread trails from the beginning to set up the trick ending that is right in front of our eyes the entire time. The best trick endings shouldn't come out of nowhere; it should have been in plain sight.

Nine minutes into the film, Morgan Freeman delivers a voice-over about him having to smuggle Rita Hayworth into the prison for Tim Robbins. It is delivered as a joke, a play on words. How could this felon smuggle a movie star into the prison? Thirty-three minutes later, the joke returns when Tim Robbins asks Morgan Freeman to get him Rita Hayworth. Freeman responds, "I don't have her stuffed down the front of my pants right now, I'm sorry to say." But that isn't the only dialogue they exchange. The scene begins with the repeatable line of "I understand you're a man who knows how to get things," and Freeman responds with "I've been known to locate certain things from time to time," because even when Darabont is hiding his trick ending, which is the point of making the Rita Hayworth request seem like a joke, he is also staying within his rule of prison talk is repetition. Even when he needs to grab the viewers by the lapels and say "Look at my left hand" while he secretly plants a seed with his right hand, he doesn't drop the entire world he created to do it. He creates his misdirection *within* the rules of the world he created. Once we see the poster of Rita Hayworth, and then later as the posters change to Marylin Monroe and to Raquel Welch, we think, "Oh, they were just using a play on words at the beginning to make me think it was ACTUALLY Rita Hayworth, not a poster." Then we think, "Oh, the posters are in the film to show us the passage of time and that cultures are changing while they are in prison." We aren't thinking, "I bet that son of a bitch dug a tunnel behind that poster and is gonna escape at the end." Darabont cleverly follows the request for the poster with the most harrowing scene of the entire movie, when the sisters finally corner Tim Robbins and demand oral sex. When he tells them anything that goes in his mouth is gonna get bitten off, they beat him senseless. We don't want to see Andy go through this moment; it has been our fear since that first night he entered prison. It is the perfect placement of this disturbing scene right after the Rita request so that we don't focus on the poster. When Andy gets out of the infirmary and the poster is waiting, it is there to show us Red is truly his friend. The number of plot pillars that poster is holding up is incredible. But the main one—that it is hiding his escape route—doesn't occur to us. It is the best way to hide a trick. I abhor when a camera zooms in on a prop, be it a gun, a pack of pills, a car key, and we all go, "Yep, that is coming back in Act 3." If you really want to make us forget about a prop, then have it reoccur before its true come back. Darabont does this better than any film I can think of. We are played by a master throughout the entire script.

I have seen this movie a million times over the years, but for this rewatch, there was a moment I was a little nervous about because I couldn't quite remember how it played out. One of my major pet peeves about new storytelling is that the writer or director thinks they want to do the out of order storytelling used in *Pulp Fiction* but they aren't as respectful of the audience to assume we will follow the story, so they show us the exact same scene twice. While *Pulp Fiction* does circle back to Samuel L. Jackson's big "I will strike you down" speech about two hours after we have seen it once, but the scene is shown from a completely different perspective. I don't just mean that we have a different perspective in what is going on with the plot, but we are actually in a different perspective because we are now in the bathroom with the gunman, whom we didn't know was there. It is not the exact-same scene shown again. In fact, another scene in *Pulp* that we come back to is when Honeybun and Pumpkin say, "Alright, everybody be cool, this a robbery." They actually say different dialogue when we see it for the second time, so that also isn't a scene we have to watch twice. I lose faith in a director who makes me watch something at the beginning of the movie and then makes me watch it all again at the end of the film like I am too dumb to remember what I saw or, even worse, that the director thought their film was so complex I couldn't possibly get what they did without seeing the same scene twice. While watching *Shawshank* this time, at fifty minutes into the picture, the warden (Bob Gunton) tosses Andy's cell, and I remembered Andy was hiding the rock hammer in the Bible. Darabont doesn't tip this. He doesn't show us Andy putting the rock hammer in the Bible or let us know he is worrying that his rock hammer will be confiscated. There is no wide-eyed Tim Robbins panicking about his Bible, thank God. The warden takes the Bible from Andy and starts to leave, but then remembers he has it, comes back, hands it to Andy, and says, "Salvation lies within." A lesser director would scream at us, "THE HAMMER IS IN THERE! GET IT???" Darabont made this movie to be watched over and over. He has this scene play this way so you can be nervous the second or third time you watch the film. He knows some first-time viewers might have forgotten about the rock hammer, and some might guess where it is hidden, or they might incorrectly think Andy has it in his coat. Either way, he doesn't want to tell you about it yet, so he doesn't tip his hand. That is for later. But it was later I was worried about.

As the movie played out, I started to wonder if Darabont was going to make me watch this scene again, once Andy escaped, and we knew he dug a hole in the wall with the rock hammer, and it must have been hidden in the Bible. If he showed me this scene again, even for a moment, it would mean Frank Darabont didn't think that I, Scott Ryan, was smart enough to remember the part when the warden slipped the Bible back through the bars and back into Andy's hands. Have no fear. Darabont respected me and, I suppose, you too. He doesn't show us that scene again. Instead, the warden, who realizes the jig is up, opens the safe to see Andy has taken all the records and left him with only Andy's Bible. He opens the Bible, which has been hollowed out to hold the rock hammer. Andy inscribed the Bible with "Dear Warden, You were right. Salvation lay within." I wouldn't be surprised if an editor or an executive said, "Should we do a quick edit showing the warden shoving the Bible back into Andy's hands?" You know, just to beat the viewer over the head like the guards at Shawshank do? I don't know if Darabont had to fight for me or not, but either way, he didn't talk down to any of us, and the scene sure works. His art of deception with the Bible/rock hammer makes this movie a perfect example of how to not show your cards before you're ready.

His respect for his viewers is why this movie is so exhilarating and why it became a classic that people watch over and over. Oh, you can feel the hand of the writer the entire film, but always incorrectly. You think it is doing one thing; it is doing another. He is leading you down a path you don't see coming. The King novella is a smaller tale told more through the eyes of Red, so the twist is not as much of a buildup. In the film, which has put many of its characters through such hardships, such as Brooks's death, Andy's rape, Red's denial of parole, and every beating the guards give, that a happy ending is the last thing expected by the viewer. The entire film just plays like there is no way anything good is ever going to happen to Andy or Red. All the deception and repetition is there to make us not expect that they will ever have a moment of freedom, let alone a lifetime of friendship without a wall in sight. The friendship of our main characters is what brings us back to rewatch this film. I can honestly say the friends I made at those horrible corporate jobs are the ones I hold nearest and dearest to me. Heck, I married one of them. I can say without a doubt that going through a prison-like experience only makes us feel more free when we finally step back into the world where we are supposed to be, whether you walk out the front door or crawl through five hundred yards of pure shit.

B: *Pulp Fiction*

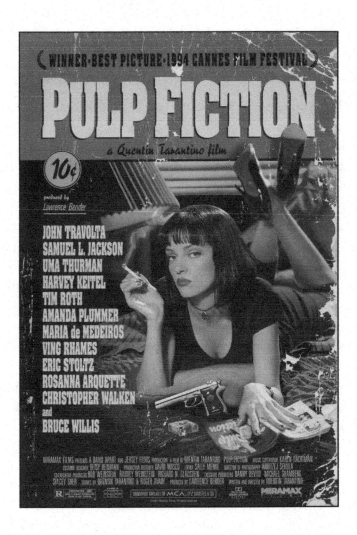

"AIN'T QUITE TIME YET. COME ON, LET'S HANG BACK."

When you are watching over 160 films from the nineties and you get up to *Pulp Fiction*, the film still leaves you staring in a daze like you are mesmerized by the glow of a mob boss's briefcase. *Pulp Fiction* is just as fresh and new as the day it was made, despite everyone trying to copy it for years to follow. In the nineties, there was BP and AP. Before *Pulp* and After *Pulp*. By 1994, independent films were starting to make ripples (*The Piano, The Crying Game, Clerks*), but AP it was all waves. Every film that wasn't original just felt out of step. The eighties were a decade of happy endings and glossy, studio, crowd-pleasing movies. A decade where the bad guys were punished and the good guys always won. Hell, I don't even have an idea who the good guys are in *Pulp Fiction*. The first part of the nineties started to blur that line, and Tarantino played a part in cracking that mold with his directorial debut, 1992's *Reservoir Dogs,* which was only filled with bad guys—Mr. Blonde, being the number one most badass bad guy, and Mr. White being the least bad guy. AP, it was no longer the norm to tell a linear story in art house films, the characters didn't have to be moral, and your film better be unique, gritty, and above all things: new. In the past, industry-changing films weren't embraced right out of the gate. They had to fail on arrival, have a tumultuous history, and be discovered years later. A *Citizen Kane, The Wizard of Oz, It's a Wonderful Life,* or *Casablanca* had to wait a generation to find its place at the top of a list of the best films of all-time. Not Quentin Tarantino's *Pulp Fiction*. It exploded right out of the gate and made every movie made before it look simple and became the standard for everything in front of it. I remember hearing about *Pulp* from the moment it played at the Cannes film festival. I didn't know what the plot was, but I knew it was a movie I had to see as soon as possible in the theater. The buzz for this film was louder than Dick Dale's opening credits guitar solo.

In the seventies, filmmakers like Coppola, Hopper, and Scorsese inspired cinephiles. In the nineties, it was Quentin Tarantino. Here was a fellow video store clerk who hit it big. His backstory, his knowledge of film, and his "fuck you" attitude spoke to my generation like the Beatles spoke to my parent's generation. I knew he was just like me, and nothing like me because he was actually out there getting it done. Believe me, every person who worked in a video store thought they knew everything about film and they would be the perfect person to direct the next great movie to change Hollywood forever. Only one did.

You Never Can Tell

So why did *Pulp Fiction* change the world for cinephiles like myself in 1994? For this I can finally fulfill something I mentioned in the introduction. I promised you another from-the-theater story. I saw *Pulp Fiction* for the first time in a movie theater in a strip mall on a Wednesday morning matinee with my former manager from Video Time, Michelle Kling. Movie theaters had such a monopoly on our entertainment, and there were so many movies coming to malls in small-town America that they used to split old movie theaters in half so they could show more movies. The screen, which used to be sixty feet, was now twenty feet, tops. I mean, the screen I saw *Pulp Fiction* on the first time was probably smaller than most television screens that hang in bars at BW3s today. There were only ten rows of seats, and you could hear the sounds from the screen next door whenever there were loud explosions because the makeshift walls were crappily installed. So in this small closet of a theater was Michelle and I, a gray-haired couple two rows in front of us and an old man sitting a row behind us. Five human beings were there. Now to be fair, it was 11:00 a.m. on a workday in a small Ohio town, so I guess the sparseness could be expected. The film wasn't a hit yet. It was still rolling out on screens here and there, which was how Miramax used to create buzz for their art house films. I had no idea what the film was about; I just knew my *Entertainment Weekly* had talked about it nonstop and put it on the cover for their 1994 fall movie issue. Plus, it had Bruce Willis in it, and I was still rewatching *Moonlighting* all the time. I was there for any movie that was getting buzz with David Addison.

During the opening scene, where Pumpkin (Tim Roth) and Honeybun (Amanda Plummer) methodically plan the best way to increase profits and decrease the dangers in their small business enterprise of robbing liquor stores, I stifled a few laughs as I enjoyed the immaculately crafted dialogue. ("What have we been talking about? Yeah, no more liquor stores.") The completely logical way they broke down the idea of making more money by robbing the patrons just thrilled me. A logical criminal. Nice. But since there were only five people in the audience, the scene played to silence because back in the nineties, people understood the difference between being at their home and being in a movie theater. We respected strangers. Now that was *my* reason for not laughing out loud. I kind of suspect the three older people just weren't laughing. Michelle might have been laughing, but the truth is, I forgot about her right around the moment the waitress responded with "Garçon means boy." I knew I was watching a movie that was WRITTEN, and I was soaking it all in.

In the following scene, where John Travolta and Samuel L. Jackson have the discussion about fast food differences in Europe and move on to the intimacy of a foot massage, I forgot there were any other people in the room with me. I was laughing so hard and so loud I was like a crazy person. I had tears pouring down my face, and I was gasping for air. The older people weren't making a sound. When Travolta said, "Fine, would you give a foot massage to a man?" and Jackson responds, "Fuck you," I was howling like it was *Blazing Saddles* and a bunch of cowboys just ate some baked beans. I assure you, I was the lone laugher at that volume. With these two opening scenes, I became a lifelong Tarantino fan. He is still my all-time favorite film writer/director and always will be.

It was just a few seconds later when I went from laughing to being absolutely dazzled at being in the hands of a skilled director. After ribbing Jackson about the foot massage, they stand in an extra close tight shot in front of a door. They realize they are just a bit early and they need to "hang back" for a second. They walk down the hall, away from the door, and stand in an extra faraway shot. This is all done in one take. They now pick up the foot massage discussion and bring it to a logical conclusion about how a foot massage is actually an undercover sexual act but we pretend it isn't. They come to an understanding and walk back to the door. The final line of the conversation is "Come on, let's get into character." This oner lets us know this is an aside to the story. The conversation taking place down the hall is never intercut with a typical close-up of each of the actors. That is because it is not part of the story. This is a cinematic footnote about a foot massage. I was immediately impressed with the skill of this director. I knew I was in the presence of an expert. He knew the story, and the audience wanted to know what and who was behind that door. Why did they feel they needed shotguns? What are they there for? But for a moment, all in one take, he just wanted to finish up this foot massage idea. Later, this conversation is brought up again, between John Travolta and Uma Thurman. We will actually find out if the foot massage mattered or not. From a directing standpoint, the shot of Travolta and Jackson having this conversation down the hall is my favorite shot in the film, but to end the scene by having a character say "Let's get into character" just tickled the writer in me.

The staging of this scene lets us know that this conversation is off to the side of the plot of the film. (Photo courtesy of Jersey Films)

A quick coda to seeing *Pulp Fiction* in the theater. While I specifically remember the silence of how that film played the first time I saw it—and trust me, I know those three older people damn sure believed I was either drunk or on drugs—I wasn't sure what the rest of the world would think of that movie. All I knew was it was the most mind-opening, alive film I had ever seen in my life. Three months later, I saw it again, in a different theater on a different night, with a remarkably different audience. This time, it was a Friday night at 9:00 pm on the campus of my alma mater, Akron University. It was a superlarge screen, and every chair in the five hundred-seat theater was filled with college kids. *Pulp Fiction* played like it was an Eddie Murphy stand-up special. This crowd reacted to Travolta's "I could use a foot massage right now" attitude exactly like I did. Oh, I laughed just about as hard, but no one noticed. There were plenty of lines of dialogue you couldn't even hear over the laughter. When Bruce Willis is tearing his hotel room apart trying to find his special gold watch, that we all know his girlfriend (Maria de Medeiros) left back at home, and he asks her, "Where the fuck is it?" someone screamed, "Check up her ass" (a wonderful callback to the Christopher Walken scene). It was that kind of audience. They loved the film. It really displayed how this film was going to create a splinter in what people were going to be looking for in movies. Those older viewers may not have gotten it, but for a while, these kinds of films were all they were gonna get, because people who were gonna fill a movie theater were the kinds of viewers who wanted a story where someone might just keep a gold watch up their ass for a few years.

Jungle Boogie

Before *Pulp Fiction*, I, and everyone, of course, loved movies. We knew what a movie was; we saw them all the time. Going to the movies was like streaming Netflix. It was what everyone did with their free time. Yes, some of the movies tricked us; some of them didn't. But even when they tricked us, we knew the film would either go this way or that way. The lovers would either get together or they wouldn't. They would either blow up the Death Star or they wouldn't. They would win the game or they would lose. The movie might be well written, it might be interesting, it might engage us, but things changed AP. Because of what Tarantino did in *Pulp Fiction*, it wasn't just that a movie could go *this* way or *that* way. It was now the choice of *this* way, *that* way, or *the biggest, baddest, scariest character could be taken in a back room, handcuffed, ball-mouth gagged, and get fucked up the ass by a hillbilly* way. I didn't know that was an option before I saw *Pulp Fiction*. And now, I wanted every movie to have that third option. It was the unthinkable option. It was the option I didn't see coming, I couldn't predict, and I never would have even considered as an option. For me, AP is all about that third option. And it changed cinema for me, forever. But it unfortunately only changed cinema itself for about six or seven years. For the following few years, for a glorious time in cinema, for the most inspiring film time of my life, we were all looking for movies to fuck us up the ass with a red neck. Wait. I might be able to phrase that idea better than that. For a while, the most popular films, the ones that everyone was talking about and everyone was seeing, were the movies that were original, independent, fearless, creative, brave, and happy to make you uncomfortable as hell. For this brief moment in time, you weren't the thing studios were trying to please. Story was.

In his wonderful book *Cinema Speculation*, Tarantino tries to explain to young people why *Rocky* changed film in the seventies. He correctly explains how no one watching *Rocky* today can ever be as shocked by the ending as he was in 1976 because today's young audience didn't live through all the unhappy endings of the movies that came out from 1970-1976. This is how I feel about *Pulp Fiction*. You had to live through all the bland movies of the eighties to understand what we were accustomed to. It wasn't just endings that changed with *Pulp Fiction*. It was that everything about movies changed. They were suddenly dangerous in a creative way for the first time in my era. Here are the words Tarantino wrote about *Rocky*, but read them and think of *Pulp Fiction*: "Now that type of audience innocence would be practically impossible to duplicate for somebody just discovering the movie today." I was most certainly innocent when Bruce Willis and Ving Rhames woke up in the back of the pawn shop, tied, gagged, and bloodied. I remember feeling so very unsure. I am not saying I was unsure what was going to happen to them next. I am saying I wasn't sure what was going to happen to *me* next. I was actually afraid, unsettled, and scared for my safety. *Bring out the gimp!* What the fuck is a gimp and why are we bringing it out? I felt like someone took my movie away from me. When are we going to get back to John Travolta and Uma Thurman dancing like Batman? It wasn't just that Tarantino was delivering a surprising script, it was that by this point in the film, I had laughed at things I shouldn't have laughed at. I basically became Rosanna Arquette giggling uncomfortably when Travolta pierced Uma Thurman's heart with adrenaline. I liked that Jackson washed his bite of burger down with a tasty beverage, and I was glad when he shot the kid for saying "What?" too many times. Now I was being punished for aligning myself with these bad guys. I wasn't safe anymore, because Tarantino didn't just corrupt us by breaking the rules of storytelling he corrupted our very morals by making us love every gangster in this film.

Tarantino had this to say about how a director can play with our morals in a film, "The director has always confronted the audience with lead characters you're drawn to despite on-screen evidence of their troubling nature, and deeds. Lead protagonist he makes it difficult to root for, but, ultimately, you root for them nonetheless. Which goes to prove what I've always believe, '*It takes a magnificent filmmaker to thoroughly corrupt an audience.*'" No, Tarantino wasn't talking about himself, or *Pulp Fiction*; he was talking about Don Siegel and the film *Dirty Harry*, but it sure sums up what he did to audiences in the nineties and beyond. I loved *Pulp Fiction* so much, I bought five posters, three T-shirts, the CD, the VHS, the DVD, then the Blu-ray, and I have seen every Tarantino movie on opening day since 1994. I wasn't the only one from my generation who felt this way. Most certainly, that boisterous audience on the Akron University campus loved the movie and bought a trinket or two from the movie. But he didn't just corrupt us. He corrupted other generations as well. This was a movie my mom and dad loved too. My parents, who balked at the violence in David Lynch's *Wild at Heart* and found nothing funny about a botched kidnapping in *Fargo*, were walking around talking about a "Royale with cheese" and dancing the Batdance at their New

Year's Eve parties. *Pulp Fiction* didn't just change things for young writers like myself or every video clerk who thought they had a hit independent movie in them; it changed cinema for the people who were used to *Dirty Harry* just shooting punks to make his day. Those film punks who were storing Clint Eastwood's and Charles Bronson's bullets in films of the past were now the front-and-center heroes of film. There isn't a "good guy," also known as a police officer, anywhere near *Pulp Fiction*. You have bad guy Travolta, working for bad guy Ving Rhames, who is paying bad guy Bruce Willis to take a dive who ends up shooting bad guy Travolta after newly reformed bad guy Samuel L. Jackson gets in a Mexican standoff with bad guys Tim Roth and Amanda Plummer. A movie filled with bad guys has no bad guys in it. By his own description, Tarantino must be a magnificent filmmaker because he thoroughly corrupted all of art in 1994. Tarantino ended his chapter on *Dirty Harry* by saying, "Every audience member of *Dirty Harry* entered the cinema with an innocent view. An innocence we would soon lose." These words describe audiences in 1994. But it wasn't the innocence of a movies with violence; it was the end of the innocence of watching bland movies and average choices in movie scripts. The movies that came BP are simpler and formulaic, and there is no doubt that the formula snapped right back into place after the 2000s, but AP movies like *Boogie Nights*, *Buffalo 66*, *Trainspotting*, and *Out of Sight* were demanded. I would never put forth the idea that there was ever a decade in Hollywood where decisions weren't made by money. It just happened that in the nineties, creativity was commercial.

I suspect Tarantino himself would disagree that nineties movies were better than seventies movies. But remember, my contention was never to talk about better. My contention is two pronged. Yes, it is about creativity, but it was also about technology, and the movies of the seventies *feel* old to me. There is nothing old about *Pulp Fiction* today. When my children watched it, they were as shocked and uneasy as I was when Uma Thurman slumped to the floor with white foam and blood rolling down her face. By the time the proprietor and the security guard says, "Bring out the gimp," we all know for sure what is going to happen: something that we can't predict. That is the kind of predictability that I long for. Anything can and will happen in a Tarantino movie. That recklessness that pours out of the script made films like *Forrest Gump* or *The Fugitive* or *Disclosure* feel like they were from a Hollywood that was now DOA.

Son of a Preacher Man

It was mostly in the 2000s when other films tried to do the *Pulp Fiction* idea of telling their story out of order, but what hack studio executives didn't understand was that *Pulp Fiction* isn't actually told out of order. The film is a meditation on redemption and is told in the proper order based on that theme. Each character is on the path to redemption. We start with Honeybun and Pumpkin. They want to rob the coffee shop. (This is another movie that has a wonderful LA coffee shop: *Reality Bites*, *Short Cuts*, *Lost Highway*, *Heat*, and *Pulp Fiction* all have these wonderful paradise-like shops that I never got to visit before they were all paved over and put up a bunch of pointless parking lots.)

The film then follows John Travolta and Samuel L. Jackson, who retrieve a case. Then we see the date with Uma Thurman. Her story ends with being saved from her night of coke. She is saved and redeemed, but Travolta hasn't learned his lesson, despite being shot at earlier and survived. We meet the fighter, Bruce Willis, and follow his story. During his story, he kills Travolta, in what is technically the middle of the film, an idea that is counterintuitive to the rules of how to get the most out of your money when casting a movie star. He dies in the middle because he should have been redeemed earlier, when he retrieved the suitcase and was saved by a miracle when the bullets missed him. Jackson understood and left the business; he was redeemed. He got out of the story alive. A miracle saved Thurman with the heart-piercing adrenal; she gets out of the movie alive. Bruce Willis is redeemed by Ving Rhames when he goes back to save him from the hillbillies. He gets out of the movie alive. Travolta didn't take his redemptive path out, so he dies. It makes most sense to circle back to Roth and Plummer to see what Jackson learned from his experience to understand his redemption, and also to save Honeybun and Pumpkin, who are therefore redeemed by the same miracle that

Jackson experienced. They would be killed by Jackson on any other day. They don't confront him; they back down, therefore they get out of the movie alive. The film ends with Jackson's redemption as Travolta and him walk out to deliver the case to Wallace. If the film was told in chronological order, we wouldn't have all the redemptions: the boxer, the wife, the gangster, the mob boss, the common criminal couple happen in the back half of the story when we are ready to care about those redemptions. The film is about bad guys, yes, but bad guys who are trying to be the shepherd of goodness, not darkness.

A movie can't just start with the end and end with the middle. A writer has to follow the story. People wonder what is in the briefcase, as if that is the point of the movie. It isn't what is in the case that matters; it is what is within you. The path of the righteous man is beset on all sides. Can you be redeemed? That depends on you and your reaction to the world and others around you. Redemption doesn't come from a briefcase full of gold. (Plus, come on, we all know it's really gold in there. That's why it shines.)

C: Reality Bites

"There's no secret handshake. There's an IQ prerequisite."

In the introduction, I explained how when I went to the movie theaters to see *Reality Bites* in 1994 for the first time, I felt like I was seen in my boxer shorts by the entire audience. Somehow, screenwriter Helen Childress and director Ben Stiller managed to take everything I felt, feared, and revered and put it on-screen for the world to see. It was this movie that taught me I was part of a generation. It's true that Cameron Crowe had done a similar thing in 1992's *Singles*, but I wasn't in a rock band, and I think those characters were a year or two older than I was. When I saw *Reality Bites*, I was one year out of college, and I was resisting corporate America and the materialistic world that I saw everywhere around me. When Winona Ryder reluctantly admits in the opening credits, "I know it's cornball, but I'd like to somehow make a difference in people's lives." That was a sentiment that I wholeheartedly believed, but more importantly it was a sentence I would never utter to anyone, including my fiancée, who was sitting right next to me as we watched Winona shyly admit my secret. But I wouldn't say it was that line that makes this movie a Gen X classic; it is actually Ethan Hawke's follow-up line that sets it apart from *Singles*. Because while I would never have been brave enough, or uncool enough, to admit what Ryder admitted, I would always be the one to deliver Hawke's mocking response of "And I, I would like to buy them all a Coke." Here he is, taking the mantra from the previous generation, which was all about supporting corporations' bottom lines and spending money on things that won't truly help anyone—in fact it will give everyone diabetes—and landing a joke using a popular slogan from their youth. Hawke plays Troy Dyer, and he is the coolest cat who ever didn't care if he was the coolest cat while secretly only caring that you think he is the coolest cat. He doesn't really want to buy everyone a Coke, but he has been raised on television and has no choice but to speak in metaphors from commercials, classic movies, and sitcoms.

The concept behind *Reality Bites* is a classic love triangle. At the center of the triangle, and the film, is the female character of Lelaina Pierce (Winona Ryder). She was valedictorian of her college, but she can't find a job she isn't either overqualified or underqualified for. She has two suitors. Option A: Ethan Hawke's Troy Dyer. He's in a band. He smokes. He is greasier than Danny Zuko and is Lelaina's best friend. He's an artist, an asshole, and knows that all they need is a cigarette, a cup of coffee, and conversation to live a meaningful life. Option B: Ben Stiller plays Michael Grates. He works at In Your Face TV (an MTV knockoff). He has a fancy car, always wears a suit, can help Lelaina get her documentary seen, and has never been cool, despite that he can also talk in TV sitcoms, discuss pop music and is more than happy to share a Big Gulp from 7-Eleven. For years, I have shown this movie to people and then paused the film before the final act, and asked them which character they think Lelaina should pick. It's a great litmus test for if a person thinks security is more important than passion. There has never been a doubt in my mind that I was always #TeamTroy. (Since I saw this movie in 1994, I guess that would read as number sign TeamTroy. Man, I am old.) The problem was my fiancée thought Troy was a horrible choice and was all in for Michael and Lelaina. Don't worry, we still got married . . . and then divorced. Should we have seen the signs that it was never going to work because of our opposite opinions about a rom-com? Duh, yes. This movie is the rare romantic comedy that actually creates two viable choices for the main character. Is anyone really rooting for Bill Pullman over Tom Hanks in *Sleepless in Seattle*? Not a chance. Pullman is merely there as a plot device. Are there actually people out there hoping Dermot Mulroney marries Cameron Diaz instead of Julia Roberts in *My Best Friend's Wedding*? No. These types of films are always created with an obvious choice, but Michael and Troy represent the two paths diverging in Lelaina's woods. She could viably choose either of them, and it would make sense. Yes, I have a friend (I'm looking at you, Courtenay) who says they are both jerks and Lelaina should just be on her own, but that tells us more about this friend—that making decisions is rough for them. Lelaina isn't ambivalent. She is a woman who makes choices and makes things happen.

You Try to Tell Me That I'm Clever

Reality Bites is a love story triangle, but it's a comedy first and foremost. Ben Stiller shows his promise with this directorial debut. He adds some great visual moments to the end of scenes that get a laugh. When Ryder is arguing with Janeane Garofalo in their apartment, Garofalo stomps off to her room and slams the door in Ryder's face, revealing that she has a life-size poster of Shaun Cassidy on her door. It's a well-staged comic bit of directing. He does an expert job of adding these visual buttons to the ends of scenes. Another example is with the use of the Big Gulp cups and their straws getting in the way of Michael and Lelaina's first kiss. He adds an extra burst of air from an airbag

The Big Gulp cups go from connections to comic props at the hands of Ben Stiller the director. (Photos courtesy of Jersey Films)

during a fender bender. It is evident that comedy is in his blood, and so is directing. All of this comes from a comic intelligence. One of the things I dislike about most comedies is that they mine comedy from dumb guys, which is so easy, with little reward. None of our main characters are unintelligent. They are all highly educated and smart. Lelaina is making a documentary on her own volition. Michael is an executive at an up-and-coming television network. Troy is said to have a high IQ and his vocabulary, and his ability to win every verbal confrontation backs this up. Garofalo's Vickie is the manager of The Gap. She improves sales by 20 percent. Steve Zahn's Sammy Gray is the character who would normally have been turned into the group idiot. (Think Matt Dillon in *Singles*.) While he is the least developed character, he is never played for easy jokes. In fact, when we discover that he is gay, at about three-quarters through the movie, his story of coming out to his mother is very moving. He sits outside of his mom's house talking about how hard it was, but how fulfilling it was to finally come out. He ends by saying he just hopes he is allowed back in the house and gives a small smile. Anyone who can make a joke in a scary moment of their life shows signs of intelligence. The way this film handles homophobia and the AIDS crisis is so subtle. There are no lessons and no judgments when Garofalo's character is waiting on an AIDS test and feels the pressure of wondering if she will live or die. None of the characters treat Zahn's character differently because he is gay. Everyone is accepted and part of the family, just like they saw on the sitcoms they watched growing up.

Stiller stages a few scenes using the one-take technique which was a staple of the nineties. Stiller truly displays shades of the excellent director he will become on *Severance* and *Escape from Dannemora*. The first exceptional oner is when Ryder and Stiller are sitting in the back seat of his convertible talking about Big Gulps, astronomy, and how materialistic things don't matter to the materialistic Michael. (He is the only one in the film with a cellular phone, although he does use it in a phone booth.) But it is not the discussion that matters. It is the approaching first kiss that is brought to life by filming this scene in one take. The anticipation of the kiss starts to build, and the camera slowly moves forward, almost imperceptibly, during their entire conversation.

Winona Ryder, who does her career-best work in this film, truly does such an amazing acting job of falling for Michael during these two minutes. It actually made me wonder if Ben Stiller ever got confused and thought, "Wow, I think the *Beetlejuice* girl is actually in love with me!" I sure know I would have. By never cutting to a close up or to a different shot, the audience never gets a reprieve from the sexual tension vortex that is created. (Yes, I just made that term up; let's make it a thing now. I want to have a sexual tension vortex with Winona Ryder too.) Constant cutting and crafting a romantic scene in editing loses the realism for an audience. No one cuts to a different shot for us in real life when we fall in love. And remember, this oner is staged for the character who *doesn't* get the girl. This is another example of how they crafted a movie where Lelaina could have chosen either guy. Later, when Michael and Lelaina meet up for an afternoon encounter in a hotel, (by the way, they never tell us they are in a hotel, you figure it out by the location, the robes, and the slippers Ryder is wearing. This movie respects every scene and every moment. There is no exposition delivered by characters.) Stiller crafts a scene where they start on the bed, he gets up to go off screen while we watch Ryder talk, he comes back to the screen to deliver his lines, she then reappears behind him, and they end the scene with them laughing about her Filofax (Damn, do I miss those. Screw you Google calendar), and they fall back onto the bed off-screen. It is a wonderfully staged scene that again brings the realism to their life and conversation. A oner doesn't mean that the camera doesn't change positions and that the actors don't move around, that is what makes them work, they don't grow stale, they stay fresh with logical movements and having the actor who is most important standing center stage. Coverage is all fine and good for the executives, but when a talented director stages a oner that allows the actors to craft their performance, it is so much better than letting an outside force decide where to make the cuts. That person might not understand the character arcs as well as the actors. This cast didn't need a safety net.

I Only Hear What I Want To

I have been preaching about the idea of showing versus telling throughout this book. As audiences have gotten lazier or more uneducated, lines of dialogue are placed throughout newer movies to explain the relationship between two friends with words that no friend would ever say to a best friend. I never say to my best friend, "Wow, I am so glad that we can talk about my sister who is an alcoholic who left her kids with my mom when she lost her leg in a baking accident." My best friend would know all those details. This movie never tells you how long the four principal friends have known each other. For all we know, Vickie and Lelaina could be cousins. Sammy and Troy could be stepbrothers or preschool best friends. Attention future screenwriters: everything you feel you want to tell the audience, write that down in your notes and then throw them away. Create a backstory for your characters in your mind and then proceed with that inner information but keep it yourself. That backstory should inform your character, not be spoken by them. If you want to tell a story about four friends, then you can't have any of the four explain their history to each other. Here are some things that are *not* directly explained in *Reality Bites*.

1. How any of them met.
2. How long they have known each other.
3. What game they are playing when Ben Stiller enters.
4. What sexual orientation Steve Zahn's character is.
5. When Winona started working on her documentary or what her plans for it were.
6. Who "him" is.

That is not a list of things we don't *know*. It is a list of things we are not directly told. The best written line of this entire movie comes when Lelaina and Troy are fighting and she says to Troy, "You're on the inside track to Loserville, USA. Just like *him*." Now I would bet my vinyl record of the *Reality Bites* soundtrack that if this line was in a movie today, someone—and what breaks my little heart is it would probably be the writer when I so badly want to blame it on an executive— would change this line to: "You're on the inside track to Loserville, USA. Just like *your dad*." I'm betting even someone educated in a small-town homeschool taught by the local conspiracy nutjob could figure out that when she says "him," she means his dad. His dad came up in the very first real scene of the movie. They discussed him in the documentary, and they mentioned him in an earlier fight. We know who the "him" is that makes Troy afraid to actually put himself out there in the world. And yes, for a brief second, especially the first time someone watches the film, the viewer has to think for a fraction of a second, "Who?" Pause. Think. And then: "Oh, his dad." That half a second of having to think gives me more dopamine than any space laser that shoots from the Millennium Falcon. It is okay to wonder. It is okay to not know for a second. It's even okay to not know till you watch the entire movie for a second or third time. It's more than okay. She doesn't have to say the words "your dad" because the two of them have discussed this over coffee and cigarettes a million times since the day they first met. Only the person who knows you inside and out can tear your heart out with just a small word. This knowledge shows us how much she truly knows Troy. It also allows us to understand why Troy is the way he is. He is making every choice to avoid becoming his father, just like Lelaina is trying so hard not to become her parents. You know, just like all of us.

The best written scene in the film and the one I am going to use in my screenwriting class that you are all signing up for occurs nineteen minutes into the picture and lasts two and a half minutes. It is a marvel in writing dialogue. Lelaina comes home from work; the gang is getting high and watching *One Day at a Time*. This scene has the friends just hanging with each other. The overall point of the scene plotwise is for Michael to call Lelaina on the phone and ask her out on a date, for us to see that it makes Troy jealous, and to deliver the information that Vickie got promoted at the Gap. So later when Lelaina is fired, we can discover the unspoken rift between Vickie and Lelaina about their career paths. But none of that is said. The dialogue is all the kind of crazy crap you say with your friends. They rhyme ("It's not easy. Sure, I make it look easy"). They want a pizza and we follow this scene with one of the best uses of music scenes in the nineties when they dance to the Knack's "My Sharona" in the gas station. How popular was this film's soundtrack? Just because of this short use of the song, it caused The Knack to chart "My Sharona" for the second time, fifteen years after its release. This film gives us the feeling that few films can ever achieve: the feeling that we are actually hanging out with our friends. It is the warm feeling that only happens when you are saying nothing and everything to the people who matter the most to you. It is the love of our chosen family. We wanna dance with them, watch old sitcoms with them, and talk all night long with them. These characters are real people because they interact with each other in code, care, and no bullshit. They talk to each other; not at each other.

I have no doubt that someone looking back at this film will want more people of color, want the gay character to be more out, dislike some of the slang words they use, and hate that the characters smoke. But when a film takes a step forward, we can't be mad at them for not taking six steps forward. I think all involved deserve major props for giving the AIDS scare to the female straight character, over having it be the gay character that fears being infected. In 1994, people were starting to talk about AIDS more, but remember the first true Hollywood film (*Philadelphia*) about it came out only one year earlier, and it was a gay man who got the disease. By having a straight girl worry about getting AIDS, it brought the crisis more to the mainstream. Having Steve Zahn's "Sammy" be a homosexual, and it not be a plot point or a big deal to any of them, was progress. Zahn mentions in the bonus features that there were more scenes with his character that got cut. It would have been nice to have his character fleshed out a bit more, but a movie has to go where the main story goes. Just having a gay character who wasn't a stereotypically gay man was a step forward. The lack of color in the characters is just honest. These characters grew up in the shadow of segregation, first by law, then self-imposed by the cultures. It is unlikely that they would be interacting with people outside their race. *Friends* debuted the same year as *Reality Bites*. They also were a group of people that were all the same race. That was where the culture was in the early nineties. I am very glad that all races are mixed together in films and television series now. I think the world has moved to a place where segregation isn't enforced by law or culture anymore. The issues now are all economics. It is unlikely that anyone from the one percent is going to be yucking it up with the rest of us who have three jobs and rent out a bedroom to strangers on the weekend. But in the nineties, at that moment, this group of friends from Houston, Texas, is as real and true to history as the group of friends from LA in *Menace II Society*. The real place where the film truly makes a leap forward is by having a female protagonist. It is a female who is worrying about her career, trying to live up to a career standard and not worrying about becoming a mom or a girlfriend. Yes, the film is a love triangle, but the main concern for Lelaina is finding a place for her art, not her heart.

I'm Only Hearing Negative

The film wasn't a hit. It wasn't a success, and I was really shocked to see it has a super low score on IMDb, if that even means anything. (I'm pretty sure it doesn't.) From my perspective, it was the first and last movie that actually covered my generation, and specifically me. I remember hearing at the time that no one from Gen X wanted to be categorized, so no one went to see it because we were all too cool for that. We saw how excited our parents were to see themselves in *The Big Chill*, so we publicly passed. The strange thing is, I don't know anyone my age who didn't love this movie and watched it on repeat. So just like Gen X was supposed to, we pretended we didn't care, but we sure as hell bought it on VHS and quietly watched it. Even one of the film's stars didn't want the film to be associated with Gen X. Janeane Garofalo said on her *Late Show with David Letterman* appearance for the film, "They are going to try to market it as a Generation X story, which is just the stupidest thing. It is not. It's just that that cast happens to be in their twenties and the director was in his twenties. It is just a love triangle story. It is just a normal small story. It's not Generation X or it's not whatever the studio's deciding whatever buzzword they are going to try to hook in to and market to." I think studios just stopped making films about us and that directly reflected us because they couldn't make money off a group that didn't trust corporations. So much of the film is about a generation that turned its back on what I like to call America's version of a monarchy: the multimillion-dollar corporations. Remember, Lelaina isn't mad when Michael lies to her about not being materialistic; she is mad when he lets Pizza Hut sponsor her documentary. This film reconfirmed my secret beliefs, and did again on this rewatch, that I must take every chance I can get to fight against corporations, greed, sponsorship, and anything that tries to take something beautiful and monetize it.

I started this essay by saying I went to see this movie one year after graduating college. It was 1994. You want to know what year I got my first corporate job? 2008. That was fourteen years later. I could feel Troy judging me. I could see Vickie mocking me for what I picked out to wear on my first day of work answering phones in a call center where every policy was centered around not helping any caller who wasn't trying to place a new order. I didn't want to have lunch in the cafeteria with Michael-esque supervisors who would incorrectly quote lines from *Seinfeld* to pretend to bond with me before they let me know I was talking too long to the customers on the phone. The only good part was when I would lock eyes with a fellow Lelaina and knew that we were both just saving this money, creating art after work, and hoping that someday we could convince In Your Face to distribute our work to the world. I only had to sell my soul for ten years in corporate America until I finally got my first book published. Luckily, it wasn't sponsored by Pizza Hut. It was mine. When Lelaina says, "I worked so hard" when she is talking about her documentary and how disappointed she is that it wasn't good enough to please the masses. I feel for her. Or does she feel for me? In so many ways, we are one and the same. We both had dreams of changing the world with our art. Neither of us did. Although she at least had an excuse for being so shocked that hard work not only doesn't pay off, it doesn't pay anything. She didn't have fair warning, but I was warned when I was twenty-four years old. Lelaina prepared me for what lay ahead with that one constant, honest, life fact that she whispered to me in a dark roomful of strangers sitting around me, "Reality bites."

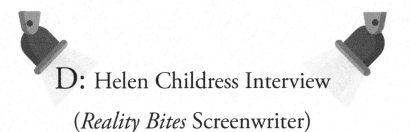

D: Helen Childress Interview

(*Reality Bites* Screenwriter)

"THERE WAS A SENSE OF SORT OF IMPENDING DOOM, BUT WE WERE KIND OF FUNNY ABOUT IT AND, LIKE, SARCASTIC ABOUT IT."

Scott Ryan: What do you think of when you think of the nineties?

Helen Childress: I was in my twenties for the nineties. I was born in 1969, when Woodstock happened, and I turned eighteen literally on the day of the stock market crash, which I think is the most Gen X thing ever, like, "Welcome to the world. It's over." But if I look back at the nineties, it's so funny, because I think there's such a parallel with today in many ways. The whole politically correct movement back then and the woke movement now. I have two daughters. They're seventeen and twenty-one. My oldest is older than I was when I started writing *Reality Bites*, but I see them going through kind of the same stuff. I'm not equating George Floyd with Rodney King, but it was sort of an awakening for the culture in terms of dealing with systemic inequality. And then we're talking about COVID all the time, the way that we talked about AIDS back then, and then the financial collapse in the early nineties. If you go back and look at the nineties, it's when, in my opinion, the country starts to split. I see my kids' generation and my joke is "I get canceled every night at dinner because I say the wrong thing." I mean, I say things like, "Wait a minute. How can that be wrong to say?" But it's like everything is wrong. It's all inappropriate. I can't say anything.

Ryan: Don't worry, my kids do the same thing. They don't have that Gen X way of just not caring what others think. When I first saw *Reality Bites*, I never heard of Gen X. I didn't know I was part of it. I had never been seen in a movie. All the movies were about my parents. They weren't about me, and then "Holy crap. I'm part of a generation."

Childress: Oh, right, it was because there was no internet.

Ryan: So it's interesting to hear you talk like a Gen Xer. That was the whole thing about being Gen X; we didn't put ourselves in boxes. We loved debate, and so my kids cancel me every night too. But I'm like, "It's okay for us to argue and be on the other side of an issue and still be best friends." You certainly couldn't have thought when you sat down to write this movie "I'm going to write about Gen X."

Childress: Not at all, and that's really because I started writing this in the summer of 1990. So the Generation X book hadn't come out yet [*Generation X: Tales for an Accelerated Culture* by Douglas Coupland, 1991]. The movie was called *Untitled Baby Busters Project,* because the generation at that point had been sort of named baby busters, because we were different from the baby boomers. The studio just trusted me. I was just like, "Hey, I'm twenty. Here's what me and my friends are talking about, and here's how we kind of hang out." A lot of times we sat around trying to remember what the lyrics were to *Schoolhouse Rock.* There was a sense of sort of impending doom, but we were kind of funny about it and, like, sarcastic about it. And there was a sense that you really couldn't change anything, anyway. There was a sense that we were probably not going to be as well off as our parents for the first time in modern history.

Ryan: Exactly, and there just weren't many movies being made about that at the time.

Childress: I guess *Singles* came out in 1992, but it seemed to be about older people, because they all had jobs. I love *Singles*. I read that script, and I died laughing. It's like one of the funniest, best scripts I ever read. But I didn't relate to it as much as *Clerks*. *Singles* seemed to be about people who had it together—like she got her keys and she threw them in a bowl, and she had a garage door opener, and I was like "I don't know anyone who lives like this." But I still love the movie, but it just wasn't it. It seemed to be more about the *Dazed and Confused* generation than our generation.

Ryan: I love that you are saying that because I agree. There is a different level of coolness in those movies that doesn't quite seem like me or my generation. I think you and I are the same age. Have you shown your children *Reality Bites*?

Childress: Yes, but I probably showed it to them too early. My youngest was ten and my older daughter was thirteen, and they were kind of embarrassed because they knew it was about me and their dad. I don't know if they liked it so much. I mean, I'm kind of embarrassed when I watch it, because it's like "Wow, they filmed my diary."

Ryan: So you wrote it about a relationship that you actually had? And that's either Troy or Michael?

Childress: Yes, it's really kind of based on my husband, and Michael was just kind of a composite of other guys that I had dated.

Ryan: Wait a minute. We have to just pause for one second because you realize that what we're finding out is pretty damn big here, because if I'm getting what you are saying here, this means Lelaina and Troy are still together!

Childress: [Laughs.] They are.

Ryan: I knew it! My wife and I just did a rewatch and afterwards she said, "They are gonna break up in a few years." And I was like, "No, they are meant for each other." One of the things I noticed this time is that Troy goes to dinner with Lelaina and her parents before the love triangle begins, and to me this shows that they really do care for each other and he knew she needed him, so he went. Now, when the romance starts happening, he does some squirrely things, but in the moment, he was there for her. So I think he's the one.

Childress: Yeah, that's it. You are so on the money. That's because my husband and I were friends in college for four years before we started dating, and we bonded a lot over having broken families. We were just there for each other, and he helped me deal with my sister. My sister actually played Lelaina's sister in the movie. She plays a character called Patty. I just basically modeled it on my own family. And so you're a hundred percent right. We're still together.

Ryan: This is exciting because I've shown this movie to my kids when they turned sixteen. Before the end of the movie, I pause it and ask them who Lelaina should be with.

Childress: Oh my God!

Ryan: Because I think this movie is a litmus test on what you care more about. If you pick Michael, then you care about security. If you pick Troy, then you care more about love. So you can learn a lot about them from who they choose. Did you create it with that mind?

Childress: Wait. I want to hear their answers.

Ryan: The ones who are passionate liked Troy, and two of the kids are very studious, very detail oriented; they liked Michael. So many people think Troy is a jerk.

Childress: Yeah.

Ryan: But Troy says, "Sometimes I will not do what you want me to do, and I will hurt you." I feel like it's laid out there. But we'll get to that. But as a writer, was that your idea? To pit passion versus possession?

Childress: When I started writing it, there was still kind of the holdover from the eighties, and Michael was kind of a yuppie. Really, it's funny when you look at that character now. Michael really ended up being a lot of Ben Stiller. He and I improvised a lot of that dialogue. The intention was she could choose a path of security and maybe not that much passion and nothing that was sort of transcendent, but something that could kind of take care of her. Or choose an equal partner in crime. Someone who really understood her and got her in a way that would support her and her art.

Ryan: Tell me about Michael in your original script, before Ben Stiller came on to the project.

Childress: He was an advertising executive who was doing market research on how to market to young people. He was trying to figure out how to make a commercial for this candy bar. And Troy in the script is a lot less of a jerk. He's just funnier and a little bit softer. In 1991, I gave Lelaina a video camera and she started taping her friends, and that gave her a goal to do something authentic with these videos. From that it just made sense that Michael would be in a position to basically co-op that video. And so that's kind of how that was born. Then Ben had done a character on his television show that was an agent character, which was so funny. He kind of took a little bit of that and then a lot of himself as an actor and just sort of gave him a new dimension. Suddenly Michael was really vulnerable, and he made the character super charming, almost too sweet, because people didn't like that she chose Troy.

Ryan: Looking at the film critically, I think it's the best triangle of any movie. Did you have a romantic comedy that you loved or you were inspired by?

Childress: There's two of them. The main inspiration was *Reds* (1981), the Warren Beatty movie.

Ryan: I love that *Reality Bites* comes from *Reds*, like this is what I'm saying about nineties movies. It was all intellectual. Can you imagine one of these current franchise movies being based on *Reds*? I just needed to get that out. I'm so sorry for interrupting.

Childress: First of all, I love that you love *Reds*. I love that you know *Reds,* because most people don't. A lot of younger people have never heard of it.

Ryan: We're the same age. I feel like we're brother and sister somewhere down the line.

Childress: We're comrades. [We both laugh.] *Reds* is one of those movies I saw, along with *The Elephant Man* (1980), in the theater when I was about eleven, and they just blew my mind. *The Elephant Man* changed my life. It was just the greatest. With *Reds,* I just thought the love triangle was so amazing with Jack Nicholson, Warren Beatty, and Diane Keaton. I didn't even understand what it was really about. But it was such a good story and such a good movie that I didn't need to understand which Communist Party was going to be recognized by Russia and America. So that was definitely one of the influences. And then the other one was *Broadcast News* (1987).

Ryan: DAMMIT! So I really wanted to start this interview by saying, "Your favorite movie is *Broadcast News,* isn't it?" But I didn't want to mess up the interview nexus if I was wrong, but I knew I wasn't.

Childress: I've seen it like fifty times. I idolized it.

Ryan: "I can sing while I read . . ."

Childress and Ryan: "I am singing and reading, BOOOOOTTHH."

Childress: I've memorized that movie.

Ryan: It's the greatest movie ever made.

Childress: I really agree with you. I was even just watching *Succession* the other night when Shiv scheduled her grief.

Ryan: It was Holly Hunter unplugging the phone . . .

Childress and Ryan: And wrapping the cord around it.

Ryan: I've never gone to a hotel and not said, [as Albert Brooks doing Arnold Schwarzenneger] "I'll meet you in the lobbies." You came up with great answers, and I just knew that you liked *Broadcast News.* But, of course, Holly Hunter doesn't choose either guy.

Childress: I remember at the time there was a lot of writing that the ending was anti-feminist because she gets punished for being a successful career woman and she doesn't end up with either guy. But at the end of the day, neither of those men were really perfect for her.

Ryan: You really don't know who Lelaina is going to pick. She could have picked either guy, because they are both viable.

Childress: I guess that's true. I mean I always knew she was picking Troy.

Ryan: Well, rumor has it you wrote the movie, so that could be why. By the way, I'm having a lot of fun.

Childress: I know, me too. This is really fun. My kids are sick of hearing about *Reality Bites.*

Ryan: So the other thing about your writing that is just a marvel to me is this movie has no exposition in its dialogue. This is a thing that drives me crazy now. We don't call our best friend and say, "Hi! It's Scott, who you worked with at Arby's from 1986 to 1990." Nobody talks that way. You never have a character express information to another character in your script.

Childress: I'm so flattered you're noticing that. Thank you.

Ryan: I want to talk about this one line. When Winona and Ethan have their big fight and she says, "You are on a one-way track to Loserville, USA. Just like him," you didn't write "Just like your dad," and no executive made you add that.

Childress: You're right. I never even thought about that. I got super lucky. I was never replaced. I was never rewritten. They never brought another writer on, anything like that. And I do remember writing that monologue, because that was my favorite monologue. It's just how people fight. It just felt like a real fight to me. The producers, Michael Shamberg and Stacey Sher, brought Quentin Tarantino to a wider audience. They got behind *Pulp Fiction*, and they pushed it. They put *Pulp Fiction* and *Reality Bites* into turnaround and made sure they both got made. They have incredible taste and incredible respect for audiences. Michael produced *The Big Chill* (1983) and *A Fish Called Wanda* (1988). I think *The Big Chill* is a great example of not overexplaining anything. And then also, obviously, Ben Stiller. He's a really serious person, and he really loves dramatic stuff even more than the comedy stuff.

Ryan: Do you remember thinking that it should be "your dad?"

Childress: I don't know. My husband and I went to the program at USC that was specifically for screenwriting. So literally all we did for four years was study screenplays, and they were good screenplays. We studied Ring Lardner, Jr., Paddy Chayefsky, Abe Polonsky, and Stewart Stern, and when you read those screenplays, they're like stage plays. There's so much taste and respect, and economy. For me, in a way, it's hard to write the other way, just because I'm always sensitive to any character who says, "I can't believe it's been two weeks since we talked last."

Ryan: That's exactly what I'm talking about.

Childress: It drives me crazy. So I don't think I ever had a draft that said "your dad." You're entirely right. The whole scene hinges on "him," because that's how well she knows Troy.

Ryan: Well, only someone who loves you, and knows everything about you, can slice you open so fast you don't even see it coming.

Childress: Oh my God, yeah. I've been married for thirty-three years. You're exactly right. Today they would probably add an ADR [automated dialogue replacement] where you cut away to the back of her head and you'd hear "your dad" looped in. I don't think it's even that screenwriters are writing to the lowest common denominator. They're writing to what the studio executives *think* is the lowest common denominator. People are so much smarter than they get credit for.

Ryan: And that's why people love *Reality Bites*, and quote it, and are still fighting about these characters.

Childress: You are so nice. I'm humbled. I mean honestly the film didn't really do that well. When it came out it was like, it opened at number five, and then it kind of went away. No one really talked about it for ten or fifteen years, and then people went, "Hey, that kind of captured the nineties a little bit," and they sort of started to remember it.

Ryan: How did that make you feel? When it didn't do well?

Childress: Well. It was bad. Stacey Sher said she figured it out: the people that we had written the movie for actually couldn't afford to go see it because everyone was broke. But the soundtrack did really well, so I was happy that it got popular.

[Scott Ryan picks up his vinyl copy of the *Reality Bites* soundtrack and holds it up.]

Ryan: Do you have the vinyl?

Childress: [Laughs.] I don't. It's such a great soundtrack. The music supervisor worked closely with Ben, and there were some songs that we both picked.

Ryan: What songs were in the script?

Childress: "Baby, I Love Your Way" and "My Sharona" were in the script. All the *Schoolhouse Rock* songs were in the script. The Violent Femmes song was in the script.

Ryan: Was U2's "All I Want Is You" in there?

Childress: No, that was Ben's genius. He wanted that song and pitched Bono on what the movie meant and described it to him. I don't know if he showed him the film or not. I can't remember. But it's really perfect. Ben also got Lenny Kravitz to do "Spinning Around Over You."

Ryan: What's your favorite song that was not in the script?

Childress: Well, I guess the obvious answer would be "Stay," which was not in the script. Oh, the song "I'm Nuthin'" was in the script. We got three different musicians to compose the song. I can't remember who chose it, but we picked David Baerwald's version. But at the same time, Lisa Loeb, who was a friend of Ethan's, wrote a version of "I'm Nuthin'," which I actually still have on cassette.

Ryan: What? I need to hear that. I love Lisa Loeb.

Childress: She's from Texas, and she's just a great girl. On that same tape she recorded "I'm Nuthin'" was "Stay." Ben's assistant Elise said, "I think you should really listen to this." And Ben did, and we were like, "Oh my God! That's a great song." And there you have it. It went on the soundtrack and put her in the stratosphere. But I love, I love that song, actually.

Ryan: So you're saying "I'm Nuthin'" was written specifically for the film? The lyrics are just perfect for Gen X. Especially when I was twenty-four, they meant everything to me. That's exactly how I felt.

Childress: I didn't write all the lyrics, but I think that the sentiment was there, and the first couple lines were in the script. Don't quote me on that, but I remember that the spirit of it was in the script.

Ryan: One of the cool things is that all the songs on the soundtrack are copyrighted from 1993 or 1994 except "All I Want Is You" which is from 1988.

Childress: What about "My Sharona"?

Ryan: The version on the soundtrack is copyrighted 1994. It does say remix. So they must have rerecorded it due to rights. I do remember it was released as a single.

Childress: With "Baby, I Love Your Way," the original is in the film, and then I think the deal struck with Universal was that we could use the original, Peter Frampton version in the film but that Ben had to include the Big Mountain version on the soundtrack, which I loved just as well. In fact, the funny thing is I took my daughter a few years ago to see the *Jumanji* remake, and the Big Mountain version featured very prominently in the film, and my daughter really liked that song, and I was like, "It's from the movie I wrote." She was like, "What?" I mean, the music was just a huge part of the film. I had something to do with it in the screenplay, but I do credit Ben, the producers, and the music supervisor, Karyn Rachtman, for pulling that all together. I think a lot of people had the soundtrack and never saw the movie at the time.

Ryan: Everyone I know loves the movie. I don't know anyone who doesn't watch it and knows everything about it, so it never went away.

That might not have been how it felt for you, but everyone secretly bought the VHS and watched it all the time. We were Gen X. We weren't going to broadcast to the world that we loved it or anything.

Childress: It felt like we'd made a movie and I threw it down a well because people kind of either didn't like it and were pretty vocal about not liking it—if I was at a party—or they hadn't seen it at all. I think people like it now, because there's a certain degree of nostalgia, and it's not threatening. It's not trying to say "Here's who you are." It's more like "Hey, here's a version of what you might have been." And there's a huge nostalgia factor.

Ryan: I don't see it that way at all. I don't like it because of some sense of nostalgia for the Clinton era or something. It's an actual good character movie.

Childress: Thanks. That is nice to hear. I do remember it came out and I was twenty-four, and it sort of failed, and I thought my life was over. I was like, "Okay, that's it. I tried, and I'm gonna keep working, but that was it." And it was incredibly depressing. I even considered moving back to Houston. It just seemed like I had just put all this effort into something and nothing really came from it.

Ryan: Right. Well as Lelaina says after her documentary gets ruined, "I worked so hard." And what else did you think would happen? You wrote the movie. I mean, come on. You knew they were gonna slap a Pizza Hut logo on there.

Childress: [Laughs.] "I knew it wasn't going to cure cancer, but it meant something to me."

Ryan: [Laughs.] Sorry. But this is why I've always wanted to interview you, in the same way I always wanted to interview Sheryl Lee from *Fire Walk With Me*. No one ever knows what will happen when you put art out into the world and how it can make it all the way to my little town in Massillon, Ohio, where I knew I wasn't doing what I was supposed to be doing. I mean, the idea that someday I'd be writing books about David Lynch movies and interviewing you, that was not gonna happen for me. And so to see your movie where Lelaina is struggling was everything to me. I was part her and part Troy. I was never Michael, but we see their struggles, and that's what we need to see. That is why artists need to create this type of art.

Childress: There wasn't really a way for people to reach each other back then. I remember going on AOL bulletin boards on the internet, but that wasn't until 1995, so the film was already over. But I've read a couple of times that the film was the first time people saw a gay person on film who was treated like just a member of the group. There was a writer from Georgia who came up to me and he said, just like you if you're in a small town in Georgia, *Reality Bites* was the first time he saw a "normal" gay guy as just part of a group—Sammy [Steve Zahn], who had his own deal and wasn't made fun of, or was like the butt of every joke. This is just a person who's gay, and I'm super proud of that. When I look back on it, it means a lot to me if it even helped one person feel comfortable with themselves or feel like they were okay.

Ryan: It is even more than that, because you gave the AIDS scare to the straight white girl.

Childress: Yeah, exactly. Well, that was the thing; he hadn't come out. He wasn't as comfortable getting into relationships, although at the end of the movie, he's sitting at the counter with his new boyfriend, Lance, who is actually played by my husband.

Ryan: Oh, so we can find the real Troy by taking a look at Lance?

Childress: He became friends over the shoot with Steve Zahn. We knew we wanted to include AIDS, and it seemed like a very *Melrose Place* thing to do to give the AIDS storyline to the gay guy, and Sammy wasn't sleeping around and Vicky was, and so it just seemed natural that it would be sort of Vicky's arc. I had friends, male and female, gay and straight, who had to get an AIDS test.

Ryan: "PFLAG, I'm beginning to like the sound of that."

Childress: That line came from the fact that my best friend from high school is a lesbian, and when she came out to her sister, who was a very conservative Christian woman in Texas, her sister wanted to support her but didn't know what to do. So she joined PFLAG. So that's what that scene was about. And Steve and Janeane are so good together.

Ryan: They really are. One of my friends and I reenact that scene. It is good there was no pushback on adding the AIDS and gay storyline.

Childress: We had more trouble with a story, and I'm pretty sure we filmed it, where Lelaina was working to get signatures for a pro-choice movement. She had a ball cap on that said "Choice." It was mine actually. And they made us cut that. So there was more trouble talking about abortion than there was talking about AIDS. So that scene got cut. Although we did sneak in the comment about the owner of Domino's. I cannot fucking believe we got away with that. It was one of those things where I had seen a *60 Minutes* report where they did an exposé on how much the owner of Domino's supported Operation Rescue [an anti-abortion group]. But there was no tape on it. So they just had to trust me that there was this segment where he said he supported it, and I still can't believe we got away with it.

Ryan: Let's talk about Winona Ryder, because we haven't yet, which seems ridiculous. Her performance is so incredible in this movie. I think it's her best performance ever, even down to when she's at the coffee shop and they announce her name over the loudspeaker and she looks so embarrassed. What did she bring to Lelaina that you didn't have on the page?

Childress: First of all, she is why the movie got made. She is why the money showed up. She was coming off of *House of Spirits* and *Age of Innocence*. She and I just bonded. We were very similar. We're the kind of people who apologized for everything. If a wrong number called us, we'll be like, "I'm sorry." We hate confrontation, but we're secretly angry and had a few of the same ticks back then. She added a whole layer of vulnerability, a softened sharpness, because sometimes the dialogue can be really kind of cutting. She just knew how to soften that. I can't say enough about her as an actress, because she has so many layers. At first you meet Winona and she is supersweet, kind of shy, and then you kind of get a layer beneath that and she's got a dark sense of humor, and then you get a little bit beneath that and it's like, "Oh, actually, she's really intelligent." As Janeane Garofalo used to say, "Everyone loved her. The geeks. The jocks. Everyone." She's just so beautiful. Winona loved Vickie and Lelaina. She once joked that she thought they should get together as a couple

Ryan: What did Ethan Hawke bring to Troy?

Childress: So much. He brought himself. I think he wore his own wardrobe. He brought like an intelligence beyond even what I was expecting for the role, and also a vulnerability, that kind of wasn't all there in the writing. He brought a romanticism to the role that did surprise me. He's so good in it. I love him.

Ryan: Now here's such a specific question. Please forgive me. But I say this line almost every time we leave the house. I've been saying it for thirty years, and I embarrassingly even wrote a song named after it. I'm curious if this is your line or a Garofalo improv, but when she is leaving, she says, "Let's locomote."

Childress: That's in the script. I think I had a friend, Elizabeth, who said that, and I just wrote it down.

Ryan: This line had to break your heart for it to be cut, and I just want to talk about it because it's such a wonderful line that Lelaina says to her parents in a deleted scene: "Who am I if I'm not taking out the trash?" That one hurt you that it got cut.

Childress: That honestly . . . [sighs in pain]. I know Ben agonized over it. He was contractually obligated to turn in a cut that was a certain number of minutes, and the problem is you couldn't just stick the family therapy scene in there without having the predicate scene of meeting Patty, the sister, because it wouldn't make sense. It just went over the time that we had. It was the one thing we could pull out and the movie still kind of worked. Although I will say I think if we could have left it, it would have given it an exponential depth, because it really does go into something more serious. The cut scene is the family getting therapy. It really deals with the generational trauma that happened to a lot of us, which is basically the epidemic of divorce in the seventies. I think that really informed Troy and Lelaina's whole relationship. It did break my heart. I wish it could have been left in, but at the end of the day, it's on the deleted scenes. I always tease Ben that maybe he'll do a director's cut.

Ryan: Yes, please. My guess is that "Who am I if I'm not taking out the trash?" isn't just Lelaina, but it's you as well?

Childress: Yeah, I think it's a lot of people. It's probably an older-daughter syndrome when your family breaks up. Usually there's an older sibling who kind of assumed the parental role, and that was me. And that's what that line was all about. Winona acted that scene so well, and my sister's performance as Patty just blew us all away.

Ryan: Where does that scene go in the movie?

Childress: It goes right before Lelaina goes home and starts packing to go to Chicago. So that was kind of the arc there, because basically her journey was more like being willing to step out of that role of fixing everything and being responsible for everybody else at the expense of her own happiness. And so that to me was kind of her journey, to break apart from the family of origin and be willing to risk starting a relationship and a new life with someone she loved.

Ryan: Ben Stiller has become one of the best directors working today. *Severance* is amazing. What can say about him as a director?

Childress: When I think of Ben, it always strikes me that one of his favorite movies is *Picnic at Hanging Rock*, the early Peter Weir film. It's so not what you would think would be Ben Stiller's favorite movie, and it just shows his depth and his degree of really absorbing film. He sort of came out fully formed. He storyboarded all those shots, and he just somehow knew how to do it. The hardest thing is to put yourself in a movie that you're directing. We had a great cinematographer, Emmanuel Lubezki [*Birdman, Gravity*], and he's known as one of the great DPs of all time.

Ryan: I can't help thinking that you have it wrong. I don't think you realize how much people love this movie. Yes, I love the movie. But I'm telling you, all my friends are so excited that I'm talking to you today, and they quote the movie all the time. This movie really and truly matters to people my age.

Childress: I mean, I couldn't be more touched. It's hard, you know. I work a lot in TV now, and that's very satisfying. And I love working with other people. But it's like, and I've worked every single quarter since then, I've never stopped working. It was the only movie that I ever got made. And so the fact that it means something to people is incredibly moving and humbling and touching, and you know, because that's the one I wrote, and that's it.

Ryan: But it's a masterpiece, and it captures this moment perfectly. And even beyond that, I've been studying 160 movies from the nineties. And this movie stands right alongside any of them. *Pulp Fiction, Shawshank Redemption*, and *Reality Bites*.

Childress: Those are great. When I was writing *Reality Bites*, some of the time I was at Jersey Films, at their offices on the Sony lot, and Quentin Tarantino was there too. Quentin and I had offices side by side, and he was writing *Pulp Fiction*. He went to Amsterdam to write it, but he came back to rewrite it, and so he was in one office and I was in the office next door. I will never forget he came in, and he read me a monologue. It was the one where Marsellus Wallace gets raped. In Quentin's first draft, the guy gets raped to "Grandpa, Tell Me 'bout the Good Old Days" by the Judds. I never forgot that, because I remember he read it and I died laughing. It was really an amazing time.

Ryan: Before I ask you my last question, is there a memory or a story that we're leaving behind?

Childress: This is gonna sound corny, but it's probably my friendship with Ben, just because it's really rare to meet someone when you're twenty-two and still be friends with them in Hollywood when you're fifty-three. He always wanted me there, and the first day of shooting was the scene where Winona and Ben go on their date. It was shot at Urth Caffé, and he really wanted me to play the waitress. This was a big deal, because you had to Taft-Hartley someone into the union. It cost $1,500, and I was broke almost the entire time of writing and shooting. I got paid $75,000 to write it, but over three years. So I never had any money. Ben and Stacy went into the petty cash, and they paid my initiation fee to get into SAG that morning so I could play the waitress, because he just really wanted me to be part of the film. And to me, that's just really sweet.

Ryan: Well, isn't that just wonderful. You blew my last question! My question was going to be "Who's that bad actress that plays the waitress in the movie?" Real nice, because I knew it was you.

Childress: Oh, no! It was the perfect last question, but we were psychically connected. We had a mind meld.

Ryan: I'm so embarrassed. I have to wipe my flop sweat off my forehead with this towel.

[Ryan brings out a *Reality Bites* beach towel and wipes his face.]

Childress: Oh my God! Where did you even get that?

We ended our interview with me showing Helen Childress my towel, and her ready to throw in the towel and end this obsessive fan's list of questions.

Ryan: Do you not have a *Reality Bites* beach towel?

Childress: I didn't even know there was such a thing.

Ryan: It goes with my vinyl and my movie poster.

Childress: Honestly, I'm gonna cry. This means so much to me that anyone would like the movie that much.

Ryan: We better end it here. I am Barbara Waltersing you.

Childress: This has been such a pleasure and such a joy to talk to you. It's meant so much to me.

Chapter 6
Intermission

How to Watch a Movie Nineties Style

Movies were created for the masses. From the beginning, going to a movie theater was always cheap entertainment. A buffalo nickel to watch a silent film sounds as close to the value menu at Taco Bell as one could get in the early 1900s. Later on, there were matinees for people to go to the newest blockbusters earlier in the day for a cheaper price. When I was a kid, I didn't even know movies were shown at night. I think the first time I ever paid full price for a movie ticket was when I went to see Edward Zwick's *The Last Samurai* in 2003. I had gone to dinner with some friends at a very expensive steak house. Since they bought dinner, I said I would get the movie tickets. I remember saying, "I'll take three for *The Last Samurai.*" The ticket seller said, "That'll be $31.75." I replied, "Will Mr. Tom Cruise be watching the movie with us?" They weren't amused either. Slowly but surely, the industry has tried to make the movie-watching experience as horrible as possible and expensive as hell. They added a ton of commercials and turned the volume up to a ridiculous degree to make the people in the theater talk louder so they can be heard over the film, because almost every movie watcher has no idea they are not watching the movie at their home. In 2023, AMC announced they would look into charging a premium price for the good seats in the theater. I love this. It reminds me of how you have to pay extra for food that isn't poisoned with chemicals. "Oh, you didn't want this food to kill you? That'll be extra." You wanted your hot dogs to fit in the bun? You have to pay extra for bun length. And now it's the same with movies, "Oh, you wanted to sit somewhere you can see the movie? Pay up." Who knows what rules will be in place by the time this book gets published. Maybe they will charge extra if the movie is good. Soon you will have to pay more to hear the audio. The ticket will just get you the ability to see the picture. I am sure some executive will find a way to squeeze money out of the industry even as it kills the very tree that produces the fruit they survive on.

Once major corporations started owning theaters, instead of a local townsperson whom you went to church with, saw at the barber shop or the grocery store, then it became a lot easier to jack up the price and lower the services they offered. The person making these decisions will never have to look any ticket buyer in the face at the closest Walmart, mostly because they don't ever have to shop at that store. Once movie theaters were owned by companies that were used to making millions of dollars for any product they sell, well then, hell, there was no reason not to raise the prices and make it an *experience* that costs more and offers less. Maybe the problem started when movies became a product and not art. Corporations will always find a way to price poor people out of consuming a product. Since the nineties, prices have started to get ridiculous for Broadway shows, live concert tickets, and now movies. All these events, which used to be for everyone, have been priced to make the filthy rich even filthier.

The last new film I went to see in a theater on opening day was Tarantino's *Once Upon a Time in Hollywood* (2019). The movie was wonderful, but the experience was horrible. Everyone was on their phones, there were at least forty minutes of commercials in front of the film, and every preview was an affront to my intelligence. It sure seemed like every upcoming movie had a computer-generated creature belch. Each expulsion of gas got a loud guffaw from the audience.

And this was in a Tarantino crowd. They should be demanding better. Maybe everyone else just accepts what they are given. It makes me think of what Michael J. Fox said in *The American President*, "When they discover there's no water, they'll drink the sand." I never really liked drinking sand, so that is why I basically gave up on new movies and went back to watching older films. I suppose there might be a new movie that will come out some day that will make me go see a new movie in the theater, but I doubt it. It isn't just the theater experience that is bad, it is the human experience. It feels to me that people have just plain forgotten how to watch a movie.

For me, the experience of watching a movie begins before you even see the movie. So much of the experience is knowing what the right movie is to select. I just realized that sharing this might seem like I expect other people to be like me, and I don't. I just figured halfway through this book you might as well get a scary peak at what goes on in this movie connoisseur's brain. The first thing you must know is to stay the hell away from previews. I stopped watching previews in the nineties because that is when they just started to ruin movies. I have heard many people say that previews give away the best parts. I disagree. If a movie can give away its best parts in a two-minute preview, the movie wasn't very good to begin with. The danger of most previews is that they are likely to give away a plot point that will ruin the end. If you are a writer or someone with an eye for story, these things can be troublesome. Hell, sometimes it's the poster that gives things away. *The Prince of Tides* shows Barbra Streisand and Nick Nolte in bed together. Hmm, wonder if they will get together in the movie? *The Shawshank Redemption* shows Tim Robbins standing free with his arms spread wide in the pouring rain. If we can't trust the poster, how can we trust a preview? The truth is a preview is for the masses who are longing to laugh at cartoon burps. The best way to select a movie to watch is by doing research. (Ugh. You mean it has to be work? I'm out.)

Before I watch any movie, I have to hear about it from three different sources. They have to all be positive comments and have to, in some way, mention that the movie is different from every other movie. Therefore, if I read something that says "The next *Rain Man*."

or "This year's *Boyhood*," I'm passing. The three sources can be one person I know, one tweet that is specific in its praise, and an article that gave it a positive review. This is usually how I chose the one new movie I watch each year. I have a friend (you know it's you, Josh) who loves every film or TV show he watches. His bar that a movie has to cross is just that he had to see it. So his endorsement doesn't weigh as high as someone whose taste is similar to mine. Same goes with the review. I used to trust when a movie was mentioned by David Letterman on his show. Today, if Seth Meyers does a joke about it in his "Closer Look" segment, then I know it is crossing over to the pop culture zeitgeist and I might want to take a look if I hear about the film from two more sources. As for late night talk show appearances, I will often times mute when the actors start talking about a film I want to see because that could lead to spoilers. When *Once Upon a Time in Hollywood* was released, I didn't watch any of those appearances. I never watched a preview, never read an article because I knew I was going to see the movie. I follow Fox Mulder rules when it comes to previews or publicity for a movie before I see it: trust no one.

And this leads me to the main way I select movies today, as well as how I did back when I was working at Video Time. I pay attention to who wrote and directed the film. For years I have read the opening credits of every film I watched. I pay attention to them with the same devotion my daughters stare at Instagram. I always know who wrote and directed a film before I see it. That is how I learned that I liked Mike Nichols's films. Back in the eighties, I loved *Working Girl,* and I remembered his name. This was why I went to see *Postcards from the Edge* in the theater when it came out in 1990. That led me to going back to watch *The Graduate* and then moving forward to see *The Birdcage.* Over time, I knew that if the director was Mike Nichols, then the film was going to be funny and take its main characters seriously. It was also going to have a plot that was for grown-ups. I have always been more likely to go see a movie in the theater because of the director over the actor. Quentin Tarantino, Steven Spielberg, Amy Heckerling, Paul Thomas Anderson, Alexander Payne, David Lynch, Tony Scott, Greta Gerwig, Mike Nichols, Rob Reiner, Robert Altman, Jodie Foster, Spike Lee, and Martin Scorsese are directors

I will watch everything they release because I know it is going to be worth my time. For writers, (yes, I know some of these are also directors) it is Charlie Kaufman, Carrie Fisher, Martin McDonagh, Nora Ephron, James L. Brooks, Elaine May, Cameron Crowe, Aaron Sorkin, Richard Linklater, Lowell Ganz, and Babaloo Mandel. There are very few actors whom I follow from picture to picture over a writer or director. Be educated in the movies you watch, because it is the craft of filmmaking that is key to enjoyment. Previews are for the masses; credits are for the cinephiles.

Here is the tip you all have been waiting for since the moment you saw the title of this chapter. Are you ready? Of course you are. Put. Your. Fucking. Phone. The. FUCK. DOWN. Oh, you can't because you are watching the movie on your phone? Here, I will let David Lynch take this one. He said, "Now if you are playing the movie on a telephone, you will never in a trillion years experience the film. You'll think you have experienced it, but you'll be cheated. It's such a sadness that you think you've seen a film on your fucking telephone. Get real." Who are we to argue with the maestro? But of course you can't watch a movie on your phone. A movie is larger than life. It is supposed to be forty feet high, not 5G wide. You can't have a notification pop up that says: the *New York Times* just posted an article about global warming just as Idgie and Ruth are cooking up BBQ out of a violent man at the Whistle Stop Cafe in *Fried Green Tomatoes*. I can't even imagine what kind of human can doom scroll Instagram while watching *Schindler's List*, besides Jerry Seinfeld. Do you really need to know that @ScottLuckStory tweeted about his next book just as Bruce Willis realizes why Haley Joel Osment's mom has not been paying his psychiatrist bills in *The Sixth Sense*? No. Who cares what's going on in the news, what people are posting on Facebook, or that your kid is texting you to find out how long they should bake a pizza? Let them burn it or eat it raw. None of it matters for two hours. Get lost in the world of the plight of Meg Ryan's bookstore in *You've Got Mail*. Forget your troubles when The Wonders hear their song on the radio for the first time in *That Thing You Do!* There is no way you will cry if you have been checking your email when the older version of Alicia Witt shows up to play the clarinet in *Mr. Holland's Opus*. When I saw *E.T.*

in the theater in 1982, I cried so hard the person sitting in front of me literally drowned in my tears. I had to serve a prison term of five years in juvie for involuntary manslaughter for crying so hard at that movie. There is no way I could have cried like that had I, even for a moment, dipped back into real life. Your phone, your notifications, your likes, your texts, your emails, your family do not matter more than a movie. If they do, then don't watch it. At least two hundred humans worked together for at least a year to bring you this film; respect their time. Nothing annoys me more than when someone tells me a movie that I know is an emotional beating was just fine and that they didn't cry. Then I ask them if they were on their phone while they watched, which is a waste of a question because everyone is on their phone.

My phone is not touched during a movie. It isn't looked at or glanced at. If we pause at some point to get a snack, or go to the bathroom, sure, take a quick look, but not while the movie is playing. This is one of the reasons I think movies are getting dumbed down. Filmmakers know you are on your phone, so they have to keep having characters restate the plot because they know people aren't paying attention the entire time.

If the kind of movies you watch are the kind where you can do two things at once, then you are not watching well-crafted, deep, intelligent, hard-to-follow movies. In the nineties, movies were made to make your brain cells fire on all cylinders. They were made to be experienced in a theater, or at home on a VHS tape that was hard to navigate or skip around. You pushed play, you forgot your life, and then you reluctantly went back to it with a new understanding of a way of life that wasn't a part of you before. Let go of now and get lost in the story.

The main way I watched most of the movies covered in this book for the first time was at home. Whether it was on VHS or DVD, it was so great to watch movies at home. Fast forward through those previews. Set up your VCR to another VCR and copy the movie on a Fuji VHS tape that you bought for $1.99. I mean, who cared if it sometimes had tracking issues? Who cared if it had those colored wavy lines at the top? It didn't matter, you owned a copy of *Groundhog Day* and you were thrilled. If those FBI warnings were true, I'd be so in debt you would think I was the national government. When DVDs came around, studios started to include bonus features. For a nerd like me, that was better than free popcorn at a matinee. Man, do I miss bonus features, commentaries, deleted scenes, and interviews with the writers and directors. That is how I learned so much about film. Also, a ton of the quotes from this book came from those bonus features. The *Clueless* DVD alone is incredible. Here is a movie made for teenagers, yet they have segments on production design, wardrobe, writing, directing, and even the DP. No one at Paramount thought, "Let's skip covering the bones of the movie; all they want is to see Alicia Silverstone." Even the bonus features showed us respect in the last decade of cinema. That is all gone with streaming. You hardly can even find a streaming service that will allow you to watch the end credits, let alone give you a bonus feature about the director of photography. Two seconds after the screen goes to black (and God help me, sometimes two seconds BEFORE the screen goes to black, screw you, HBO or HBO Max or Max or whatever stupid thing you are calling yourself; just let us watch what we picked to stream) here comes the Skip button to bring up the next thing for you to consume. Dear Lord, don't we even get a second to think about what you just saw? Just devour this next crappy movie we are suggesting to you because no one will watch this one and we paid for it. Maybe after watching all that is the beautifully crafted *Magnolia*, I might need a moment to think about if what I just saw drop from the sky actually did drop from the sky.

Streaming services are never happy that you are watching something; they only want you to watch the NEXT thing. I'm not saying I watch the entire end credits to every movie, but many times that is how I learned who sang that song I really enjoyed. Reading credits on a VHS was like trying to decode my handwriting. I remember for years I wanted to know what songs were not on the released soundtrack from David Lynch's *Fire Walk With Me*. The text was so small, and pausing didn't help. Pausing made the screen have more lines in it than an accountant's spreadsheet. There was no IMDb to look things up; you had to figure them out for yourself. But I backed up those credits over and over. "Ooh, 'Deer Meadow Shuffle.' How do I get that song?"

Credits are research. Research leads to smarter choices and teaches us how to become better movie watchers.

I am saddened that today, people don't even have DVD players anymore. So many of the films covered in this book are not streaming. There are no video rental stores, and no one has a machine to play anything on. How is anyone going to discover *Citizen Ruth*, *Muriel's Wedding*, *Defending Your Life*, or *Beautiful Girls*? I discovered the classics from the seventies by renting them at Video Time, and it turned me into a cinephile. Is anyone out there a stream-a-phile? No way. Streaming isn't about learning; it's about binging. Consumption of product, not the widening of an education. I can't say it better than David Lynch did: Get real.

Okay. Now I am thoroughly depressed. Intermission over. Check your phone and see what horrific event happened in the world and then move on to 1995.

Chapter 7
1995

A: *Before Sunrise*

"DO YOU HAVE ANY IDEA WHAT THEY WERE ARGUING ABOUT?"

What could be more fun than to fall in love with a stranger on a train? There can't be a more romantic place to lock eyes with someone and quickly look away. Add in the facts that this train is rolling through Europe and the two people locking eyes are Ethan Hawke and Julie Delpy and you have the film ingredients for *Before Sunrise*. Where are you gonna fall in love today that tops that? Not in line while Southwest Airlines partitions you into class-based letters and sections. No one in the A group is going to lock eyes with someone with C group status. What if they don't have TSA precheck? Are you gonna fall in love with a stranger in an Uber car? No. We all have our heads down, AirPods in, and the outside world is totally shut out. The film reminds us of a time before we sealed ourselves in our own private bubbles, back when we were open to strangers, or when we left our homes. We get to see two twentysomethings meet on a train rolling through the old towns of Europe on its way to Vienna. "Vienna waits for you," sang Billy Joel on *The Stranger*. Richard Linklater, with cowriter Kim Krizan, and a major assist from the attractive cast of Ethan Hawke (Jesse) and Julie Delpy (Céline), sets *Before Sunrise* in Vienna, and love waits for everyone who watches this midnineties romance.

Before Sunrise is basically an all-talk movie, which, if you haven't noticed yet, is my favorite type of movie. Plot is overrated in a film. If you can create two true-to-life characters, set them up with a running clock, and add great conversation, what else do you need? When I was a little kid, I used to watch the 1978 Alan Alda and Ellen Burstyn movie *Same Time, Next Year* all the time on HBO. They were the only two people in the movie. They meet every year on the same weekend and have a lifelong affair. All they do is talk. I have no idea why I loved the movie as a kid, but it reminds me of the same feelings I have for *Before Sunrise*. Both movies are right up my alley. The idea of finding someone who would want to debate and discuss the finer points of life, past loves, their lack of belief in God, and their fears for their future is about as close to film Gen X foreplay porn as a movie can get. The idea that I could find a girl as beautiful as Julie Delpy (Céline) who wanted to talk about the collapse of the environment and the government is an aphrodisiac to a person like me, who loves talk. She also calls Ethan Hawke (Jesse) on every piece of bullshit he tries to sling past her. She has no trouble busting his balls when he makes fun of romance only a few moments after saying how romantic it would be to kiss her during their Ferris wheel ride. She is also way smarter than he is. When she discusses Georges Seurat's art, you can tell he has no idea who she is talking about. Kudos to Ethan Hawke for allowing these acting moments to come through. He knows she is out of his league, and he is doing what all guys do in that situation: just try not to be found out. She is a perfect specimen of a dream girl from the nineties. It isn't to say Hawke's Jesse isn't well-developed. He also is a dream, for a woman who wants a sensitive man who can discuss the finer points of life and isn't trying nonstop to get into her pants while he is actively trying nonstop to get into her pants. A friend of mine really wanted this book to be all personal stories from my twenties that tie to the movies I watched. Hot damn, do I wish I had a story to go with this movie, but I have never picked up a sexy French woman on a plane, train, or automobile. Hell, I couldn't even pick up John Candy on one of those. No, this film is all fantasy: meeting someone and then allowing the talk, discussion, and debate be all the sexual tension you could ever need. Our parents had *Basic Instinct* in the nineties, and we had *Before Sunrise*.

Come Here

The nineties was the last decade where romantic comedies were a staple at the cinema, with *You've Got Mail, Pretty Woman, Ghost,*

Sleepless in Seattle, *While You Were Sleeping*, and *The Wedding Singer* to name just a few. I say you can pick whatever you think is the most romantic, hottest moment in any of those films and compare it to the record store scene with Hawke and Delpy and *Sunrise* will win. The couple grab a record and take it into a listening booth. The room barely fits two people. They stand very close to each other and listen to Kath Bloom's "Come Here." When her soprano voice is first heard, Hawke lets a sly smile appear on his face. We can imagine this isn't his kind of music, but he isn't going to spoil this moment by laughing at the vocals. Each person glances at the other person just after the other looks away. They do this so perfectly it amazes me each time. Their eyes dance from staring to being shy with such precision, it feels like their glances were choreographed by Twyla Tharp. Was director Linklater calling out, "Look away. Now, Ethan, look at her. Now Julie"? I don't know, and I don't wanna know. I want to believe they just sensed the passion between each other. While moviegoers today are enthralled with one person shooting down twenty faceless guards as they break into the Hall of Justice, I am enthralled by watching two actors create the moment when you want to kiss someone so badly it is the only reason you exist in life. Should we take that leap? Will it ruin the relationship? Can I take the risk? Do they feel the same way as I do? Are they out of my league? But then passion takes over, and they steal one last look, hoping the other is staring back at them, but it never happens. This is why romantic comedies succeeded in the nineties. These two really have a reason to be afraid to make the leap. They have this moment, this one evening, and that is all. He has to get on a plane and go back to America tomorrow. She lives in France. This is all the time they have in the world, and every moment matters. You can have Sharon Stone crossing and uncrossing her legs. I'll take stolen glances and the fear of moments missed any day.

This is just one scene in a movie filled with romance. The film didn't set out to capture the time, but it sure did. There are no cell phones, no Facebook, no mention of the internet. The characters are worried about the environment, governments, and the fall of society, but every generation worries about that. The simplicity of the film is a staple of Richard Linklater's best work, but in this film, it works as a genre as well as matches the story. When two people fall in love, the rest of the world really doesn't matter. The only thing that matters is the thoughts and feelings of that other person. This isn't a new concept in movie love stories. You can go all the way back to *Casablanca* (1942) and get a love story set in the worry of the crumbing world around them. "Ilsa, I'm no good at being noble, but it doesn't take much to see that the problems of three little people don't amount to a hill of beans in this crazy world." The hill of beans will always be there, but watching *Before Sunrise* today shows just how damn innocent we were in the nineties. Political issues are evergreen, but from *Casablanca* through *Sunrise*, human contact and connection were still the mode of communication. Would the movie have to be called *Before Swiping Left* if it were made today?

The talking does take a back seat when they finally kiss a few scenes after the record store, and it is the female who initiates the kiss. Her character has all the power. The reason everything feels so real in this script is because the actors helped craft the characters and the dialogue. Julie Delpy said, "Ethan and I basically rewrote most of the dialogue—89 percent. There are maybe three scenes left from the original screenplay." Hawke said, "The movie had to be an expression of ourselves. For it to feel substantive, there has to really be a connection. We had to kind of find out where was the intersection of Ethan and Julie? And then create a connection of Jesse and Céline and blur the line." Allowing the actors to craft the words their characters spoke makes the entire film feel real.

Ethan Hawke mocks religion, mocks the palm reader, mocks the poet. He doesn't believe in anything. A young man in his early twenties fears anything that is uncertain. Delpy says later in the film, "I believe if there is any kind of God, it wouldn't be in any of us. Not you or me. But just this little space in between. If there's any kind of magic in this world, it must be in the attempt of someone sharing something." What a beautiful, thoughtful idea. Something only a confident female could share this early in a relationship. Hawke and all his maleness would never let his guard down to share this beautiful idea. She, just like him, is longing for a connection in this world, but she is ready to share herself. What else is there but the attempt to share our inner feelings with someone else? That space between us can be filled with love or contempt. This film is all about the decision to fill that space with love. Both are attempting to settle down and feel love, but how much are they willing to share and trust a stranger to get it and to let them in? This is an action-adventure film because it covers the scariest thing a human can do: trust. The gift that this film gives romantics is the joy of watching two people struggle in making a life decision. Life isn't about whether we succeed or fail; life is the chance to constantly have the gift of attempting something. Richard Linklater was attempting something he would do over and over again in his films: try to capture as close to real life on film as he can. He succeeded in *Before Sunrise*.

Linklater had already created a name for himself with his breakthrough 1990 film, *Slacker*. This had the same kind of buzz Kevin Smith's *Clerks* had in 1994. Both were underground, independent director heroes. It was 1993's *Dazed and Confused* that gave Linklater a hit movie. (*Mallrats* didn't do that for Smith.) Linklater would take the concept of *Before Sunrise* and turn that into 2014's *Boyhood*. See, and you thought I hated all films made outside of the nineties. Nonsense. While *Sunrise* is certainly one of the best films of the nineties, *Boyhood* is Linklater's masterpiece. While *Sunrise* captures one evening, *Boyhood* follows the growth of a child from age six to eighteen. They filmed one week a every year from 2002-2013. As of the writing of this book, he is currently pulling the same trick of following a story over decades, allowing the actors to age and mature, with Stephen Sondheim's *Merrily We Roll Along*. He basically took what he learned in *Sunrise* and has stretched the idea out from one night to a lifetime with characters, allowing them to age naturally. Linklater wants to capture life in real time, but also is careful to be sure the plot, shots, and characters are still interesting. Like I have pointed out in many other of these films, he also has a ton of oners. One of the really long takes is shot on a bus where a discussion lasts for six minutes without a cut. This is the way he makes it all feel like real life. He gives the actors the chance to tell their story and keep the scenes so alive.

Two-thirds of the way through the movie, there are several

conversations containing strangers in a coffee shop, where most of the dialogue is in another language with no subtitles provided. We don't need to know what the strangers are saying. We actually just need a little break from conversation, and Linklater decides we get that break by hearing more conversation, just the kind we can't comprehend. When we get back to our couple, they are placed on opposite sides of a booth, and the film has its most rom-com moment when each character pretends to call their imaginary friend and to tell them about each other. The scene is sold by the absolute charm that each actor brings to this moment. While I was rewatching the film, I bet myself a trip to Vienna that this was the scene the movie trailer was based around. (I'm booking my ticket as I type this.) This moment of them pretending to talk to their friend but actually telling the other person how they truly feel about them is adorable and works perfectly because we had an hourlong buildup of getting to know how they felt before we see this typical movie scene. The conversations up to this point have all been philosophical and deep, but here we are treated to a moment of whimsy and fun. In doing research for this essay, I learned the original script didn't have this scene written but just had a note that said the café scene had to be the best scene in the film. No pressure there. There aren't a ton of cutesy "Meg Ryan/Tom Hanks" moments in the film, but it's nice to have one of them, especially when it's been earned.

Let's get to the real reason this movie is picked. It's the badass ending of the film. With only twenty-four minutes remaining, the characters finally discuss what we have been wondering the entire time. Will they ever see each other again? After a scene where they decide there is no point in exchanging information because that will cheapen the moment, they decide they will never see each other again. They will just create a lifetime of memories in one night. A few scenes later, they are laying down on some grass in the middle of the night. Céline suggests they should not have sex, since they are never gonna see each other again. He tries to convince her, but she says no. Then she starts making out with him, and the camera pans up. We have no proof whether they had sex or not. The following morning, a few moments before boarding her train, they make the decision to meet up again at this exact spot in six months. He heads to the airport; she gets on the train. Will they meet again? Will they stay in love forever? Did they have sex? We will never know. The movie ends.

It is rare in any decade to have an ambiguous ending. It was not a cliffhanger. It was an open ending because YOU have to decide. If you are a romantic, you might think they had sex and they met up in six months. If you are a pessimist, you might think they had sex and they don't meet up. There would be some viewers who might think they didn't have sex but do meet up. It was there for you and your friends to debate, to wonder. What is the answer? The text from the film doesn't tell us, but you know what you think, and that is all that matters. Here is a movie whose only plot point is about if these two characters fall in love and live happily ever after, and the film won't even tell you that. I remember having a ton of arguments with my friends about how it played out. But I don't remember anyone being upset that they didn't explain it. In an interview with Bobbie Wygant in 1995, Linklater said, "I think they do meet again. I think we all have this capacity to be very romantic and project romance. I think they would spend the next six months thinking, 'I can't wait to see them again.'" It was just his opinion; there is no proof. The fact that he was answering this in 1995 shows that he had no intention of ever continuing the story. The ending left you to wonder about so many things, and that bravery was so very nineties. I can't imagine how angry audiences would be today, or how certain everyone would be that these characters were just created for the sole purpose of continuing the story to another movie. But *Before Sunrise* wasn't created during the time of franchises, IPs, or sequels. This was just one night of romance followed by a gloriously unrequited lifetime to hope, to wonder, and to fall in love for the first time night after night after night.

A.5: *Before Sunrise* (Coda)

Was it killing you that I wasn't mentioning *Before Sunset* or *Before Midnight*? Did my little trick work? Were you saying, "This guy doesn't know anything about movies. He thinks we don't know what happened? They made two more films. We know exactly what happened!" But we didn't know that in the nineties. No one was thinking there would be more. Not even Linklater, who said on the Criterion release, "After the first movie, there was no one in the world asking for a sequel." Julie Delpy said, "The idea that the character would want to meet him again came from me. Because the original screenplay was like that, they would have this night and then never see each other again. So the idea of a sequel really came from this idea. For me, what is interesting in these films is this conversation between this love that keeps on going."

I wanted to write about *Before Sunrise* as it played in the nineties—when there was no hope or even an idea that they would make another of these films. It was just a romantic litmus test. Once we know there are two more movies, the original ending is destroyed. The bravery is gone. The new bravery is in following a lifelong relationship and how one can keep that fire alive. I think that is a very important topic. It's a different topic, and does ruin the ending, but it's a worthy topic. I am not upset that they made a trilogy out of the film. In fact, I am hoping there will be a total of five films. Because the idea of seeing them growing older would tell a wonderful story. Once they took away the litmus test, which made it a nineties classic, the only thing left to do is to continue on with the story. Hopefully we see them in their sixties and then their eighties. These two characters are there to take us through a lifetime of love, devotion, and what all that means. All three movies are beautiful in their own way, but it only works if they take it all the way to the conclusion of their lifetime. To leave five films behind of what each of these decades were like would be worthy of the mystery of love that Jesse and Céline unknowingly found on that train ride to Vienna.

B: *To Die For*

"You're not anyone in America unless you are on TV."

It all happens in Little Hope, New Hampshire. And if there was little hope for the culture in 1995, when it came to undeserving people wanting fame at any cost, there is certainly no hope today. There are movies that age poorly because times change and the slang characters use in movies becomes outdated, or is seen as inappropriate or classless. Then there are movies that age badly because they are too sweet, and their warnings for how things are getting bad weren't anywhere near harsh enough. *Broadcast News* tried to say news was becoming too commercial in 1987, when news was still not taking political sides. Today, the movie seems like a fairy tale. In 1995's *The American President*, Michael Douglas is actually trying to pass a bill where political parties are not just voting along party lines. *The American President*, while being cute, seems so outdated now it's like a child wrote it, and it was written by one of the best writers of the nineties, Aaron Sorkin. *Wag The Dog* seemed like too far of a stretch in 1997 to have the media promote a war to help a president change the news cycle. That's child's play compared to the modernday media tactics news divisions use now to ensure viewers don't flip the channel. Heck, the media would gladly help start a war just to increase their ratings. So many movies tried to sound a warning bell of where the culture could head only to be drowned out by the loud clang of the American dream clinging and ringing as it tumbles down the cavern of the Grand Canyon with no one looking, or caring.

To Die For tried, with a wild story, to warn us of what a person might become when a television camera turns its uncaring eye toward a person who wants nothing more than to be famous. Kinda cute, huh? This movie didn't even consider what would happen once everyone would have access to carrying around their own camera to broadcast their own lives for nothing more than a like—a digital thumbs-up. At the time, the film might have seemed like a stretch, or an over-the-top look at the burgeoning desire for televised fame, but it didn't even scratch the surface of the culture's insatiable desire for acknowledgement from total strangers. Director Gus Van Sant and writer Buck Henry (based on the book by Joyce Maynard) crafted a fun-filled tale of murder, deception, and characters filled with utter stupidity.

The film mocked the rising tides of daytime tabloid shows, and the then new idea of sensational news stories creating celebrity. In 1993, John and Lorena Bobbitt became huge stars. Were they in the latest great movie? How about, did they write a song for Boyz II Men? Maybe they wrote a bestselling book about the NAFTA legislation? Nope. They were famous because one of them cut off the other's penis and the other had their penis cut off. It launched them both into stardom. Similar things happened with Joey Buttafuoco, Tonya Harding, Heidi Fleiss, and the king daddy of destroying the seriousness of news, O. J. Simpson. His birth into global fame actually occurred during the filming of *To Die For*. Van Sant said, "I remember a very funny moment when we were doing a wide shot of Joaquin [Phoenix] in the jail cell. There were bright lights on him, so he couldn't see us behind the camera. One by one, people started leaving the set, and for a while Joaquin didn't realize he was all alone. He was trying to stay in character but asked, 'So are we gonna shoot?' and nobody answered. He walks into the adjacent room, and everyone had gathered around a TV to watch the O. J. Bronco chase on the freeway. Surreal." Even the crew of a movie about how the media shouldn't give unearned attention to a murderer got caught up in a taste of a tabloid and faux-news stew. There really was little hope.

Dirty Laundry

The character Suzanne Stone (Nicole Kidman) is our tabloid avatar; a weather girl whose husband (Matt Dillon) is murdered and becomes a national sensation. Well, she isn't really a weather girl; she is just on public access and bullied her way into that job. Her husband isn't just randomly murdered; she cons some high school kids into committing the murder for her. She just wants to be famous, and after trying so hard to make it as a journalist with absolutely no talent, she settles for the attention the media gladly gives her once they realize this story has murder, teenage sex, and a hot woman at the center. No story, all sizzle. This was what *To Die For* took aim at. What happens when the media focuses on stories and subjects that truly don't matter? The insidious part of major news organizations focusing on a simple murder is that they pull the resources away from uncovering events that actually matter. If every reporter is worrying about a small-town idiot, they are not keeping up their end of the bargain in the delicate soup of checks and balances. The more the media slipped away from covering what local politicians and businesses were doing, the easier it became for the powerful to circumvent democracy, but hey, viewers got to see a hot chick on the news.

It isn't just Suzanne who gets caught up in the glory of the television camera. Her parents and in-laws go on a daytime Maury Povich-type show to display their grief and anger in front of a studio audience. The opening credits of the film is a montage of newspaper and grocery store checkout line magazine stories this small-town murder inspired. This also seems quaint. There was a time when there was an active print media. It is interesting to think about how much newspapers mattered in order to uncover local political scandals. Newspapers started covering tabloid stories in the late nineties, they said in order to stay in business, but they went out of business anyway. That was the thing about these sensational sex stories that took over journalism— it wasn't just the crappy daytime shows that covered them. It was the newspapers and major network news that started to devote columns and minutes to covering murder and affairs. This switch just "happened" to coincide with the fact that by the end of the nineties, all three major networks moved to trying to make a profit during the nightly news. In an article detailing this trend, Marc Gunther wrote, "The newscasts anchored by ABC's Peter Jennings, NBC's Tom Brokaw, and CBS's Dan Rather are reporting fewer 'headline' stories, preferring to highlight in-depth stories, live interviews, and news-you-can-use." *To Die For* saw this desire for news to become sensational and tried to warn us, but the warning went as unheard as it had in the previous decade's *Broadcast News*.

The brilliance of Buck Henry's script is that none of what I have written about so far is mentioned, acknowledged, or really even part of the movie. The movie is really just a comedy about an uneducated woman who kills her husband. The film is funny, deliciously written by a comedy legend who wrote *Heaven Can Wait* (1978), *The Graduate* (1967), and *What's Up Doc?* (1972). The characters are so well-developed that all the humor comes out of situations where we just know how the characters are going to react. We know these simple, small-town characters. The film isn't trying to make a sweeping indictment of the news at the time. That is just what I see when I watch the film. Henry and Van Sant leave all that up to the viewer. They can walk away laughing or crying; it depends how important you think these things are. That is what nineties films did—gave you a choice.

Nothing from Nothing

Sometimes a movie has a scene in it that is better than the entire movie. It isn't a put-down; it just means there can be a scene that rises to a higher level of writing or captures something so perfectly it burns into your brain. It happens in *True Romance* with the torture scene and Sicilian monologue between Christopher Walken and Dennis Hopper. It happens in this movie at one hour and sixteen-minutes into the picture. After Matt Dillon is murdered and the police are at the scene of the crime, Nicole Kidman's house, her family surrounds her and the television is on. The local channel ends its programming. A policeman is dusting the TV screen for fingerprints as an American flag waves on the screen and the orchestra plays the notes for "Oh, say can you see." The cop dusting for fingerprints is so on point. They have the true killer right there—television. The national anthem plays as Nicole Kidman sees something from outside. It is a bright, hot, white spotlight coming in through the window from outside. All the windows fill with the lights of the media congregating in her front

Suzanne (Nicole Kidman) is drawn like a moth to the flame to the lights of the press. (Photo courtesy of Columbia Pictures)

yard. The trumpets blare the section of the song "And the rocket's red glare, the bombs bursting in air." She moves closer to the front door. A police officer in the house says, "You don't have to talk to those people if you don't want to." Kidman shoots the officer a look of pure disgust. Why wouldn't she talk to the press? In slow motion, she sees the reporters outside; her eyes are wide open; the lights for the cameras turn on; she checks her hair and makeup and steps outside as the anthem ends. Americana to perfection. The pulse of the nation is shown in the consumption of murder for entertainment while "The Stars Spangled Banner" plays. Van Sant even wanted the scene to go further. He said, "One idea I'm glad Buck [Henry] did talk me out of: I wanted Suzanne to hand out 8-by-10 glossy photographs of herself to the press the night of Larry's murder, but Buck thought that was too much. He was right." I'm not sure whether it would be too much or not. They would have taken them and gladly put them on as the lead story.

This wasn't the first time Van Sant has played with a patriotic musical theme in one of his films. One of my favorite scenes in Van Sant's 1991 *My Own Private Idaho* is when he uses "America the Beautiful" as a counterpoint to the poor street hustlers sidestepping the American dream. The film ends with River Phoenix, who is narcoleptic, asleep in the middle of a road that runs through a cornfield on the way to nowhere in Idaho. Two white men, who are in better financial situations than Phoenix is, stop their car, pull over, and steal everything he has, including his shoes. They leave him stranded in the middle of nowhere as the instrumental patriotic theme plays "O beautiful for spacious skies." This is the America Gus Van Sant sees, leaving a queer man, who has nothing, on the side of the room to fend for himself. The AIDS epidemic was very much going on in 1991, when he made this film. He knew that the country was happy to just let gay men die in the middle of America. To juxtapose patriotism with actual America is so much fun to watch. Van Sant takes his AIDS statement from *Idaho* and does the same thing in *To Die For* with the latest nineties epidemic: the desire to be famous at any cost. In one of the *Real World*-esque interviews that happen throughout the film, Nicole Kidman says, "Because what's the point of doing anything worthwhile if nobody is watching? And if people are watching, it makes you a better person."

To Die For came out three years after MTV debuted *The Real World,* and reality TV was just starting to infect the culture. The film has characters talking directly to the camera, just like reality TV. Who cares if this brand of television teaches us to not empathize with those we don't know? Who cares if it makes money off people of moral ambiguity? Who cares if we laugh at people who can't sing, those who have to eat bugs, or those who pretend to be powerful businessmen on fake reality TV shows? What's the worst that could happen? It's not like one of those incompetent people could ever become president of the United States of America or something. It's just a lark. It's just a movie. It's just another American product to die for.

C: *Clueless*

"AS IF!"

The kids of America were buying movie tickets in the nineties, and they were buying tickets for movies that were made with them in mind. In the summer of 1995, grown-ups could go see *Apollo 13*, little kids could go see *Pocahontas*, romantics could see *The Bridges of Madison County*, and teenagers could see director Amy Heckerling's *Clueless*. Teenage movies were abundant in the nineties, especially after *Clueless*. Those types of movies, ones that focused on high school, might have come of age in the eighties with John Hughes, but in the nineties, it wasn't just one director making movies for the awkward age of life. Just some of the quality teenage nineties movies were *Pump Up the Volume, Cruel Intentions, Can't Hardly Wait, 10 Things I Hate About You, She's All That*, and *Dazed and Confused*. I could have picked any of these films to focus on, but there are just a few things that set *Clueless* apart from the other films. It starts with the film being based on the Jane Austen novel *Emma*. It says so much about the quality of nineties films when even the teenage movies were born from novels published in 1815. Teenage movies of the nineties were not watered down, dumbed down, or bringing us down. They were fun, moving, important, and most definitely smart.

Rollin' with My Homies

I was not the targeted demographic for *Clueless*. I rented it when it was released on video. I remember liking it. I, of course, already had the CD. Some of my favorite songs of the decade came from soundtracks to movies I hadn't seen yet. I had the soundtracks for *Clueless, Singles, The Crow*, and *Sleepless in Seattle* long before I ever saw the films. (You might ask, where's the best-selling soundtrack of the decade: *The*

Bodyguard? Well, that was never a part of my music collection for a very simple reason—no one should listen to "I Will Always Love You" unless it is sung by Dolly Parton from *The Best Little Whorehouse in Texas* (1982). And we will never speak of it again.) I can't imagine that compiling original music from a plethora of pop artists would serve today's music industry that just wants people streaming songs and not albums, but soundtracks were so crucial to my music experience in the nineties. I discovered so many wonderful artists whom I never would have found if they didn't have one track on a soundtrack that I obsessed over. I still listen to Jill Sobule's "Supermodel," and became a huge fan of hers after hearing her on the *Clueless* soundtrack. I am still annoyed that Jewel's cover version of "All By Myself" isn't on this soundtrack and still has never been released on any album. So many great tracks from these films just faded away into the great jukebox in the sky. My lifelong fandom for artists I discovered from films also happened with Lisa Loeb, Harry Connick Jr., and the Cranberries.

While over the past thirty years I have many times put on the CD of the *Clueless* soundtrack, I had never popped in the DVD and rewatched the film since it was released. In rewatching it for my studies, I was really taken with the spirit of the film. It truly made me laugh. I bought in on the "will they/won't they" between Alicia Silverstone and Paul Rudd, and it made me feel good about life while I watched it. I was curious how much of the story truly came from Austen's book, so the following night I watched 1996's *Emma* with Gwyneth Paltrow. Both movies were very charming and were led by their respective star-making lead actresses. But man, *Clueless* just really popped off the screen. Alicia Silverstone plays Cher, which is the Emma role. Heckerling had to change the name so she could get in her joke about being named after former pop stars who hawk products on television now. Cher's best friend is Dionne (Stacey Dash), allowing her to make the home shopping joke about Cher and Dionne. Let's face it, any movie for teenagers that is brave enough to do a Dionne Warwick joke in its first few minutes is alright with me. It is pretty obvious that Amy Heckerling's script has no intention of talking down to anyone.

This is a movie called *Clueless,* but is built around a character who is anything but. Cher is actually well-read, college bound, and isn't about to throw her future away on a boy. Does she know everything exactly correctly? No, of course not. But if you compare this comedy to similar comedies that were crafted around male leads, think *Billy Madison*, *Wayne's World*, or *Tommy Boy*, the lead characters were always stupid. There is nothing intrinsically wrong with mining comedy out of dumb, but a smart comedy will always feel fresher and has a better chance of becoming a classic. The truly amazing thing about Heckerling's script is she is able to pull off both brands of comedy and sometimes within the same damn sentence. The girls are trying to coax two teachers to fall in love, so they send one of the teachers an excerpt from Shakespeare's "Sonnet 18." Dionne asks Cher if she wrote the iconic poem. Cher responds, "Duh, it's like a famous quote." See, our lead character is smart. But she also is a kid. Kids think they know everything, but they don't. Heckerling stays true to this concept and pulls a joke out of that. When Dionne asks where the quote is from, Cher, confident as ever, replies, "Cliffs Notes." That is a quality joke, chased down with a perfect button. Dionne doesn't know Cher is wrong, but we do. This allows Cher to keep her confidence high, even though we know she is a bit more clueless than she thinks she is. Have you ever been around a teenager? Trust me, four of them came through the ranks of my home. They know everything, even when they are in the midst of the blowback from doing something that was all due to their stupidity. A smart character, while being a ton harder to write for, will have people caring for the main characters years after whatever pop references are stuffed into the script fade away. The other wonderful thing about this joke is there is a good chance many of the teenagers who are watching this movie may not get the joke, but Heckerling knows grown-ups will be watching too. Smart jokes will always age better than lowbrow jokes. The same youngins who watched *Clueless* in 1995 might just get that joke when they came back from college in 1999. I remember watching *Grease* for the first time as an adult. I was like, "Holy crap. That is why they say Rizzo is a defective typewriter? Because she skipped a period." That joke flew way over my head for years.

There are no one-sided, one-dimensional characters in *Clueless*. Probably no character embodies this more than Dan Hedaya's character of Cher's Dad. Can we just take a moment to look at Hedaya's films in 1995? He had to be the hottest actor of that year. Not only did he crush it in *Clueless*, he also is in *The Usual Suspects* and *To Die For*. All three films had an impact on culture that summer. I wonder if he was on the cover of any magazines that year? Probably not, but he should have been. Most dads in teenager movies are either absent (*Welcome to the Dollhouse*), bumbling idiots (*10 Things I Hate About You*), or totally unhip while thinking they are hip (*Pump Up the Volume*.) Hedaya plays a smart, powerful attorney. It wouldn't make sense that his daughter could outsmart him, and she never does. He knows she is falling in love with Paul Rudd's character way before either of them knows. He actually knows what is going on the entire film. Cher is certainly a really well-written character, but it is the attention to details in the writing for the dad that truly impressed me. It would have been easy to have Hedaya play a version of his *Cheers* character and mine humor out of that one note. But in having him be an actual human being, we care about Cher's relationship with him. Remember, this is based on the Jane Austen novel where Emma considers sacrificing her love life for the purpose of caring for her father. The relationship is central to the story, so it is nice to see a writer that doesn't jettison that pillar of the story for a few dumb jokes. Heckerling had this to say about his character in the DVD extras, "When I envisioned the character of the father, I thought, I wanted to cast somebody that would normally be cast as a hitman in movies." She wanted him to appear scary and stereo-typical, but then for audiences to discover he actually loves Cher. A film that allows parents to be close, but also strict is a rare thing in any film, but rarer still in a teenage genre comedy.

Kids in America

There have been plenty of films that just happened to be released to coincide with a moment in pop culture. Examples are *Saturday Night Fever* (disco), *Perfect* (exercise craze), *Urban Cowboy* (electric bull riding); wait a minute, there has to be ones without John Travolta in them, right? *Swingers* (swing music), *Easy Rider* (free love), and *Gleaming the Cube* (skateboarding). *Clueless* is even rarer still because it did not coincide with any pop culture trend; it actually created

The fashion, language, and style of *Clueless* can't be discounted. The film didn't reflect the culture, it shaped the culture. (Photo courtesy of Paramount Pictures.)

its own. In 1995, grunge was where it was at. No one was dressing like Cher or Dionne. No one was talking like them. But after the movie was released, everyone was. Costume designer Mona May was as influential on the success of this film as Patricia Field was with *Sex and the City*. Those two women might have more to do with late-nineties fashion trends than anyone else. *Clueless* wasn't mirroring; it was creating. Heckerling wanted to create a colorful, stylized, fantasy world. She did the same thing with language. The film brought to pop culture a ton of sayings including: As if, Betty (a hot chick), Barney (a boring guy), Audi (out of here), Monet (ugly up close, pretty from far away), Jeepin' (making out in the back of the car), Baldwin (hot guy), and most famously, "whatever" (while making a W with your two hands).

These were not being said by kids before the release of the film, these were things Heckerling created on her own. She mentions in the bonus features that for years she studied slang and kept track of things she heard people say that were just a little different. The rest she just made up. It is always fun when a movie creates its own language. And I'm not talking about Jar Jar Binks. When we hang out with our friends, we all start talking the same way. When I was in high school and any of my friends would see each other at the beginning of the day, we always said "Moanin'." Why? Because no one else was. It made us stand out. Probably it made us look stupid, but that is what high school is all about: trying not to look stupid within your group and learning to not give a rat's ass what you look like outside of your group.

With all the lingo, the smart dialogue, the smart characters, and that the film has three female leads, it's hard to imagine how this movie ever got made. It started out as something called *No Worries*, and it was a television script. Heckerling expanded her original sitcom idea into a feature film. With her pedigree of writing and directing *Fast Times at Ridgemont High*, I am sure people were expecting a different kind of movie. But she wanted to make a happy movie. She said, "I think people like happy movies, and I don't think I was treating that age group with disrespect." Both those concepts are such an important difference to what is being written today. Movies about kids are always about how horrible they are. Or the parents are horrible parents, and the kids are running the entire household. It is doubtful that either extreme is what is actually going on, but why would we want to watch either version? No one thinks *Clueless* is a documentary. The same year this film was released, *Welcome to the Dollhouse* was released which is a harrowing look at middle school. The life of that film's main character, Dawn Wiener, is a hell of a lot closer to what my school days were actually like more than the life Cher was living. In 1993, *Dazed and Confused* was released, but just like *Dollhouse*, it contains a bullying storyline of the older kids hazing the middle schoolers. Both films might be more representational to what high school was actually like, but it's a lot less fun to watch. I am glad that there are movies that show both versions of high school: the real and the fantasy. I believe the lasting success of this film is all tied to the happiness it creates in and out of the film.

Alicia Silverstone brings happiness, positivity, and an honest-to-goodness charm to every second she is on the screen. Her performance is not to be dismissed just because she is adorable. There are very few female characters who are given this kind of role and screen time. It really is amazing to see a young female character created with not the goal of falling in love and finding a man, but instead to have the goal to spread kindness, find love for those who need it, and also to donate a pair of unused skis to the Pismo Beach disaster relief. This film has three female leads, a female writer and director, and a female costume designer. They all combined to create one of the happiest, most pleasing, well-written comedies of the decade. Lots of clones would come, but when they weren't as well written, most people just said, "Whatever."

Chapter 8
1996

A: *Swingers*

"VEGAS, BABY."

If you took a trip to Las Vegas before 1996, you probably at some point said, "What happens in Vegas stays in Vegas." If you visited the City of Sin after 1996 and you saw *Swingers*, there is no way you didn't say, "Vegas, baby" about a million times to the annoyance of everyone around you. Few movies put a stamp on pop culture in the nineties like *Swingers* did. Yes, there were films like *Singles*, *Reality Bites*, *Clerks*, or *Empire Records*, but those movies *reflected* the culture; *Swingers* created a whole brand-new one. It would be easy to say the film just happened to hit at the moment when the character's tastes displayed in the film became popular, but that isn't the case. The film reflects a very small corner of LA that no one outside that corner knew until this film was watched by every cool cat around. No one was saying "You're so money," telling each other they were "all growns up," or looking for "beautiful babies" before *Swingers* came along. Yes, the swing music scene might have been rocking the Dresden or some underground bars in LA, but after this film hit, swing music was in the mainstream. Big Bad Voodoo Daddy, Royal Crown Revue, and Squirrel Nut Zippers were finding their way into every hipster's CD collection. *Swingers* arrived in 1996 and dominated the conversation, pretty much like the Vince Vaughn character does in the film. Let's see you try to get a word in edgewise while that guy is around.

Jon Favreau moved to LA after completing a role in *Rudy*. His friends back East thought he had made it, and so did he. After finding out Hollywood didn't have a place for him, Favreau decided to take his future in his own hands and sat down to write a semi-autobiographical script about him and his friends. At the time, he was going out to clubs where swing music was playing in the background.

He watched his friend, fellow out-of-work actor Vince Vaughn, do well with the ladies while he struggled with a broken heart. All of these moments, including the cadence and phraseology of Vaughn, made its way into a script called *Swingers*. This was the nineties, when everyone was looking for the next small picture to burst into a big picture and make unknown actors the next well-known actor. The script started to get interest, but like always, the studio executives wanted to change everything that was interesting about it. Favreau thought maybe his ragtag group of friends could do a reading to show people what the script could do. The cast we see in the film did the reading. Doug Liman convinced Favreau to sell him the script for one dollar and said he would direct it without changes.

I Get Paid for Lovin'

A film that rocked the entire industry in 1996 was made for only $250,000. Favreau said, "We used a very small French camera called the Aaton 35 on 35mm, but it looks like a 16mm. We didn't have enough money to light things, so we used a sensitive film stock, Kodak 528." The film even references other films from the nineties but makes fun of their large budgets. They mention how Scorsese took four days to light the scene in *Goodfellas* covered in Chapter 1 where they do the long oner. Later in *Swingers*, they also do a oner of the boys going into a club through the back entrance of one of their hangouts. It's a wonderful microcosm of everything that makes *Swingers* a classic. The characters truly believe what they are doing is just as good as the *Goodfellas* scene, but while it has the twists and turns and is filmed in one take, it doesn't have all the finesse and cast extras of *Goodfellas*. That's because it's not supposed to. It has charm, and it's funny. The people they are saying hi to as they walk through the kitchen are not amused by it. They don't even know why these guys are walking into the club this way. There is no reason for it. But that describes the characters of the film perfectly. They want so badly to *be somebody*. But they are just everybody. This isn't an attack on the film or the scene; it's a perfect example about how art inspires us. These male characters are lost at this moment of their lives. They want so much more, and they are nowhere near ready to give up their dreams of being goodfellas themselves. They are going to do what makes them feel important. As long as they keep doing that, everything will be money. It is also a great jab at filmmaking. Wannabe filmmakers who have a script always say they could make something as good as Scorsese, but hardly anyone ever tries. Doug Liman knows this scene isn't the same, but it's close enough, and it has heart. This was the essence of the independent film movement of the era. They didn't need the big-budget lighting, the extras, the multiple takes; they had heart, love of film, and a whole lot of charisma.

"We had good music, good performances, and the rest of the stuff sort of fell into place around it," said Favreau. I watched the film on an old DVD copy, not a Blu-ray. A few days later, I bought the Blu-ray, and I didn't like seeing the film in high-def. There is something so charming about the way Liman captured it. It isn't that the quality is poor; it just isn't perfect. Costar Heather Graham talked about how many people thought they were shooting a documentary when they shot scenes at the Derby nightclub. Graham said, "We shot in a bar that was open. We'd be filming, and we tried to keep the camera incognito, and there was a seat open next to me, and like a regular bar patron would sit next to me and we'd be like, 'No, no, no we are filming.' So if you look at the extras in that movie, they are just all real people at the bar that night." Moments like that can't be recreated on a computer or in a controlled green screen studio.

Even when the film was completed it was a hard sell to major studios, because none of the cast were stars. This seems crazy now, when Jon Favreau has become the go-to action director (is there anything sadder?), Vince Vaughn is a comedy icon, and Ron Livingston made *Office Space*, a movie everyone remembers. But when they were trying to get a distributor for the film, no one wanted it because they didn't think it could open or do well on video without a household name. Favreau said back in 1996, when the film was just coming out, "They need to know that they can sell video units if they can't sell the movie." It is great to find a quote like that from back in the day. It is another fact that backs up why movies like *Swingers* don't get made anymore. The video home market was a huge source of revenue for a film like this. In a DVD extra, Favreau said that it was when the movie hit video that he truly became a star. That avenue is as outdated today as swing music was in the early nineties. Soundtracks were also a great source of income for movies. Miramax ended up picking up the film, and I am sure it had to be one of their best investments ever. The soundtrack went Gold and even spawned a sequel soundtrack. Movies used to have a few chances to recoup their money, even for a movie that only cost $250,000 to make. The studio needed those ancillary products to make the investment worthwhile. Favreau said the finished film cost closer to a million once they paid for music rights and cleaned up the footage.

Go Daddy-O

The film is so very deliciously male. It feels refreshing and almost naughty to watch a film in 2023 where young men behave like men in a truthful way. We are in an unbalanced time where true maleness has been swept away to give the female perspective of life more space. That is a needed thing because men and the male agenda dominated the film conversation for too long, and it was mostly the culture of White men, to boot. There should have always been space for all genders and cultures to tell their story, and in a perfect world they would all be as truthful as this tale that just happens to focus on a small group of men. *Swingers* doesn't represent anyone else but these four or five guys, but you can't help but smile and enjoy watching their world. Watching it this time, I thought I was so relieved that I wasn't living their life of going from bar to bar trying to con women into giving me their digits. But you don't have to directly relate or envy the actions of movie characters to be interested in a story. Sometimes it is just nice to see a different world other than your own and have it be honestly told, not filtered through a social media review board. It would be nice if a new independent film would try to truly capture what it is like to be a male in today's culture. Maybe truly dig into the complexities of gender stereotypes and what it means to have a choice as to which gender people want to identify as. This film takes on the male gender with all its issues and benefits. It would be great for the current generation to have a movie like *Swingers* to reflect what is going on with them. I hope it's out there. Lucky for me, I'm too damn old to find it or know what streaming platform it's on. I can't remember all those passwords anyway.

One of the main emotions Mikey (Jon Favreau) displays that is just gone from modern film is shame. Comedy now loves to have a dumb guy who doesn't know he is embarrassing himself. The idea has become to push a scene so far to where it is above and beyond any logical comprehension. That can be funny, but when a writer does that, he sacrifices the audience's empathy for the character. Mikey knows very well he is digging himself a hole when he is interacting with women, and he doesn't know how to stop it. The entire time he digs that hole, he wears his shame on his face. Yes, audiences cringe during his phone message scene. Yes, it is over the top, but that is what comedy does best. It makes us see us at our most vulnerable while making us laugh at it, because in the end, we are all human. Plus, who hasn't left a rambling phone message that you wish you could take back? (Okay, for you young people, replace that with a text.) But Mikey *knows* he is a walking mess. He knows he says too much to the two girls Trent (Vince Vaughn) and Mikey meet in Vegas. He wishes he wouldn't have made the pancake joke to the waitress. He is self-aware. That is a key component to comedy that sets this movie apart. It is why the movie makes viewers relate and feel for the leads in a way that just isn't going to happen in *Deuce Bigalow*.

The other impressive aspect of the script is the friendship these guys have. I am not sure there has ever been a male friend in a movie who supported another male friend to the level that Trent does for Mikey. The number of times he builds him up is incredible. I want Trent to fluff me up before leaving the house even if I'm just going to the post office. Trent is introduced to the audience as a god among men. He is full of confidence, knows what to say every second, and has never made a mistake in front of the opposite sex in his life. Mikey is shown as the polar opposite. But as the film goes on, we slowly see both sides change. What is even more fun is that we don't notice it is happening until it happens. It does, at first, appear to the audience that when Trent keeps saying Mikey is so money, that he is mocking him. But Mikey actually *is* money. He just forgot. He needed a friend to remind him, and he has one. It is why we don't write off the character of Trent.

We can see he isn't just a two-dimensional horndog.

In the Blu-ray bonus features, Favreau says, "The big skill of writing and filmmaking is cutting away the stuff that is not interesting and keeping the facts that are quirky or help drive the story." This quote takes us all the way back to *Unforgiven* where Clint Eastwood said a similar thing. It is the quirky stuff that is jettisoned from films today. Now, art that is generated from the belly of corporate algorithms is created to make us feel the same, to be all-inclusive, and to hide anything that screams out different or risky. The goal for all pop art today is to feel calm, not challenged. In the final scene of the film, their positions are comically reversed as Trent misreads the cues of a woman across the restaurant, but it is actually the acting of Vince Vaughn and Jon Favreau during the entire scene, plus the hour-and-a-half journey we have been on, that lets us already know they actually haven't grown or changed their overall character. The film was a blip in time when their positions were reversed. Mikey was always an all-around better guy than Trent. The truth was always that Trent, while being a load of fun, was never going to get the kind of girl who lasts longer than one night. Despite all the pitfalls and horrible word choices the entire film, Mikey really was so money. *Swingers* is as well. It's a little gem of a movie that shouldn't be just remembered whenever you pass through Las Vegas and everyone in unison says, "Vegas, baby."

B: *Citizen Ruth*

"WHAT'S THE MATTER? ARE YOU FUCKING PEOPLE DEAF? I SAID I WANT AN ABORTION."

I have been waiting to write about this movie for the entire project, and we are finally here. If you noticed, not once have I told you to watch any of the movies I selected for these essays. I was saving that for this film. IF you have read this entire book up to this point AND you think the idea of watching a comedy about abortion is even halfway intriguing, then let me say for the first time in 198 pages that you really should watch this movie. It is truly unique, funny, heartbreaking, and thought-provoking. So, basically a nineties movie.

In 1996, somehow, Alexander Payne (whom you know from *Sideways*, *About Schmidt*, or *Election*) made his first major motion picture, and it was a comedy about abortion. Miramax bought it and released it. (Well, kind of, but we will get to that.) But what is even more amazing is that the film is actually really funny. It's not one of those political movies like *Wag the Dog* or *Bulworth* that tries to be funny while using social, hot-button ideas as a substitute for comedy. No, this movie has actual laugh-out-loud moments that are created from character, plot, and situation. But it also has a lot to say about the way America deals with its major political issues. Yes, this movie happens to be about abortion, but it could have easily been about global warming, racism, hunger, homelessness, or any other issue where there are two sides that can't even begin to see the other side's point of view. The topic of abortion was just as dangerous to discuss in 1996 as it is today, although at least the right was legal. But while the topic might be abortion, the real focus of the movie centers around (and in) the womb of one Ruth Stoops (Laura Dern), who is aptly named because there is literally nothing she will not stoop to.

Moon Mother

Laura Dern was probably best known for *Jurassic Park* to most American filmgoers in the nineties (that's the saddest sentence I have ever typed), but to a David Lynch fan like myself, it was *Blue Velvet* and *Wild at Heart* that brought Laura Dern into my life. After seeing her as Lula Fortune in *Wild at Heart*, I committed to watching everything Dern was in, even if that meant I would have to watch a bunch of comput-a-saurs in *Jurassic Park*. In the nineties, Dern did an amazing job of bouncing from independent films (*Rambling Rose*), to blockbusters (*Park*), to even doing television (*Ellen*, *The Larry Sanders Show*). Only a fool would pick out one film from her astonishing career and say it was her best performance. Good thing everyone knows I'm a fool. Laura Dern's best performance is in *Citizen Ruth*. It is an acting seminar on how not to judge the character you are playing, how important it is to commit to the motivations of your character, and how not trying to be funny can be absolutely hilarious. The buzzword to describe every male character after Tony Soprano hit the small screen was always that overused, and misplaced description of antihero. You want to see an antihero? How about starting with a mother who doesn't give one thought about her unborn or born children. Tony cared so much about his kids that he let them become monsters. There is no monster in this film bigger than the society that created Ruth. Her character is so well-defined, her motivation is so transparent that the viewer has no choice but to laugh and not get upset with the pro-life or pro-choice side of this debate because you just can't forget that this person is not worth all this trouble. Her character is so low, it becomes absurd that these two unbendable sides are fighting over this absolute piece of shit person.

If she was an upstanding, moral, likable character, we could start buying into what was going on. We could start thinking that the rules around abortion were set up to help someone. When the person who is going through the situation doesn't care what happens, it shows how silly it is for strangers to invest this much interest in a private act that truly doesn't affect them. When Laura Dern crafted Ruth, she didn't give a damn what you thought of her. She is not judging any decision that Ruth makes, mostly because Ruth is only doing what she can to survive. Alexander Payne and Jim Taylor's script makes one thing clear—judging isn't part of their plan, and it makes all the difference. You won't want to have Ruth over for dinner, but you certainly understand her. You get why she does each despicable thing she does. They are true to her character, and when a writer does that, a viewer will follow their farce no matter where it leads. In *Citizen Ruth*, you always believe the journey; Ruth, however, believes in nothing.

Ruth Stoops is addicted to drugs. If you haven't seen the movie, I bet you think you have an idea of what that means, huh? Not in this movie. She isn't addicted to crack, heroin, or meth. That would be too simple for our girl Ruth. She is addicted to huffing paint, cement sealant (the same brand is in Payne's follow-up film, *Election*), or anything she can find in an aerosol spray can. Watching her suck the air out of a paper bag filled with spray paint, with only her wide eyes to show us the high she is achieving, brings out a laugh at the same moment I feel an absolute disgust with her. When she passes out, she is left with a blue paint stain around her mouth. It lets viewers know right from the start—no one gets out of this story without getting dirty.

Ruth (Laura Dern) sleeps off a huffing session with a blue tint around her mouth. (Photo courtesy of Miramax Pictures.)

After passing out from huffing, Ruth gets arrested, and the court discovers she is pregnant for the fourth time. Her other kids have been taken away from her for being an unfit parent by the state. The judge in the case tells her privately that if she gets an abortion, he will not send her to jail for the drug charge. The truth is, any logical person would agree with this decision. There is no way this person should have another kid. There is no way that baby wouldn't be born with major birth defects as a side effect from all the drugs and alcohol Ruth takes in. But once the Baby Savers (led by Mary Kay Place and Kurtwood Smith) get even the smallest huff of this behind-closed-doors ruling, they decide to make an example of her and this case. The first forty-five minutes of the film gives us the Christian/Baby Savers's side of the issue.

The film doesn't judge the Baby Savers any more than it judges Ruth. It presents their side: they are devout Christians, and they want to save every child. They achieve this by spending their free time going to abortion clinics and yelling at young girls who are having to deal with a very personal issue. The script mines comedy out of this in the best way. The writers add mundane, everyday activities in between the Savers screaming "Baby killers" at strangers. Watching the Baby Savers go from eating donuts on the side of the road outside an abortion clinic to running to the fence to yell at these women in dire straits shows the absurdity of the situation. This little moment, taking this action and putting it in context of real life, shows how yelling slogans at someone, anyone, in any situation, is pointless as hell. We just can't picture Jesus attacking these women. Even the security guard who knows all the protesters' names, just calmly sends them back across the street, as he does every day. He knows this isn't going to change anything; it's just everyone doing their job. There is no animosity at all. He allows these baby-saving activists to pointlessly fight the system to the end.

Through comical events that I won't spoil here, the pro-choice activists get a hold of Ruth. Now we get to see the other side that wants to be sure Ruth makes the choice she wants . . . only because it happens to coincide with their beliefs. They want Ruth to get the abortion she wants and save her from jail because they battle the other side. Once someone from the Baby Savers offers Ruth $15,000 to have the baby, in a scene that has more comic-frenetic energy coming out of Laura Dern than a Robin Williams stand-up special, you watch those pro-choice activists jettison their idea that Ruth is free to make a choice. How quickly the pro-choice group forgets that the freedom of choice means a woman has the right to choose even for the wrong reason. As the issue gets media attention and higher-up activists start to descend on the scene, it becomes clear how both sides are less and less interested in Ruth, her choice, or her baby, and are just interested in winning. (Remember when I said this could be any political cause in American politics? Winning at any cost. Sound like two parties you might have heard of before?) At one point, Ruth's mother, played by Diane Ladd, Dern's real-life mother, calls out to Ruth, "What if I would have aborted you?" Fair question. But I assure you that Dern's response to that question is the single funniest line I have ever heard in any movie, and that is not hyperbole. I invite you, if you have never seen the movie, to write down twenty responses you think Ruth says back to her mother, and I assure you that you will not have stumbled upon the response. Trust me, this film is a comedy.

Another moment that shows Dern staying true to her character is when Ruth explains to the pro-choice activists that she can't afford to pay for the abortion. The activists (played by Swoosie Kurtz and Kelly Preston) say with such pride and giving sacrifice, "Don't worry, we can find a way to take care of it." Dern shrugs her shoulders and says, "Whatever," with not even the slightest bit of thought, appreciation, understanding, or anything. She doesn't give the smallest fuck whether they help her or not. She knows someone will take care of her because someone always does. This is whom both sides have put all their faith in. The two sides are set up, and it all goes crazy from there. I won't give away how it ends, because I am pretty sure you have not seen this movie, because basically no one did.

Obviously, a movie about abortion that is this honest and funny could never be made today. If it would be, at a minimum, one of the sides would be slanted to whatever political persuasion the writer had. "It was right there, and it was so radical and mean and vulnerable and the best example of an equal-opportunity-offender script I'd read," said Laura Dern in 2021. But somehow the movie got made; it just didn't really get a wide release. The film only opened on twelve screens and there was no ad campaign for the film outside of festivals. This is another great example of how video stores leveled the playing field and how important it was for video stores to be locally owned. Video Time got *Citizen Ruth*, and because Laura Dern was in it, I rented it. I don't know if Blockbuster made the video available for rent, but I doubt it. I didn't know what the film was about when I rented it. I saw the cover and I rented it, loved it, and became a lifelong fan of Alexander Payne. Three years later, he made a much bigger splash with *Election*, which is covered in the epilogue of this book, but *Citizen Ruth* is an example of brave filmmaking that was alive and well in the nineties. This movie shouldn't offend anyone. It can make you angry at how we treat addiction, might upset you about the way the judicial system treats the poor, but the topic of abortion shouldn't offend anyone in this film. No one involved is trying to change your mind about your belief about abortion, and that includes me writing this. That decision is one of the most personal decisions anyone should make. The film isn't getting involved with any of that. It is telling a human story and it does it so well. With all that is going on with Roe v. Wade today, and how difficult it is for any two-sided issue to see even the smallest human commonality between one side and the other, everyone should rent this movie, watch it, and we should all be able to come together with the united front that Ruth Stoops is an absolute piece of shit and we love her for it.

C: Alexander Payne Interview
(*Citizen Ruth* Writer/Director)

"IN GENERAL, IN HOLLYWOOD, THE A PICTURES AND THE B PICTURES HAVE SWITCHED."

Scott Ryan: Thank you so much for speaking with me today. *Citizen Ruth* has always been one of my favorite movies.

Alexander Payne: What is your interest in this film? Why do you like that movie so much?

Ryan: The first thing is that it is funny. So many films try to have a concept but forget that comedy comes from character. Also, Laura Dern's performance is one for the ages. Why did you want this topic to be what your first major film is about?

Payne: I don't think Jim Taylor and I were interested in making a movie about a topic. We liked the ridiculousness of the characters and the situation. I didn't really want this to be my first movie. The first feature script I wrote out of UCLA film school was called *The Coward* that eleven years later became *About Schmidt*. I wanted to come back to Omaha and shoot something about a dude who retired and realized he had wasted his life. I wrote that but hadn't quite cracked the third act. I was setting about to rewrite when Jim Taylor and I were living together in Los Angeles, and we subscribed to the *New York Times*. Jim had circled an article in the paper and asked if I had read it. It was a story that suggested *Citizen Ruth*. It took place in Fargo,

North Dakota. It didn't tell the story of the movie, but it presented us a premise of the movie: A standoff between antiabortion and pro-women's rights characters. To me, it suggested Billy Wilder's *Ace in the Hole*, one of my favorite movies. Have you seen it?

Ryan: No.

Payne: After his big success in 1950 with *Sunset Boulevard*, Paramount gave him carte blanche, and he made an extremely good movie about someone in trouble, and everyone is fighting about the person in trouble, but only for their own interests. I thought it suggested a very good black comedy. The setting is the abortion war, but what it is really about is people acting out their own physiological dramas in the public arena and caring more about their own cause than about the football that is being passed between them. We wanted the audience to understand and sympathize with Ruth Stoops and then kind of make fun of everyone else. We got criticized at the time by liberal critics for not being pro-choice enough. They accused the film of trying to have it both ways. I think in terms of your word "topic," you can easily see what Jim and I think, but it was not meant to be a screed. Perhaps that is why it survives and someone like you still likes it.

Ryan: How did you get Laura Dern? I think this is her best role.

Payne: She would agree with you. She is in her "legendary" phase of her career now, and when she is asked about a favorite role, the first thing out of her mouth is usually *Citizen Ruth*. She is extremely proud of the film. The producer Cary Woods put money out of his own pocket and got me a casting director. That is what you have to do to get a movie made—just start making it. That starts with casting. Even if you don't have financing, you have to start spending money to make it. Somehow Jeff Goldblum got the script, and he was living with Laura Dern at the time. Jeff read it and thought this would be a terrific role for Laura. She had never occurred to me. She read it and flipped for it. I was flattered because I thought she was a terrific actress but was skeptical that she was the right ticket for this role. We met for lunch, and her understanding and enthusiasm for the material were very impressive.

Ryan: What she does in the film is she never judges Ruth ever. She plays Ruth.

Payne: None of us do. In fact, we love her. She's our favorite.

Ryan: You understand where she is coming from. Some actresses might have been afraid to be such a piece of shit. Ruth is way down; she doesn't love her kids. For a woman to not take care of her kids was a very brave choice for an actress to do, even in the nineties. Don't you think?

Payne: For Laura Dern, it isn't brave. It's just who she is. She did *Blue Velvet* when she was barely of age, so that stuff has never occurred to her. We heard that a lot at the time, "Oh, it's such a brave performance." I never got it. I appreciate your saying it, and I understand the compliment implied in it. It's a good part. Twenty years later, I directed her dad in *Nebraska,* and the dad is also fearless as all get-out. Those Derns want to go to all four corners of the human room. Why not? That is where the fun lies. Is it fun to play it safe? Nuh-uh. "Oh it's such an unvain performance." The truth is always beautiful. Also, we are making a comedy, man.

Ryan: [Laughs.] Well, also, you directed the whole family, because you have Laura Dern's mom, Diane Ladd, in *Citizen Ruth* as a cameo as Ruth's mother.

Payne: Yeah, she came in for a day. That was a lot of fun.

Ryan: So we are living in a time where everyone is worried about AI writing scripts. A thousand computers could try to write the response to Diane Ladd's line of "What if I would have aborted you?" and none of them would come up with the response that you have in the movie.

Payne: Thanks for mentioning that. First of all, I hope AI can write a lot of scripts because it will save me a lot of trouble. I remember the very moment that Jim Taylor came up with that line. "Well, at least I wouldn't have had to suck your boyfriend's cock!" We were sitting in his apartment on Orchard Street in the Lower East Side when he had just begun NYU film school. I knew it was a great line because it's shocking and funny, and also, in my screenwriting career, it's so economical because in one stroke of a brutal sword, it gives a whole backstory. It's shocking to the audience, and it's shocking to the pro-lifers on the road. It's a super funny line—brutal—but also heartbreaking.

Ryan: And the follow-up line is killer. Now I laugh hardest at Diane Ladd's line, "Do you have to bring that up every time?"

Payne: Oh yeah, "I've been saved." It's funny.

Ryan: It's hard to have the double good line. Also, there is a crossover between the worlds of *Citizen Ruth* and *Election*. It is the patio sealant can. Ruth huffs it and Mr. Novotny stocks it in *Election*. Did you do that on purpose?

Payne: We had the same prop master on both movies, and he still had the patio sealant on the prop truck. So we said, "Why don't we have this guy working at a hardware store?" Thanks for catching that inside gag.

Ryan: Watching Ruth huff that paint is funny every time, with the blue coloring on her face, but it also shows such desperation. Did you guys go through other drugs for her to be addicted to or was it always huffing?

Payne: Right to huffing. It was also suggested by the real-life women on whose story it was based. She was a huffer. My brother at the time was an ER doctor and he had seen huffers. It was his line that we used in the movie. He said, "Al, I've had people in my ER that look like the

Tin Man from *The Wizard of Oz.*" That is where I got that line.

Ryan: How did you balance both sides of the movie? How did you make sure that we don't get too mad at the Christians or the pro-choice activists?

Payne: I can't guarantee that someone didn't get mad. It's a comedy. One thing is casting. I can't tell you how many people read that script when we were looking for financing and said, "She is too unsympathetic to have as a protagonist." My response was always, "She hasn't been cast yet. Are you going to read *The Godfather* and say, 'Michael Corleone kills his brother, so he isn't sympathetic and we are not going to make the movie'?" It's ridiculous. Mary Kay Place, Swoosie Kurtz, Kurtwood Smith, Kelly Preston—bless her heart—all brought such brio to their roles. That has been a comment about my earlier movies, which were a little more satirical, Leonard Maltin once said of *Election* something like it takes dead aim at his targets while avoiding being mean-spirited. It's just the style that occurs to Jim and me.

Ryan: Do you have a Burt Reynolds story for me?

Payne: When he is out on the road with the microphone and says, "Ruth, if you can hear me, we love you and your baby," if you look closely, some of the protesters standing behind him had mistakenly picked up his cue cards and are waving them as signs. So some have "Save Baby Tonya," "Don't have an abortion," cards, and others are waving his cue cards. The editor and I thought that was so funny we left it in.

Ryan: I saw this film on video. I was surprised to read that it never really had a wide release. Tell me the story of *Citizen Ruth* and Miramax.

Payne: It premiered with a lovely reception—I hesitate to say thunderous—at the Sundance Film Festival in January 1996. We thought Miramax would release the film with greater gusto, but instead they kind of dumped it. When a film doesn't have box office success, I don't want to completely blame the distributor, but we definitely felt that Miramax could have done a much better job of releasing if they were interested in doing so.

Ryan: From what I saw, it really only opened in a dozen places.

Payne: I think a few more than that. I certainly went with it to festivals around the world. In *New York* magazine, David Denby compared it to Preston Sturges. It was very well received but dumped. I remember that the producers at the time theorized that because Harvey Weinstein was trying to get in tight with the Clintons, because it was an election year, he didn't want to be perceived as having a politically questionable movie. That's just a theory. I have no idea if that is true, but they certainly didn't support it with many marketing dollars. At least it did well enough that Jim and I got work and the job of *Election* with Paramount. When that movie came out in 1999, that gave us a big boost.

Ryan: I also adore that movie. One of the things I think you do so well in your films is use real locations and actors I haven't seen before. Where do you find these people?

Payne: It started on *Citizen Ruth*. I'm still doing it to this day. It's from my taste in casting and making a movie in such an unlikely place as Omaha, Nebraska. I like a documentary approach to fiction filmmaking. I prefer locations. I also like to combine professional actors, nonprofessional actors, and people off the street. In *Citizen Ruth*, for example, the woman who plays the pro-life protester who says "They brainwashed her. They've got her all doped up," she is a dentist's wife in Omaha and a wonderful woman. John Jackson, my local casting director at the time, was performing at a dinner theater onstage and noticed her at a table. When the show was over, he ran out and grabbed her before she left and asked her to audition. When I did *Nebraska*, it had Bruce Dern, Will Forte, June Squibb, and Stacy Keach, but almost everyone after that were real Nebraska farmers. You have to get the right faces. The more real faces you have and the flatter acting style you have, which more approximates how people are in real life, it can make stars look like they are being more real too. The cops in *Citizen Ruth* are real cops; the ER doctor is actually an ER doctor.

Ryan: The two guys that play in *Nebraska* that say "Two goddamn days to drive from Billings?" were they professional actors?

Payne: One of them is in *Citizen Ruth*. The taller of the two lunkhead cousins is a wonderful local actor. He plays one of the cops outside the lesbian house who says "Ma'am, I know this woman. This is about as sober as I've ever seen her." That is Tim Driscoll. His sister Delany Driscoll plays Matthew Broderick's love interest, the married woman he has an affair with, in *Election*.

Ryan: Wow. She is my favorite actor in *Election*. You are continuing to make movies. What is the difference between nineties films and today's films? Are you struggling today to try to get your type of film made?

Payne: A bunch of us from my generation, my class, are still working: David O. Russell, Paul Thomas Anderson, Sophia Coppola, Wes Anderson, Spike Lee, David Fincher, James Mangold. We are all still working pretty much. Not all of us are still making the smaller, more human films. In general, in Hollywood, the A pictures and the B pictures have switched. Until the 1980s and 90s, it used to be that the A pictures were intelligent, adult dramas. The B pictures were the car chase and *Fast and the Furious* or horror films. As editor Kevin Tent says, "Now everybody's making Roger Corman movies and spending $200 million on them." What used to be the A movies, and certainly as a child of the movies of the 1970s, the movies that made me want to become a film director, are now relegated to having shrink-wrapped budgets. You fight for every dime, and usually you have to have a star.

Ryan: And how do you get around that?

Payne: The key is always to keep budgets low. I've made eight features, and the most expensive movie was *Downsizing*, and it didn't do so well. Among the other films, the most expensive one was *About Schmidt* and that cost thirty-two million bucks. Why? Because half of that went to Jack Nicholson. Which is fine, it's all good, but you couldn't get thirty-two million to make that movie today, which is just a character study.

Ryan: I love how human your films are. It makes a difference to a writer like me to see actual characters in a film.

Payne: You are kind to say that.

Ryan: Do you think a young writer/director could get *Citizen Ruth* made today?

Payne: The budget was maybe $2.4 million. I was non-DGA. Jim and I got WGA minimum of $52,000 for the script. Laura Dern worked for scale, which was maybe $4,500 a week. If you can get people to play ball with you and not spend a lot of dough, plus now you can make things digital, and that reduces production . . .

Ryan: Was *Nebraska* shot on 35mm or digital?

Payne: Digital.

Ryan: How do you feel about digital versus 35mm?

Payne: Whatever. [Laughs.] Do I miss film? Sure. What I miss most, however, is film projection, because flicker will always be superior to glow. But that battle is pretty much lost.

D: *The Birdcage*

"WHAT DIFFERENCE DOES IT MAKE IF I SAY YOU CAN STAY OR YOU SAY I CAN STAY?"

Don't ask, don't tell was how our queer brothers and sisters had to navigate through the nineties. President Bill Clinton implemented this idea for the military. No one should *ask* if anyone is gay, and no one should *tell* they are gay. In *The Birdcage*, "Don't ask, don't tell" is Agador's (Hank Azaria) response when Armand (Robin Williams) tells the servant he is going to have to get a uniform to serve dinner to Senator Keely (Gene Hackman), who is coming to dinner to meet the family that will become in-laws upon the engagement of the children of a conservative senator and a gay nightclub owner. This is about as political as Agador or Armand get in Mike Nichols's comedy based on *La Cage Aux Folles*. But this one throwaway line is enough to remind those of us who lived through the nineties just how in-the-closet homosexuality still was. No doubt it was worse in the eighties, and better in the aughts, but as enlightened as the nineties might have seemed, it still was "Don't ask, don't tell."

For more proof of how closeted the decade was, Robin Williams and Nathan Lane guested on Oprah Winfrey's show in 1996 to talk about the movie. I just watched the episode on YouTube and was amazed at how obvious it was that "Don't ask, don't tell" also seemed to be how Oprah was handling Nathan Lane's sexuality. Oprah asked him if he was afraid of being typecast after playing the homosexual role. Typecast as what? Who he is? Now, I don't know if Nathan Lane was out then or if he was ever in the closet. I don't ever remember finding out Nathan Lane was gay, but also, I'm not sure it was much of a secret. I had been a huge fan of his work in musicals, and it didn't matter to me either way. But the fact that she asked the question says a lot about where society was at that moment. Then add in that Oprah also did a pretaped segment with the other costar Hank Azaria where she asked him what his father thought of seeing him play a gay house servant, and you begin to fully understand just how much things have changed for LGBTQ+ society—the implication being that his father would be ashamed of his son for crushing it in a major Hollywood comedy? It's so obvious how much more common it has become to have actors playing gay characters, or straight characters, no matter their sexuality. It was nice to think of, just for a second, how far we have come, but over the last couple of years, it is so heartbreaking to realize how much we have allowed things to snap back.

We Are Family

Director Mike Nichols begins the film with one of those classic nineties long-shot oners, which brings us into the nightclub (although technically there is an edit when they open the outside door and enter the Birdcage). We go from the busy streets of Miami, with all kinds of couples, straight and gay, all kinds of men, trans, queer, and everywhere in between, and then enter the club, where trans performers are lip-synching to the disco classic "We Are Family." Everyone is smiling, having a great time, and it hit me like a ton of bricks that this club would be shut down in 2024 if it were in Tennessee. In 1996, audiences, no matter their sexual orientation or politics, loved this film. It was helmed by one of the most successful directors; written by comedy legend Elaine May; starred the biggest movie comedic actor of his time, Robin Williams; and had the supporting cast of acting giants Gene Hackman and Dianne Wiest. This was not an independent film like *My Own Private Idaho* made for only queer audiences. No, this was a major Hollywood feature film, and before the movie could even get started, it would, by today's law of the land, be shut down in America today. Somehow we went from "Don't ask, don't tell," which was offensive enough, to "Don't dance, don't sing?" Who in the hell does that protect? *The Birdcage*, which was not a controversial film by any means, didn't get treated like *Citizen Ruth*, where the film couldn't be screened anywhere. The cast was on *Oprah*. You can't get more mainstream than that in 1996. The following year, the television show *Ellen* aired the famous "Puppy Episode," in which the title character comes out, and while Ellen DeGeneres would face a temporary backlash for this, it did bring homosexuality to mainstream television. In 1998, *Will & Grace* would become a hit, and it seemed like the idea of acceptance would last forever. It has insanely rolled back over the past few years, but I think *The Birdcage*, and specifically the character of Albert, played with such humanity by Nathan Lane, had more to do with knocking down some walls than people give it credit for.

The movie, in the simplest terms, is a farce. In a farce, the writer creates well-defined characters with simple motivations, places them on opposite sides of an issue, creates chaos in a situation that neither side can get out of, and, voilà, comedy ensues. Here we have Robin Williams and Nathan Lane as a gay couple who run a drag club whose son (Dan Futterman) is engaged to Ally McBeal—um—I mean Calista Flockhart, whose father is the leading Republican senator (Gene Hackman) from the morals commission committee or some bullshit idea that only serves to make people feel bad about themselves. Obviously, there is no way the senator would ever accept his daughter marrying a man with gay parents. But Elaine May, who was the standup comedy partner of Mike Nichols for years in the sixties, knows a thing or two about how to make an audience laugh. She navigates an idea that is ripe with chances to upset people on both sides of the issue, and instead writes one of the funniest scripts of the decade. This rare, smart, adult comedy doesn't have one unintelligent character in it. What May crafts in this script is one of the hardest things to write: a comedy that isn't stupid and has logical reasons for each bit of farce to occur as our characters go deeper and deeper down the lie tunnel. Just like *Citizen Ruth* (and let's remember these scripts were written in the center of the nineties, when authors were free to write anything without fear of cultural persecutions), *The Birdcage* makes no judgments on any of its characters. May leaves all the judging to you. And if the movie works as intended, the audience will say to themselves, "Hey, there is something wrong here. These two men love their child. How is that different from how any other couple loves their child?" That is the magic trick that May pulls off in her script. I know magicians aren't supposed to reveal their tricks, but this one must be studied. So I am about to tell you how she saws off her audience's legs, I mean makes them laugh and care at the same time.

The plot of the film has Armand's son ask that Albert leaves for one evening while the senator visits. The son is certain that Albert (his de facto mother) will just be too gay, and it will ruin the evening. He asks his father to also change the entire decor of the apartment (I mean, how many penis statues does the average person have in an apartment? Fifty?), lie about their jobs, their heritage, their religion, their orientation, every bit of themselves. As the film goes on, we see the amount of pain this request causes Albert as well as the strain it puts on the relationship with Armand. Despite this, Armand never says to his son, "This is too much." Or "Hey kid, this is who we are, and you are asking us to change everything. You are hurting the people who raised you." Wouldn't a parent say that? Why doesn't Armand stand up for his right to be a couple with Albert? He could just say that they both can be who they are and just live their life the way they want to and the senator will just have to accept it. Well, the reason he doesn't is because Elaine May wants the *audience* to say that. She wants that person who is fearful of homosexuality, gender ambivalence, or drag queens to have that thought themselves. Because Nathan Lane creates a character whom everyone can recognize immediately—a mother. Viewers can't help but empathize with Albert when he realizes the son he raised as his own is embarrassed of him. Not because he is gay, although he is, not because he makes a living singing in drag, although he does, but because like all of us, the kid is embarrassed of his parents. In the same way the Calista Flockhart character is embarrassed when her parents say the wrong conservative thoughts in front of her liberal in-laws at dinner. It's a human emotion to be ashamed of where we come from, to not feel we are good enough for others, and this film uses this simple idea to try to open the closed minds of nineties audiences who were so afraid of finding out the answers to the questions if they asked and they were told.

Another reason this movie works is because the actors in this film are actually huge movie stars. Robin Williams was coming off *Mrs. Doubtfire,* which was a blockbuster hit. Nathan Lane had just done a voice in *The Lion King*, the biggest Disney movie of all time up to that point. Hank Azaria was on *The Simpsons* which was the most influential and popular television cartoon of the time. All three men were heavily steeped in pop culture at the moment. Having them play gay men invited everyone to the party. Hank Azaria said in a 2022 interview that it was wrong for him, a cis man, to play Agador, and he would never do that again. He said, "It's a role I would not play today and rightly so. Although I grew up in a Spanish-speaking household, [. . .] it would go to a genuine Latin actor and perhaps a genuinely gay actor." He went on to explain there are plenty of roles for him to compete for. He is correct that Agador would go to an actor with those real-life traits today, and it probably should. But in 1996, it was more impactful by having these major stars play the role and demonstrate that these characters are just regular people. Remember, even Oprah thought playing a gay character could make your father ashamed. That was the norm of the time. Gay = bad. Here we have three major stars saying "Who cares?" One of the greatest directors of all time saying "What's the big deal?" All that being said, it is doubtful that any actor of any race or gender could have been funnier than Hank Azaria in this film. He was perfect for the part in any time.

It is easy for the culture police who sit here safely in 2024 to judge these actors in hindsight, but they were brave for taking on these roles because it could have cost them in their careers. It isn't the place of people in the future to turn around and judge artists of the past. Having Keanu Reeves and River Phoenix play gay men in *My Own Private Idaho* and Robin Williams in this film is what was needed to move the culture forward. Now times have changed, and casting like that doesn't need to happen to move the needle forward. Today, it is the right choice to find a trans or gay actor for roles. Tomorrow, it might change. We don't know. All we can do is take art as it was intended. Unfortunately, the real place the culture needs to move forward in 2024 isn't in film; it's in our local governments. Audiences are just fine with characters of any sexual persuasion. They were back then too. It is so disheartening to me that in back-to-back movies I am covering for 1996, *Citizen Ruth* and *The Birdcage,* both have topics about rights Americans have lost in the last thirty years. That is mind-blowing. Old movies aren't supposed to be *more* progressive and have *more* freedoms than the people watching them. Can you imagine watching *Casablanca* and seeing those characters have the right to fly on an airplane, but we wouldn't have that right anymore? It isn't just weird. It's disgusting. *The Birdcage* opened the minds of people who were either close minded, or just didn't consider what was happening to queer couples.

The scene that truly breaks my heart and is a wonderful portrayal of what happens when someone is forced to not be themself is when Nathan Lane dresses as a stereotypical businessman and walks into the bedroom to show Robin Williams and Dan Futterman that he can hide who he is. The problem is Albert just looks so wrong. His posture, his face, his clothes, the lack of makeup, the voice, the hair are just all wrong. His partner and son know it. The audience knows it. And, even if I'm wrong, I want to believe the homophobic bigots know it. All of us have had to put on a face to please someone else, but asking them to put on a gender to please someone else is disgusting in a country that pretends to care about freedom. This is a story that exists back when every show didn't automatically have one gay character just to be safe. This idea, this story, needed to spread to the masses, and it did. It was important to focus on gay characters and to tell the world that we are family. All of us. There isn't anything in this movie that feels fake. It is an honest look at love and parenting.

It Takes All Kinds

A scene that delights me is the "I Could Have Danced All Night" scene. It might only be a minute long, but it displays how closely related we all are. Robin Williams and Dianne Wiest sit at the piano singing the song that, at least in 1996, every adult knew from *My Fair Lady*. Gene Hackman and Nathan Lane (who is dressed as a woman) dance; and the newly engaged couple dance as well. Everyone sings every word of the song. Even Agador comes in and sings the last line. Broadway, which is so connected to the gay community, was something everyone loved in 1964 when the film version of *My Fair Lady* was released. Of course, they all know this song, because Americans were brought together by culture and music in the sixties and that was still happening in the nineties. Seeing a group of people, whose politics put them on opposite sides, singing together is a nice remembrance of how Americans used to be connected by common music. This isn't the only Broadway connection in the film.

You didn't think I was going to forget that my favorite composer of all time wrote some songs for this film, did you? I have selected a Stephen Sondheim lyric to begin each of my books. For this book, I picked one from *A Funny Thing Happened on the Way to the Forum*, but I could have chosen a lyric from the song he wrote to begin this film; a song that got cut. Sondheim wrote a brand-new song for director Nichols called "It Takes All Kinds" for the opening-credits sequence. The title alone could be used to describe films of the nineties, as well as what gay rights activists have been trying to convince the small percentage of conservatives who still have a problem with this lifestyle: "It takes all kinds to make up the world." The song has a disco beat and describes how humanity is filled with just about every variety. "Bimbos, Dumbos, Rambos, and Columbos." The song also has a refrain that says we are all "members of the club." The club, representing Armand's Birdcage, but more widely the club of humanity.

Sondheim also wrote the song "Little Dream," which is heard for just a bit when Robin Williams is writing at the piano and then when Nathan Lane is practicing with the dancer who is chewing gum. Sondheim said, "I thought the first song was appropriate and clever [. . .] but Mike decided not to use ["It Takes All Kinds"] and only half the lyric of ["Little Dream"]." Mike Nichols also cut a production number of Nathan Lane, as his female avatar, Starina, performing the Sondheim song "Can That Boy Foxtrot!" The song was originally written for Sondheim's 1971 musical *Follies* but was cut and replaced with "I'm Still Here." (Remember when I said learning about credits and research can lead you to interesting connections to other films? The song "I'm Still Here" was used in Nichols's previous film, *Postcards from the Edge*, sung by Shirley MacLaine. Everything's connected.) Luckily, they did include "Foxtrot" on the soundtrack for the film, so at least we get to hear this comic number. Nathan Lane confirmed on *Oprah* that they did film this number, and it would have been nice if it showed up on a DVD bonus feature, but it never did.

The fourth Sondheim song used in the film is "Love Is in the Air." Christine Baranski and Robin Williams sing this song as they reminisce about performing it together in a show they were in when they were young. Here is what a Sondheim nerd I am. "Love is in the Air" was cut from *Forum*. So what show are they talking about when they say they sang it together? There really is only one option, and it's really unlikely. The song is used in a medley in the Sondheim musical review *Side by Side by Sondheim*, but that is just a collection of his songs that has a cast of only three people. Who believes these two unknown dancers would star in a musical review that has no dancing in it? See, I'm a Sondheim and film nerd.

I think Sondheim should have assumed Nichols was going to cut the songs he wrote for the film because the two songs Nichols did put in the film were cut numbers from Sondheim shows. What comes around, goes around. It is a shame that more of "Little Dream" wasn't heard in the film. Although the melody does score a scene where Williams is at the bar having a drink, the unheard lyrics have a nice callback to the scene where Williams and Lane have their moving

No green screen here. Mike Nichols had to time this shot to get the boat in the background while Nathan Lane and Robin Williams sign legal documents to make their relationship permanent.
(Photo courtesy of United Artists.)

discussion on the park bench about their future and they sign the paperwork that says they both own the club. Remember that in the film, "Little Dream" isn't a song written by the greatest songwriter of all time, Stephen Sondheim. It's supposed to be written by Armand. The lyric in the song, which is a song he is working on over these two days, references the huge ship that sails behind the two men as they sign the paperwork that connects them. Getting a contract that says they will each share the property was the only rights two men had in 1996 to legally merge their lives. They couldn't get married, but they could be co-owners of property. In the scene, Robin Williams says, "What difference does it make if I say you can stay, or you say I can stay? It's ours." Sondheim, who always writes from the character's point of view, wrote the song as if it was written by Armand later that day. I like to think Armand went home and finished the lyric he had been working on during this crucial moment in their relationship. Armand wrote these lyrics: "Are you my dream or am I yours instead? Either way, little dream, supreme, I say, 'Full steam ahead!'" It calls back the discussion, the ship in the background, and becomes a beacon for progress. America made gay marriage legal (for now), and for a while it was full steam ahead for equal rights for all Americans, until a mean-spirited roll back of laws started to target transgender and queer Americans. Let's hope, with a little dream, we can all remember that it does take all kinds to make up a world and move full steam ahead; but for real this time.

Chapter 9
1997

A: *Two Girls and a Guy*

"IS THIS HOW YOU WANT TO LIVE THE REST OF YOUR LIFE? JUST DAMAGING PEOPLE—DAMAGING YOURSELF?"

There may not be a more apropos named film from the nineties better than *Two Girls and a Guy*. It only stars two girls (Heather Graham as Carla and Natasha Gregson Wagner as Lou) and a guy (Robert Downey Jr. as Blake). The movie, which is a hundred minutes soaking wet, is a perfect microcosm of nineties film. It's a low-budget, all-talk movie where the entire story takes place inside and directly outside of a New York City loft. The loft is just about the coolest place anyone could live. It puts the *Friends* apartment to shame. It makes you want to move in there, even if you'd have to room with Downey and all of his crazy singing. This is a film that is impossible to remove outside of the time it was made, due to the fact that it was filmed in between Downey's drug arrests in 1996 and 1997. This is relevant because his character, Blake, is a perpetual liar who, once he is busted by the two women he has been two-timing for the past ten months, tries to fast-talk his way out of his infraction. Writer/ director James Toback said he wrote the script after seeing Downey, whom he had worked with before, being carted away in handcuffs. "There was something about his fragility. The absolute sense of being inoperative, the vulnerability, the loss. I thought, 'He's not going to want to (expletive deleted) up for a while. His desire is to kill himself.'" The film even has a scene where Downey fakes his suicide and holds a gun to his own head. Downey, who is today only known as an action hero, was in the prime of his acting game when he made this film. As dangerous as Brando was in the fifties or De Niro was in the seventies, Downey was in the nineties. He is an absolute marvel in this film, as well as *Home for the Holidays, Chaplin, Short Cuts, Natural Born Killers*, and more. Not in a costume made of iron, just an actor creating characters that fly off the screen and feel alive.

The film, which uses dialogue like *Star Trek* uses photon torpedoes, has a centerpiece moment in which Downey performs a soliloquy in front of a mirror where he tells himself he only has one chance left. It was this scene that had critics talking about the blurring of film and real life. Every time Graham or Wagner confronts him about his duplicitous behavior, it's hard not to wonder if the entire production wasn't an intervention for Downey. Natasha Gregson Wagner said, in an interview with me that will follow this essay, that Downey improvised parts of the mirror speech. Watching him act his way through this is one of the main joys of the film. It was heartbreaking at the time because as a fan of his, I remembered being honestly worried that this might be the last film I get to see him in. It was unlikely that he would overcome his addiction. He did and became a superhero superstar. I guess I didn't know what I should have been worried about.

You Don't Know Me

The first fifteen minutes of the film are led by Graham and Wagner as they learn of each other's existence and realize they have been duped by Downey. They decide to break into his apartment and confront him about his deception. One of my pet peeves about modern movies is how the first half hour of films are setting up the concept that the trailer already let us know was going to happen. In *Two Girls and a Guy*, the entire setup is under five minutes, and that includes two minutes of credits. The characters find out they are both dating Blake quickly, because why waste our time? The title told us if the preview didn't. Once they realize they are both dating the same man, the women do not turn on each other. They don't cry, scream, or pout. No, they remain as numb and stoic as a Gen X character should. There is no way that a hip cat like Wagner would ever show her true feelings in front of her rival, Graham. This simple decision allows each female character to begin from a point of strength instead of weakness. It also allows their eventual breakdowns, later in the film, when we know and care about them, to have much more of an impact. Once we are invested in them, that is the time for them to explain how they truly feel. This allows the characters to feel more real. In 1997, strangers didn't express their deepest feelings in front of people they didn't know. There wasn't Facebook yet. We still had shame and dignity. If the script would have started with the characters having emotional outbursts, where could the film build to? If this film was made today, which would *never* happen, studio executives would certainly have these two actresses screaming at each other at the top of their lungs from word go. That way, the audience would *know* they were upset. I mean, we wouldn't want two women to not cry to express themselves. But this film doesn't want drama with a capital "D." It has a plan, and the only way to execute that plan is to set it in a world where discussion, repartee, and cleverness is the main mode of communication and expression. This is what makes the film rewatchable. The first pass through viewers will naturally want to know what Blake did, how he did it, and what the girls will do about it. But upon repeat viewings, it's the subtle admissions the characters share within dialogue about other topics where we learn who they truly are. This is a movie about people in their twenties in the nineties. Gen Xers were about debate, discussion, and privacy. We watch Graham and Wagner develop a relationship. We see how they are the same and different. We fall in love with both of them, just like Blake did. Who wouldn't want them both? Or all three, for that matter.

The film takes the concepts of fidelity, relationships, and new love and dissects them from every direction. It's also hella funny. As the girls confront him, Downey, who plays an actor in the film, asserts that they should have known he would lie to them because all actors lie. It's their job. He asserts that all actors are untrustworthy. After a beat, Wagner deadpans a dagger to the heart of his theory: "Denzel Washington. He doesn't lie." Good answer. I'm with her. This is a moment where we truly learn about Lou. She wants to prove him wrong in this moment. She isn't concerned with the big picture; she wants to win this moment, this argument. Heather Graham's character doesn't want to go on this tangent, she wants to know why Blake lied to her. She doesn't care about Denzel Washington or any of Blake's actor nonsense. It becomes clear why each woman was attractive to

Blake. They both have desirable qualities and they are not told to us; they are shown to us within their dialogue, and the script doesn't make any comments about it. No one points out to the audience that Lou is just trying to win the argument; you have to think about it later and get to understand her character. Hot damn is that a fun thing to do while you watch a movie. You actually get to analyze what is going on and figure out who these three people are. A viewer can just laugh at the scene, or crazy people like me can think about it for days after watching it. This is such a wonderfully written scene and a lesson in how to do situational comedy. As the characters go off on this brilliant tangent, we laugh but also agree. I mean, no one would think Denzel would lie to us. When a writer can get an audience to buy into their offbeat theory and take it seriously, the writer gets big laughs. The film is a treat for viewers who enjoy good writing and listening to characters saying the things that you always wish you said to someone who was breaking your heart, but you think of them three days later. No punchline is left unsaid in this film.

If there is a word that has been overused in every movie in every decade since the seventies, it would surely be fuck. Most movies use fuck as a signal to let us know their character is edgy. Usually it is a wasted word that adds nothing to the scene. But Natasha Gregson Wagner uses it to perfection when she takes the moment to not just tell Robert Downey Jr. to fuck off, she gives him a fuck-off soliloquy that Shakespeare himself might have crafted. No doubt Spike Lee had a fuck-off rant that rivals this one in his 2002 film, *The 25th Hour*, but before 1997, no one had quite told someone to fuck off more eloquently than Wagner, and maybe no character earned it more than Downey. Back when this film came out on VHS, there was no YouTube, no memes, no sharing of audio. My cousin and I recorded this speech on a mix CD and would listen to it in between songs like it was the latest Jewel song. It was my fondest wish to someday say it to someone who broke my heart, but when my heart was broken, I didn't have the composure of Wagner to deliver it so well.

The film didn't shy away from fuck-you rants, and it didn't shy away from the then taboo topic of bisexuality and throuples. Lou's sexuality was fluid before the term existed in pop culture. Carla's sexuality is also a bit blurred. Some films from the nineties might seem dated, but this film is really ahead of its time with its subjects. It is messy, grown-up, and superlow budget. At the time of its release, I was a few years outside of working at the local video store, but I waited with bated breath to view the film. I was a huge fan of Heather Graham from *Twin Peaks* and *Swingers*. She would become a major star in a few years in *Boogie Nights*, but with this role we actually get to see her develop a well-rounded character. Where Wagner is full of spunk and emotion, Graham is cold, calculated, and reserved. She reacts slowly, thoughtfully to each moment. Each actor is an important side of the triangle of characters who come alive only through how they interact with each other. It would be easy to say this is a child of *Before Sunrise*, but it is so much more of a Pinter play, a deep dive into the psyche of three humans who share a bond and a love between them.

The film has largely been forgotten. It was written and talked about at the time primarily because of Downey's trouble with the law, but watching it in today's era, that won't be on anyone's mind. It is the work that is left. I luckily forgot how it ended and it came as a surprise to me, which is a nice thing for a small picture to do. As I have pointed out over and over, the key to good writing is for the ending to be inevitable and a shock at the same time. This film manages a surprise ending in a way that dramas rarely do. The film does not get eaten alive by its own gimmick of only having three characters in one room. It comes alive because of it. I hadn't rewatched it in over twenty years before studying it for this book. That is a mistake I will never make again.

B: Natasha Gregson Wagner Interview
(*Two Girls and a Guy* Actress)

"I WAS JUST ALWAYS SPUNKY."

Natasha Gregson Wagner: How does *Two Girls and a Guy* hold up? I haven't seen it in decades.

Scott Ryan: I hadn't seen it in twenty years. It was so good. I loved it.

NGW: Really? I should watch it again. What I remember about it was that it was Robert's comeback film after he had his substance abuse issues. When they sent me the script to have the audition, there was a lot of interest in James Toback. People were excited about him as a director. This was the time when independent film was just beginning.

Ryan: That was what the nineties was all about.

NGW: We are gonna make this movie for a million dollars, and it's gonna just be three actors in a room, and that is all it is. That kind of thing hadn't been done before. That is the way it was pitched to me. It premiered at Cannes. I can't remember why I didn't go. I think I was working on *Another Day in Paradise*. There was buzz due to Toback and Robert. Robert is so good in that movie. He was super supportive of me in the audition. I actually read with him, and I read for the part of Carla, Heather Graham's role. Kate Hudson read for my part. I remember that Robert called his wife at the time, Debbie, and they were friends with my older sister, Katie. I could hear him talking to her. He said, "I'm in the room with Katie's little sister, and she is totally awesome for the role. She just blew me away." I was like, "Oh my God. This is crazy. I am having an out-of-body experience." So by the time I got home, my sister called me and said, "I think you are gonna get this part." I didn't know, because you can never be sure about anything in acting . . . or life. So my agent called and said, "I've got good news and bad news. You are in the movie, but you are not Carla; you are playing Lou. Heather Graham is gonna play Carla." That was her name in the movie, right? Carla?

Ryan: Yes, I was really proud of you for pulling that name out of nowhere.

NGW: Me too! That just came out of my deep subconscious. [Laughs.] That is how it happened. I loved the entire experience. The other thing that was interesting is that they put us up at the Soho Grand Hotel. It was brand-new, and it seemed exciting to stay in this new downtown hotel. I was walking around the streets of New York City to feel like I lived there. I was gonna have dinner with the director. We go to this Italian restaurant and order our food. Jimmy gets up to go to the bathroom. He never comes back to the table. The food comes. The waiter says, "You might as well eat it; he won't be back for a while." So I ate my dinner. The check comes to the table, and Jimmy comes back and says, "Okay, where were we?" Now I had been sitting there for ninety minutes. I guess that was when he was gambling with horse racing a lot, which he did while we were shooting. Shooting would shut down for two hours because he was betting on horses. [Laughs.] It was insane. It was this freewheeling film. It had a real improvisational-play feeling to it.

Ryan: I am interested that you were considered for the Carla role because you are so good as Lou. What were your feelings on swapping?

NGW: At first I was a little disappointed because I had gotten my head around Carla and had a good back-and-forth with Robert in the audition. But then I reread the script and I liked it so much, and I was excited to work with Robert, and I liked Jimmy. He was easy to work with because he told you exactly what he wanted. Sometimes directors don't let you know if they are happy with what you are doing, but with Jimmy, I always knew if he liked a take or not because he was completely honest about it. I think I thrive in an environment like that because if a director doesn't like what I am doing, then I can change it.

Ryan: What was the vibe within the threesome?

NGW: Robert was so supportive of us, Heather and I. We were really a team, the three of us. It was hard because I didn't know how it was going to work out. Off camera, I really liked Heather, and we were becoming friends. But I was unclear if that was in opposition to my character. But then I thought Lou felt conflicted as well because she really liked Carla, but she was jealous of her as well.

Ryan: One of the first things that struck me was that in the opening ten minutes, before Robert joins you and Heather, you do not yell at each other. It is so refreshing. No way was Lou going to give Carla that satisfaction. How did you take that part of the script?

NGW: I was able to see the dimensionality in that idea. Maybe that is because I come from a family that is a patchwork quilt of parents. By the time I was old enough to know everything, everyone was friends. So even though there was cheating and breakups and divorces, everyone spent the holidays together. There was no animosity. I was able to understand that Lou was really devastated by the situation, but she knew it wasn't Carla. It was Robert that was the rascal. I feel that way now that I am married and have children. My daughter is almost ten, and friends are starting to break up. I feel like a lot of my girlfriends whose husbands have cheated, they are not mad at the women, they are mad at the men. It is a really mature point of view.

Ryan: Tell me about the fuck-you speech. What was it like to destroy Robert Downey Jr. and give the best fuck you in film history?

NGW: I feel like he felt the fuck you. Whatever his issues in his life were, the fuck you was meant for him. That made it easier. His eyes are so crazy expressive. When we were doing it, it was like there was this energy that was happening on the set every day. Everyone was really excited. We didn't have a lot of time. We had been rehearsing a bit, so we knew. We rehearsed the camera blocking, but not the dialogue. Some of those takes were long takes so we knew where we had to be for Barry Markowitz, the DP, to capture us. That speech just came out of me. I was like twenty-six and still devastated at the loss of my mom and angry that happened to me. It was easy for me to connect with my rage. It really helped me for that part. I was a little bit more of a firecracker then than I am now. I am much less pissed off. [Laughs.]

Ryan: Good to hear that you are better, but you do it so well when you get there. You are full of spunk in that role. I can't see you as Carla.

NGW: Genes are crazy. My daughter does so many things that remind me of me. One of the things she has is that spunky quality. At the time, I didn't like that people would say in an audition, "She is a little too spunky for the role." I was like, "What does that mean?" Now I understand it. I was just born that way. I don't know. I was just always spunky. It was a good marriage because Lou was spunky and she is very much a New York girl. She doesn't like to be messed around with. He totally blindsided her. She trusted him. She thought he was a great guy. It was the vessel for me to let all of that out.

Ryan: The mirror speech that Robert gives just breaks your heart. When he says, "You only have one more chance," I think it feels like the movie and his personal life are merging. Now he has passed through all that addiction, but back then it could have gone either way. Was that improvised?

NGW: Most of it was on the page, but here and there, Jimmy was really open to us improvising. Robert is a natural. He improvised a bit of it. It was a free-flowing thing. We would shoot something, and then they would catch Robert doing the mirror scene, and Heather and I would be in the other part of the loft waiting or talking. There were no dressing rooms. We were just all in this loft. If Jimmy needed to grab something, we would either watch or wait in the other room. It was like that for the crew. Everyone was around watching. It felt like a rehearsal for a play.

Ryan: What did you learn about acting from Robert and Heather?

NGW: Robert is very much in his skin, in his body. It doesn't feel like he turns it on and off. He can be talking to you and then they say action and he is in character. He wasn't afraid to flub his lines or throw something in. He is very free. Heather is more steady. She is very prepared. Robert was off the cuff, and that is his genius, and Heather is a good student. She is very professional. I really admired her. She had been acting for so much longer than I had. I was totally the newbie on the set. She had been carrying movies longer than I had. With Heather, there is always something mysterious about her. She doesn't ever give you it all—in work and in life. She is enigmatic. Robert is easy to know in those moments with him. You feel like you are really connected with him on camera.

Ryan: I remember this movie getting NC-17, but there isn't any nudity. Am I remembering that correctly?

NGW: I think what happened with that was in a scene with Robert and Heather, they edited something out. There was an NC-17, and Jimmy took out whatever was going to give it the NC-17. He thought it would diminish the chances at the box office.

Ryan: Do you remember what it was?

NGW: It was something with them in the bedroom. I wasn't in there, so I don't remember. It was maybe a little more graphic.

Ryan: What do you see as the main difference with nineties films?

NGW: I think there was this grittiness which was reminiscent of the seventies. They didn't have a lot of money. A lot of writers and directors were writing movies they wanted to direct, and they didn't have a lot of money to make it. Actors weren't making a lot of money on them. It felt like it was from the heart and soul. It wasn't about money the way it is now.

Ryan: My theory for my book is that after the nineties, they stopped making films for grown-ups. If you don't have a cape and you are not looking for a glowing rock, your film isn't getting made. I am over superhero movies.

NGW: Me too. I think it is really a bummer that movies like this don't get made anymore because all these huge Marvel films do. Movies have to make billions of dollars to be considered successful. Back in the nineties, they didn't have to make that much money to be considered successful.

Ryan: I don't know if you remember how *Two Girls* ends, but I was really surprised by the ending. I don't even want to spoil it for you, since you haven't seen it in a while.

NGW: I need to rewatch it, so don't tell me. I feel like I have an inkling. Like is there a third girl that comes?

Ryan: I am not gonna say. You'll have to watch it to find out.

NGW: [Laughs.]

Ryan: So I don't know how you will feel about this, but until three days ago, I didn't know you were Natalie Wood's daughter. You were always the girl from *Lost Highway* to me.

NGW: Oh my God, I love that. That makes me feel so good, because I do think it got in my way as an actress. That is why I would like to act again, because I was able to process so much about my mom after making the documentary about her [*Natalie Wood: What Remains Behind*]. I was able to put it out into the universe and let it go.

Ryan: The documentary flowed so naturally. When you ended up interviewing—if I could be permitted, I'd like to call him "Daddy Wagner," like you do in the film?

NGW: [Laughs.] Of course!

Ryan: Your interview with Daddy Wagner is just so heartbreaking. Do you mind talking about this?

NGW: Not at all. HBO said, "We are interested in making this documentary, but we want to make sure you don't shy away from the accident, so we want to see the interview with your dad first." The first day the interview wasn't going well. The director [Laurent Bouzereau] said, "We don't have it." That night, I said to my dad, "Listen, we need to go deeper. I know you like to talk about the great parts of your life with my mom, but we have to talk about what happened that night." The next morning, Scott, I am telling you, he was *right there*. He was so vulnerable. Laurent said, "What did you say to him last night?" But he wanted to make this documentary, and I was so blown away by him that day.

Ryan: How did you not just cry uncontrollably during that interview?

NGW: Every time I did an interview, I didn't want my emotion to overtake the interviewee's emotion, but at the premiere at Sundance, when the movie ended, I just burst into tears in front of the entire audience.

Ryan: I was so moved by the honesty in your beautiful documentary. It's such an emotional look at losing a parent. My dad died before I became a published author. It has to be so hard for you that your mom never got to see you as an actress.

NGW: It is so true. I am sorry for your loss. It's so hard to lose a parent. You want them there to see your accomplishments. I do truly believe that they are watching. I spoke to this medium a few years ago. She said, "Hold up a piece of paper and just write what you want to tell your mom. She is closer than you think."

Ryan: Why do you not act anymore?

NGW: I am married to an actor, and I tried acting when my daughter was seven months old. I did a movie that Tim Blake Nelson directed [*Anesthesia*], and I was just so miserable. I just didn't want to be there. I wanted to be with her. I am a hands-on mom. As much as you have to give to create a character, I just can't do it anymore. The way my brain works, I can't compartmentalize being away from her. I can't do it, because most of me is always with her.

Ryan: That is nice, but I'd like to see you in stuff.

NGW: Ruth Gordon [*Harold and Maude*] was my godmother, and she won an Oscar when she was a much older lady. And I'm not saying I would win an Oscar, but I feel like she's an example that I can go back to acting anytime. I am interested in what I would bring to my work because I'm a totally different person now. I have more gravity to bring to my work.

Ryan: And then you'll go on your first audition and they'll say, "Ugh, she had a little too much spunk."

NGW: YES! "She's a little too old to have that much spunk." [Laughs]

C: The Ice Storm

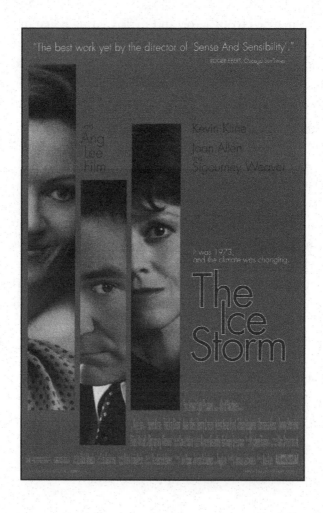

"You're Boring Me. I Have a Husband. I Don't Particularly Feel the Need for Another."

Outside, the ice crackles. Air has weight. Everything is frozen. The silence is something that can almost be heard as each branch, leaf, and electrical cable is encased behind fresh ice. It leaves a protective coating over everything it touches. Every car window looks like a Monet painting. The only thing more sterile and dead than the outside is the insides of the suburban homes of New Canaan, Connecticut. The kitchens are lime green. The women are dressed in purple jumpsuits. The men have ascots or double Windsor knots around their necks. In director Ang Lee's *The Ice Storm,* everything has been submerged under the coldness of ice. Everything is frozen in a moment. But after all, what is ice but frozen water? The moment chosen was in the midst of the scandal that finally shattered the myth of the American dream: Watergate.

The Ice Storm was incorrectly marketed in 1997 and has one of the worst trailers for any movie covered in this book. It has that old-fashioned voice-over and begins with a sentence that truly makes no sense: "Once there was a time when families were strangers." What are you talking about? There was a time when that was a thing? And are you saying that it's over now? What? That also isn't what the movie is about. In watching Siskel and Ebert review this film, which they loved, they expressed their concern that there would be no good way to market this film because there weren't ten second sound bites to put in a commercial. Amen to that. All the marketing department could do was try to focus on one of the titillating plot points of this movie:

the fact that the adult characters go to a key party. In case you have lived a bland life, like I have, I will explain what that is. It is a party where all the husbands put their car keys in a bowl, and at the end of the night, the wives pick out the keys and go home with whichever husband's keys they pick out of the bowl. But when the trailer and media focus on that idea, it makes it seem like the film is a sexual romp à la *Basic Instinct*, *The Last Seduction*, or *Eyes Wide Shut*. *The Ice Storm* isn't anywhere near those films. It is not a titillating film. It is a deep, spiritual look at disillusionment and loss of faith. But the fact that the studio focused on the married swingers plot point, and then crafted a preview as if the movie was a fun, family Thanksgiving zany look at seventies fashion, lets us understand how even in the nineties, when a film was truly a unique, grown-up, honest character study that strove to show something without telling it directly to the audience, studios didn't have any better ideas of what to do with this type of film back then than they do today. Although at least back then, they were thankfully willing to *make* these types of films. Unfortunately, instead of learning how to market a film that can't be summed up with a sentence that begins with "Once upon a time," studios just said, "What if we just put this Tobey Maguire kid in a spider costume and made that type of movie instead?"

The ironic part of watching *The Ice Storm* now is the connection to superheroes. Granted, this might just be ironic for me, since I was working on a book where I redundantly expressed how sick I am of superhero movies and totally long for movies exactly like *The Ice Storm*. The film begins with Tobey Maguire (the actor who will officially launch the superhero era of film in 2002) reading a comic book of the Fantastic Four. Maguire voices over how the family has a superpower to destroy each other as they each get more powerful. Thankfully, the comic book story stays just where it should, within the confines of the comic book that the sixteen-year-old character reads as he rides the train back from New York. It is all just an analogy for the families displayed in the film that can't stop hurting each other. There are no superheroes in this film. No one can save the parents or the children from the path they are on. While there may not be a hero in the film, there is a villain who keeps popping up: President Richard

Milhous Nixon.

Nixon and our best-named vice president ever, Spiro Agnew, are shown in prison outfits on a poster that hangs on Maguire's wall. His sister, played by Christina Ricci, is obsessed with watching Nixon on TV. She knows more about Watergate than her parents and brother combined. Every chance she gets, she turns the television on to watch Nixon lie. This film was released one year before President Clinton would go through his scandal, but watching the film in 2023, it sure feels like these characters are struggling like Americans struggled from 2016-2020 with news fatigue. But the difference between Americans today, or in the nineties, and these particular Americans of the seventies is that people in the seventies were just learning that politicians lie. They were just about to discover that a high and mighty president would and could break the law. That level of innocence might be hard for someone who is just discovering this movie today to wrap their Fox News-infected head around. No one was shocked that President Clinton lied to everyone in the nineties. Even in the split political system we have today, no one was surprised that the president of 2016 was a liar, but in 1973, the idea that the president, *any* president, would lie to the press that openly was shocking. These Americans didn't know that Kennedy snuck Marilyn Monroe into the White House yet. They didn't know that the government knew that Vietnam was unwinnable and stayed in it anyway. They didn't know that Nixon knew about the break-in at the Watergate hotel. They were innocent, and that innocence was just beginning to fade away in 1973. Rick Moody wrote a novel that tied this disillusionment of the American dream and wrapped it together with the infection of the suburbs with the idea of free love. Then screenwriter James Schamus put it all together in his perfect script.

Like all good nineties films, none of what I just said is pointed out in the movie. You have to, and you might want to hold on to something for this next sentence, you have to think on your own to understand what the film is actually about. It is all in the subtext. Subtext is like porn. It might be hard to describe, but you sure know it when you see it. This film might be the best example of how to use subtext to get your point across. This is a film where, honestly,

Subtext is the key for Kevin Kline and Joan Allen in this wonderfully acted scene. (Photo courtesy of Searchlight Pictures.)

the most heartbreaking dialogue delivered in the entire movie might just be when Joan Allen says to her husband, played by Kevin Kline, "Did you remember to pick up the cranberry sauce? You like it on your turkey sandwiches." She begins to cry while delivering the line and turns around to hide herself from her husband. When a writer can create that much subtext into a script, all writers better pay attention. Joan Allen's acting in this film is superb. She is carrying the weight of the suspicion that her husband is cheating on her with their neighbor, Sigourney Weaver. It is Thanksgiving weekend, and her son is back from boarding school, her daughter is in the next room watching television, she is not going to confront her husband as to why he smells like another woman. It is lightly implied that he has been unfaithful before. All she can bring herself to say to him, as she finally breaks down, is a question about cranberry sauce. It is a human, relatable moment. Today, that scene would have Joan Allen throwing the dishes against the wall and screaming F-words at Kevin Kline for banging the hot chick from *Alien*. This viewing was maybe the fourth time I have watched the film in twenty-six years, and it was the first time that I picked up that Kline had cheated on her before. You have to pay attention, you have to rewatch, you have to think. Man, do I love that.

Dirty Love

No disrespect to the ice storm that blankets the town of New Canaan, Connecticut, but the true source of cold in this movie is Sigourney Weaver. Despite the fact that she is having an affair with her neighbor, she is totally impenetrable. After having sex with Kevin Kline, he starts telling her about his work nemesis and their golf game. She suffers no fools and tells him plainly that she is bored and he should stop talking. When she catches Ricci playing a game of "I'll show you mine if you show me yours" with her young son, she doesn't react with anger; she just tells the girl to remember that her body is a temple. She reacts briskly to Joan Allen when Allen offers to help clean the dishes after dinner. She tells her no thanks the first time, like we all politely do, and the second time she is so abrupt that Allen practically has to be treated for frostbite. Not allowing a woman to help wash the dishes in the early seventies is akin to not giving a guest your Wi-Fi password today. It's as mean as you can be. When Weaver has a second sexual encounter with Kline and, by golly, he starts blabbing again, she simply gets out of bed, gets in her car, and leaves him alone in his underwear. Did I mention it was her house they were at? As always, there is no way I am willing to spoil the ending of this movie, but even the ending can't get a reaction out of her; she is truly frozen.

If this movie were made today, the end would totally be spoiled because there would be a content warning before the film even started listing all the twists held within. Art is made to make you feel. Surprises in art are good for everyone. If there are things you are sensitive to, I totally get that. But James Moody worked hard crafting this story, and James Schamus brought it to life in his screenplay. Their work should be honored by the groundwork they lay in the first two acts of the film and the third act should be experienced as it plays out, not by a sentence that whittles the ending down to a trigger warning. The film also deals with teenage sexuality very openly and honestly. No way would Ang Lee be allowed to use young actors to film these scenes today. Elijah Wood, Adam Hann-Byrd (who is also wonderful in *Little Man Tate*), and Christina Ricci have preteen sex scenes that are not glamorous by any means. I don't remember worrying about the child actors when I saw the film back in the nineties, but no doubt people would worry about them now. I hated myself for even thinking about it today. All the scenes are very innocent, but it is the awkwardness and truthfulness of the scenes that make you so damn uncomfortable and make the scenes seem worse than they are. To be honest, the uncomfortableness of this movie is what really makes *The Ice Storm* stand out as a film classic.

Yes, back in the day, if anyone was discussing this movie, it was the key party scene they talked about. But what they should have talked about is how uncomfortable you feel when the key party scene plays out. As soon as the wives get on one side of the room and the men on the other, everyone in the scene giggles. They fret. They worry. None of them really want to do this. Much earlier in the movie, a character says that these key parties happen all the time in California. That line is the true key to this party. These people are living in an East Coast suburb. They know this idea of free love is happening in San Francisco. It is happening in LA. It is all "California Dreamin'" on such an ice storm day. They don't want the world to pass them by, but they are giving up the trust and safety they have with their spouses. Even if that relationship is cold, it's theirs. This scene delightfully makes the viewer uncomfortable. It makes you feel awkward and dirty. Movies today do their very best to never put their audiences in a real-life uncomfortable situation. The movies are created in the bubble, for your bubble, and for the purpose of reaffirming your already held beliefs. *The Ice Storm* dares you to consider how you would feel about having to share your spouse in the most intimate way with an acquaintance at a party. What would it be like to have to watch that play out? I immediately felt protective of my wife. The idea of being at a party and being split across the room from my love and watching others pick and choose over her made me uncomfortable and made me appreciate what I have. This is how trigger warnings can diminish the experience of watching good art. Not knowing how it will all turn out allows us to put ourselves in situations that we wouldn't ever want to put ourselves in. When we are in that unwanted moment, we are forced to empathize with a situation that is outside of ourselves. We just might understand what someone else went through, and we might just be able to see over our fences that line our boundaries that falsely protect our way of life. It is good to have a safe and unpleasant experience in a film. Everyone has thought about the excitement of going to a key party, or having sex with a complete stranger, but watching it play out, knowing how these characters feel, it becomes real, it becomes dirty, and it becomes uncomfortable. Any drama that makes me want to cover my eyes like it is a horror film is alright with me.

One of the truly brilliant subplots is when a reverend (Michael Cumpsty) shows up at the key party just as Joan Allen is allowing her emotions to overtake her. She has just had her suspicions confirmed that her husband has been cheating on her with Weaver. She sees the reverend, who earlier in the film tries to pick her up, but she misconstrued his advances as him trying to save her soul, but at this party he takes a more direct approach and says, "Sometimes the shepherd needs the company of the sheep." It doesn't go over as well as he planned. This betrayal of his position of leadership makes Allen respond with the truth that all Americans were grappling with as their president betrayed his fiduciary responsibilities to his flock. She responds, "I'm going to try hard to not understand the implications of that." No one in America, in any era, ever wants to confront the implications that their leaders commit crimes, are dishonest, and that maybe the very laws that were created to protect us actually harm us. Do we confront the betrayal or do we try hard to not understand it? The reverend, unlike future politicians and religious leaders, actually experiences shame, and leaves the party immediately. His reaction is as outdated as smoking during a dinner party. Leaders feeling shame has long been eradicated from our political or religious infrastructures.

Help Me Make it Through The Night

While this is all going on for the parents, the children are fighting their own battles. Ricci, who the day after she says Nixon should be killed for lying, steals a Devil Dog treat at the local five-and-dime store. She walks in, slips the snack in her pocket, stands there, turns around, sees an older woman has witnessed it, and then just simply leaves the store. She openly committed this crime for the same reason that she is sexually experimenting with the neighborhood boys: just to feel something. To see if anything matters. To see if she will be held accountable for her actions. The rule of law doesn't apply anymore. If the president can tell a lie on national television, she sure as hell can steal a Devil Dog.

My favorite relationship in this film is between brother and sister, Maguire and Ricci. They actually like each other. They also have their own language of speaking to each other. Most of the relationships in this movie are rightly frozen. But if you make *all* the relationships exactly the same, you get the one-note emotional type of drama that is currently being made. Yes, that is easier to market. It is easier for uneducated critics to understand, but it isn't a better written film, and it isn't as enjoyable to consume. Everyone in the world is not the same; we are all different. If the writer crafts parents who are not getting along, it is nice to be able to cut to someone in the family who does get along. Also, when your parents are falling apart, it is to your siblings that you cling. Their relationship rings true to the characters and the moment. Their relationship brings the viewer momentary respite from the cold. This, along with the fact that the film is also very funny, gives us a slice of how life really is. Sometimes up. Sometimes down. I'm not saying there are jokes and one-liners throughout the movie, but there are comical moments from the characters.

The uncomfortability doesn't only exist during the key party. When Elijah Wood suits up to take a walk outside to explore the ice storm, we are immediately a nervous wreck. Especially when he stands on a diving board that is totally ice covered and jumps up and down on it, slightly slipping with each jump. Why are we so uncomfortable? Because the pool is drained beneath him. If he slips, he is going to fall onto the concrete, twelve feet below him. All the safety nets have been removed, and all the rules don't exist, not even the laws of physics. He is as reckless with his body as his parents are at the key party and as Ricci is at home with his younger brother. Throughout the movie, both of Ricci's parents catch her in a presexual situation. They each catch her immediately after being unfaithful to their spouse. When Joan Allen opens the bedroom door and sees her young daughter topless under the covers, she can't condemn her any more than her father could when he caught her dry humping the neighbor boy while wearing a Halloween mask of Richard Nixon. He literally sees the president trying to fuck his daughter—the next generation. The parents are watching their sins play out on their children. Whether it is through sexual experimentation, being reckless in an ice storm, or blowing up toys with firecrackers, it doesn't matter. Everyone knows that these children will have to pay the ultimate sacrifice for the world their parents created and the mistakes they made—America's mistakes. The children of Nixon will pay the price from a country that will sacrifice all the future children for guns, junk bonds, plastic, high fructose corn syrup, and the destruction of the ozone. The ice will cover it up and silence it for a moment, but eventually it will melt, and everyone will drown.

Chapter 10
1998

A: *The Big Lebowski*

"Were You Listening to the Dude's Story?"

Every once in a while a film comes along that creates a character who becomes the prototype for that time. The Greatest Generation had Rick Blaine. The Boomers had Butch Cassidy. The millennials had Katniss. Gen X had the Dude. Or el Duderino, if you're not into the whole brevity thing. There are movies that land at the cinema with a loud bang and dominate pop culture from the word go. Then there are movies like the Coen brothers' *The Big Lebowski* that are released in theaters, don't make much of a splash, and are destined to slink off to the video market to just fade away into film oblivion. One problem with that fate. The Dude would not abide. He needed reparations for that rug, man. It really tied the room together. *The Big Lebowski* became one of the biggest cult classics from the nineties. I don't think it's an overstatement to say it might just be the *Rocky Horror Picture Show* of the decade. It also might be the most quoted film. If we're at a bowling alley and you say "I'm throwing rocks tonight," we just became lifelong friends. If there is a group of people talking and someone interrupts the flow and a person in the group says, "Donnie, you're out of your element." Everyone laughs. Once I conducted an interview for a podcast with an actor who said, while we were in the middle of recording, that they had to go because a rug was being delivered. I responded, "This was a valued rug." For people of my generation, *The Big Lebowski* isn't just a film, it's a way of life.

Just Dropped In

Before we dive too deep into the world of cutoff toes, bowling alleys, and coffee-can funerals, let's see what condition our film condition is in at this point in the nineties. If you noticed, the first few movies selected for this book were big studio pictures (*Pretty Woman, T2*). Then it was a bunch of small-budget, independent films (*Before Sunrise, Swingers*). I am sure there were a few movies I selected for the 1995-1997 chapters that you might not have seen or maybe even heard of before. In the final two years of the decade, we are back to studio-based films with big stars and big budgets, but the plots are still focused on independent stories. The fact that true independent films could ever dominate the market for even a few years is incredible. Hollywood isn't the kind of town that likes to be left in the dark, so big studios adapted quickly and started to throw money at small, quirky ideas to try to see if they could reclaim their power. This was something that occurred in the nineties in many businesses. (Remember when Walmart was the villain of small business?) It was basically the last gasp of mom-and-pop businesses versus huge corporations. Who's up for a tangent to please my friend Em, who wants this book to be a sneaky memoir? Oh, that's right, you can't answer me. I'll just tell you.

In my hometown of Massillon, Ohio, there was a super hip record store called Quonset Hut. It was the Empire Records of my small town. It sold CDs, vinyls, T-shirts, and lots of hidden drug paraphernalia. It was the first place I ever saw a bong. (I mean, this is a chapter on *The Big Lebowski*; we need to get a bong in this story.) I loved the store because they carried a ton of CDs from artist's back catalog, not just the current pop hits. Their CDs were always $11.99, which was a great price. We heard that a new superstore was moving into the local mall called Best Buy. It was a huge structure. They sold computers, washers and dryers, televisions, stereos, VCRs, DVDs, and, as an afterthought, CDs. When they opened their doors all their CDs were $9.99. I was a poor college kid working at Video Time. That two dollar difference was huge for me. I started shopping at Best Buy. It was true they didn't carry all of Billy Joel's back catalog, but they sold his newest album, *River of Dreams*, for $8.99 the day it came out, so of course I bought it there.

In about two years, Quonset Hut was out of business. The doors were locked, the bongs were trashed, and Massillon potheads had to get their wares somewhere else. Best Buy did NOT sell bongs. About a month after the Hut was shut, Best Buy raised the prices on their CDs to $18.99. Sometimes even more. They dropped all their back catalog and unless you wanted to buy Garth Brooks or Goo Goo Dolls, you were out of luck, because there was no competition left. This was way before the internet, so now, where would I get my newest Indigo Girls CD or 10,000 Maniacs? Best Buy wasn't going to carry independent artists. They were only carrying Mariah Carey or Ace of Base. Where would I find the soundtrack to an offbeat movie like *Six Degrees of Separation*? Well, I had to drive two hours to Columbus for that. The thing about a big corporation coming in and being in charge of distributing art is that they don't care about the art. They care about the profit margins. All they want to do is sell *something*, not sell music. This is precisely what the big film studios did in the late nineties. They knew they had lost their grasp on the film audience. They watched small films snatch their product from them. But studios had something that a small company didn't have: money to burn. Best Buy didn't care that they sold all those CDs for less money for two years, because they had another store in another city that was already selling CDs for the jacked-up higher price. They could wait out Quonset Hut. They could wait until it died, and then they would make the real money. That Best Busy is still there in my small town. Now they don't carry any music. In fact, there isn't a store in the surrounding area that carries only music. So how does this apply to films of the nineties? Well, if for these few years the studios had to make a couple non-IP films, they could wait it out. They knew eventually all those bongs were gonna end up in the trash can, and soon enough they would be back to counting up all their money.

The Big Lebowski isn't the type of movie that would have gotten a large budget and big star release early in the decade, but this was a moment where a small idea could get extra money and a wide release in order to bring their vision to life. Joel and Ethan Coen were already famous thanks to the critical success of their 1987 film, *Raising Arizona,* which truly feels like it should have come out in the nineties. But once middle America, and everyone else, went all-in with their 1996 comedy, *Fargo,* about a botched kidnapping, the Coen brothers had a blank check for their next film. This brief moment where studios jumped into the independent game wouldn't last long, but it did allow there to be a blip where the types of films being made could actually have a budget to back up a creative, unique idea. It allowed us to not have to wonder what a Dude who flew through life-size bowling pins would look like. The Coen brothers had the money to make that fantasy come to life. If they wanted to add naked women jumping on trampolines in slow motion, then, by golly, they could do it.

Tumbling with the Tumbleweeds

So here we are in 1998; we have a big-budget movie; we have a movie that you actually have seen, and what is my plan for covering the film? I have decided to not actually write about the entire film, but to only focus on the first six minutes. What kind of jerk would get so artsy to do that? One who liked artsy films that took chances in the nineties. When a writer sets out to tell a story that is not going to follow the conventions of normal storytelling, the most important task for them is to set the audience up for that new experience. Even the most avant-garde stories have to set the stage early for that experience. The Coen brothers were certainly already known for making different kinds of movies, but *Lebowski* was going to exist in a very heightened reality. They knew that in order for us to accept the balance of film noir, comedy, mystery, and nonsense, they had to start off in that vein. So let's take a look at how they did it.

The movie begins with a pan of the desert while "Tumbling with the Tumbleweeds" plays and a voice-over from Sam Elliot starts with that deep Southern drawl that years later Bradley Cooper would badly imitate in the remake of *A Star Is Born*. Having a voice-over is nothing new for noir. Classic noir films like *Double Indemnity*, *Murder My Sweet*, and *Sunset Boulevard* use voice-over. Even noir films from the nineties like *The Two Jakes*, *Devil in a Blue Dress*, and *L.A. Confidential* use voice-over. One point of voice-over in noir is to keep the audience on track when the plot gets too convoluted, but also it can be used to misdirect the audience so they don't notice what the writer doesn't want them to notice yet. Usually it is the detective who does the voice-over. But here we have the Stranger doing it, because the Dude is just too damn lazy to tell his own story. The Stranger mentions early on that no one from where he is from would ever identify as the Dude.

This lets us know that the Stranger is outside of the story, outside of LA—just a narrator to guide us through the story. The opening shot matches the opening song, a tumbleweed blows across the desert and it all seems as it should, if this was a western mystery. But the camera keeps fading deeper into the depths of Los Angeles with an aerial shot, an overpass of the highway, then right down a main thoroughfare, and all the way to the beautiful Pacific ocean and all the while, that tumbleweed keeps a-turning. It is highly ridiculous that a tumbleweed could travel and blow that far, but that is the point. If you want your movie to be outside of the realm of reality, to be an analogy, and to sometimes just be plain silly, set it up from the get-go. No doubt an audience can complain—people can complain about anything—but they have been fair warned. Is this a noir? A western? A mystery? A comedy? The answer is yes.

The first time we get a look at the Dude, he enters around a grocery store corner wearing a V-neck white undershirt, a robe, long shorts, sandals, and dark sunglasses. He makes a beeline for the most important thing to a White Russian drinker—the cream. We are told that the film is set in the midst of the Iraq war (the first one) and that the Dude is the man of his time. He is set up to be the prototypical man in the early nineties and is described as quite possibly the laziest man of all time. As I said—a man from the early nineties. The Dude then writes the clerk a check for sixty-nine cents just as the narrator loses his train of thought and just trails off, like that old tumbleweed. We see a shot of President Bush (the first one), saying this "aggression" will not stand, a line we will hear echoed again from John Goodman's Vietnam vet character, who is also interested in stopping all unchecked "aggression." This movie wants viewers to remember how important it is for the American ego to stop any and all aggression. It is why we were at war in 1991. Everyone was behind it. Except the Dude. He just wants to bowl.

As he takes his half-and-half back to his apartment, he is grabbed by an assailant and his head is pushed into the toilet. The henchman asks, "Where's the money, Lebowski?" But the Dude won't talk. Mostly because he can't talk while the henchman keeps asking the question when his head is in the toilet, not giving him any chance to answer the question. When the henchman finally does give the Dude a breather from the commode and asks again, the Dude answers the question the only way he can, "It's down there somewhere; let me take another look." This is the first line of dialogue that our man of his time utters. It's sarcastic, non heroic, and pretty chill. The other henchman decides to relieve himself on the Dude's rug. The Dude reasons with them that he doesn't have a wedding ring, and his apartment doesn't look like anything but a bachelor's pad. The toilet is so dirty that the toilet seat leaves a ring of dirt from being left up so much. I'm thinking the Dude doesn't spend a lot of time scrubbing the bathroom.

The henchmen discuss how the guy they were looking for was supposed to be rich, and they head out into the world leaving a soggy Dude sitting on the toilet wearing his sunglasses, robe, and sandals, which protect his feet from the mixture of cream and toilet water. There is a quick cut to black as the title credits appear: *The Big Lebowski*. This is our setup for one of the most quoted films of the nineties and a film that has spawned a plethora of books.

The first six minutes of *The Big Lebowski* would totally be one of my lectures when I get to teach my college screenwriting class that I will never be hired to teach. So why not teach it right now to you? Everyone has seen the film; we all know why it's a classic. *The Big Lebowski* took the classic film noir mystery and added a stoner to it. The Coen brothers must have been sitting around thinking about how much they love *Chinatown* and thought, "What would you get if you took Jack Nicholson out of *Chinatown* and replace him with the Dude?" Well, you'd get a cult classic is what you'd get. You'd get a film that people would misinterpret as being written by Cheech and Chong, not Robert Towne. A rich man hires a man of lowercase in a case that involves a family member messed up with a crime that leads the man through the city inner workings of LA. Could be *Chinatown*, could be *The Big Lebowski*. But how do you hide what you want to do but also set up the world you want to explore? Well, you better have a set up that announces to the audience your intentions. The Coen brothers' script does this expertly. They set up a mystery of the men breaking into the Dude's apartment and demanding money. They set up the absurdity of the tumbleweed, the check writing, and the henchmen not knowing what a bowling ball is. They introduced the brilliant character created by Jeff Bridges, from his outfit, to his speech pattern, to his quippy retorts.

His performance is on par with Denzel Washington's in *Malcolm X*. (Yes, that's right, I just compared the two performances, and I stand by it.) I can't imagine anyone else in the world who could have brought out every "man," "um", or "whoa." Every word, thought, and action is a wonderment to the Dude. If you compare this actor to the actor in *The Fabulous Baker Boys, Tucker,* or *The Mirror Has Two Faces* you won't see how it can be the same person. Jeff Bridges is always the best thing in every movie he is in. (Okay, Michelle Pfeiffer on top of the piano might be just one tick better than him in *Baker Boys*.) Not to take anything away from the greats like Al Pacino or Robert De Niro, but they are always the same in every movie. They either get quieter, in De Niro's case, or louder, in Pacino's case, but Bridges is always a new discovery in each film. He is so effortlessly funny. He brings the comedy out of the Dude and never at the expense of the character. Most of that comes from the script, which is truly funny. Although Gene Siskel did miss the underlying humor that is all over this film when he said, "I just think the humor in *The Big Lebowski* is uninspired." Critics. Ugh. There is no doubt that the film works because Jeff Bridges was cast as the Dude. There isn't a moment where you don't believe he has been high since the seventies.

The building blocks for an experimental film have to be laid out carefully in the opening if the writers want to be accepted by a wide audience. The Coen brothers wanted to mesh a lot of genres together in one film. To do that, they needed a big budget to tell a story with dream sequences, a great actor who could totally commit to the premise and never break character, and a strong opening that would set the stage for audiences to expect something different while also buying into the world. *The Big Lebowski* does all of that, and it does it in the first six minutes. Once this is accomplished, the following 111 minutes are as satisfying as the sound of a bowling ball smacking down ten pens for a perfect strike. Just like a good rug, a writer's setup can really hold a room together.

B: *Pleasantville*

"Where's my Dinner?"

Watching *Pleasantville* today gives you a double dose of nostalgia. The film in 1998 was created to take a look at our obsession with old television series that were still being rerun in the nineties. Nick at Nite was huge. Everyone was still watching *The Brady Bunch*, *Good Times*, and *Leave it to Beaver*. Even movies were looking back to television series, with *Brady* and *Beaver* made into feature films in 1995 and 1997. But watching *Pleasantville* in 2024, the viewer gets nostalgia for when television actually was television. The film starts with the sights and sounds of flipping channels. Remember watching television instead of entering passwords, paying for twelve different streaming services, and watching what was on instead of what you wanted? The setup for the film shows us how much Tobey Maguire's character has watched the made-up classic sitcom *Pleasantville*. This is what kids in the nineties used to do: watch the same show over and over because it was repeated daily in syndication. When television icon Don Knotts shows up to fix the remote that Maguire and his on-screen sister, Reese Witherspoon, broke and gives them a remote that zaps the kids into the actual television show, viewers can incorrectly assume they are in store for another silly look at classic television. Those viewers are about to be delightfully surprised. The true charm of *Pleasantville* is how it sneaks up on you at how good it is. It also has an agenda that you just don't see coming.

Rave On

In the beginning of the film, before the kids get trapped in the world of a fifties sitcom, we see a bit of their life at school. The teachers are lecturing the students about their future. These characters, who would be known in the future as millennials, were told every day growing up that AIDS was going to spread, the ozone was depleting and global warming was coming, that the medium income would go down and they probably wouldn't be able to pay for their college loans. All these fears the teachers spout have now come to fruition. The world the boomers created, which is displayed in the sitcoms that these millennials watched, was disappearing. So why not look back at the good old days? These kids are scared of the future.

Once Maguire and Witherspoon are living in the sitcom, they immediately discover that these good old days weren't so good for everyone. Oh, make no mistake about it, it was great for white men, but that pretty much ends the list. Gary Ross, who wrote and directed the film, performs quite a magic trick with his story. In order to tell a story about when sex, women's rights issues, and honest expression of art and feelings were all voluntarily left unsaid, he lets two teenagers from the nineties be our eyes into the repressed world of the fifties; a time that was very much a political topic in the 2016 election. This film looks at the "Make America Great Again" dream before it ever became a nightmare. The calendar reads 1958, so we are smack-dab in the middle of the time when women stay home, cook the meals, raise the children, and live to serve their husbands. They sleep in separate beds, and sex isn't a thought for anyone—until Reese Witherspoon's character gets a look at the hot guy in Pleasantville.

Witherspoon, who is now pretending to be Mary Sue, asks the boy to go to Lovers' Lane. He just wants to pin her and nothing more. Even holding hands would be considered forward. Once they get up to Lovers' Lane, Mary Sue introduces the boy to something much more exciting than a pin. Letting the girl take control of the sexual situation is the first crack in the idea that the fifties was the best time in America. A nineties girl was savvy, knew what she wanted, and was fully in charge of her sexual needs and desires. But with this modern act, it allows the modern world to slip into this sitcom world and the world of black and white suddenly finds a red rose in the center of town. Just like the apple in Eden, red has entered the palette of Pleasantville.

The easy answer is the act of sex created the color disruption, and no doubt, as the boy spreads the word of sex, Lovers' Lane fills with teenagers having sex. It would be easy to imagine that is what the film is about. But it isn't about sex; it is about releasing to the world who you actually are. If committing the act of sex was enough to turn you into color, then the first question is, why does Reese Witherspoon stay in black-and-white? She herself questions this when she says that she has had more sex than any of the girls who are starting to turn to color. That is because it is always sex that is blamed for the troubles, but it rarely is. The issue is being who you are inside and society's reaction to that honesty.

When Mary Sue's mom asks her what sex is, the daughter tells her all. She even tells her about masturbation. The nineties were still a repressed society. It was controversial for schools to teach masturbation despite the fact that the AIDS crisis was killing Americans. In the early nineties, Madonna was almost arrested for simulating masturbation in concert, and her album *Erotica* was considered by critics as going too far. *Seinfeld* had an episode that couldn't mention the word. What Gary Ross was trying to point out was that while people felt repressed in the nineties, the fifties were worse. When the mom tries out what her daughter taught her, the tree in the front yard bursts into a colorful fire. Once women are free to express themself, men's control slips away, and freedom flourishes. The character whom Witherspoon creates is a strong, confident young woman. She will create two more similar characters in two films released in 1999: *Election* and *Cruel Intentions*. The films she chose as a young actress had to help inspire the same young women who would take the streets in the late 2010s when the Republican party started to try its best to go back to Pleasantville.

While there is plenty to look back and be nostalgic for in this film, there is no need to remember what oppression was like. The film was created to show the growth America, and women specifically, had made from 1958 to 1998. Now the film shows all that has been lost. The Mayor and the city's chamber of commerce are all filled with men who are still firmly in black-and-white. The future and change scare these small men in the same way they scare our current group of men who govern with a sharp eye on the past. The only difference is now women have joined the ranks of government to suppress us as well. One thing that never goes out of style is that whoever has power will do whatever they can to maintain that power. As more and more of the young folk turn into color, start listening to rock 'n' roll, and start reading books, signs start to pop up that read "No coloreds allowed." Now we get to the true point of the film. This isn't a story about nostalgia for *The Andy Griffith Show* or *Father Knows Best*; this is a morality tale about racism. Gary Ross found a way to get right inside to the bubble of the people who needed to be told this story. He created a story about racism in America with a movie that has no Black characters in it at all.

Across the Universe

So many times films are preaching to the choir with their righteous stories to the people who were already on their side. But all those people in the nineties who didn't want Blacks or gays to be as free as straight white men were tricked into watching this movie with no Blacks or gays in the film about a time when no one acknowledged Blacks or gays. This was a way to show maybe one or two of the people who were on the edge to see how ridiculous the men are when they don't have dinner on the table, or when kids can't read any of the classic literature, or how painting with color is seen as offensive. There is no doubt that as I write this sentence sitting in Florida, where books are being banned and taken out of school libraries, all those fears are still alive and well, but I think this movie does an amazing job of hiding its stories about female rights, homosexuals coming out, and the racist policies America turned into law to hold Blacks down within the fifties sitcom genre.

When Joan Allen starts turning to color, she takes it a step further and starts putting gray makeup on her so no one will know she has changed. When a character has to hide who they are inside for society, you have a perfect example of what it has to be like for transgender people today who have to hide who they are out of fear of government retribution. When Mr. Johnson (Jeff Daniels) sees an art book for the first time, any idea that this is just a silly, concept movie has long vanished from the viewer's mind. Randy Newman wrote a beautiful score to play along with the scene of him, and us, seeing the colorful, amazing, impressionist art. Daniels smiles and says, "I'll never be able to do that." None of us can live up to the art that has been created before us. All we can do is add to it. So many times in history, each advancement is met by the older generation as demonic and destructive. When Mr. Johnson creates his own art, who can be surprised when the mob destroys it and his soda shop. The mob can never create; it can only destroy. It is always the artist who moves the dial forward.

An artist who certainly moved art forward was John Lennon. The end credits of the film, and the main single from the soundtrack, is Lennon's Beatles song "Across the Universe" sung by Fiona Apple. The music video was directed by Paul Thomas Anderson, and it uses Mr. Johnson's soda shop. Fiona Apple sings, "Nothing's gonna change my world," as the mob smashes all the art, glass, and booths in the shop. She smiles and ignores the violence as she sings a song, from the same songwriter who wrote "Give Peace a Chance" and "Imagine." It is such a perfect companion to the movie. I miss music videos and how they could interpret a song into something greater than it was before. I think the sentiment for Lennon was that no matter all the violence around him, nothing was going to change his mind that the world was a good place. Sometimes when I watch the video, I wonder if the meaning isn't something else. Maybe putting on headphones and smiling and singing a peaceful song when the world is crumbling isn't the way to go. Once you see the world in your own way and decide that nothing is going to change that view, you become rigid, fearful, and the world's problems suddenly fall into two categories—black and white. But we have to remember, we live in a world of color. When looking at the colorful, beautiful art that only a handful of people have the ability to create, Mr. Johnson said it all when he said, "Must be awfully lucky to see colors like that. I bet they don't know how lucky they are." We so often forget how lucky we are to have so many colors around us. So we need art like *Pleasantville* to remind us.

Chapter 11
1999

A: *The Cider House Rules*

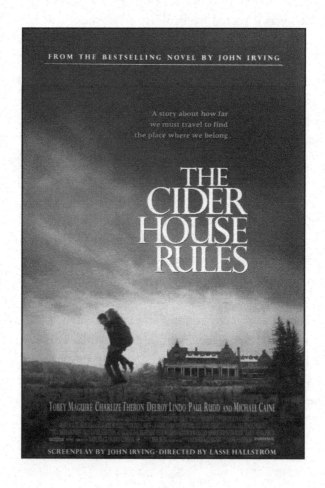

"YOU ARE MY WORK OF ART. EVERYTHING ELSE HAS JUST BEEN A JOB."

John Irving wrote his novel *The Cider House Rules* in 1985. It was twelve years after abortion was made legal in 1973. The film came out in 1999. It would be twenty-three years until abortion would be made illegal again. John Irving claimed he wrote the book because he felt the right was in danger. In 2019, he still felt that way when he wrote a *New York Times* op-ed piece and said, "If you think Roe v. Wade is safe, you're one of the reasons it isn't." In 1985 and 1999, it seemed unlikely to most that the horrors women go through in Irving's imagination would ever be unleashed on modern society again. When I read the novel and then later saw the film, I never focused on the abortion aspect of the story. Yes, the main character, Dr. Larch (Michael Caine), performs abortions in the 1930s and 1940s, when abortion was illegal, but he also runs an orphanage for women who don't want to abort their baby but can't afford to raise them. The film focuses on the lifetime of one of those orphans and sets him on the path of what happens when an orphanage becomes a permanent home for a child. While the book and the film always get caught up in the controversy that comes with abortion, the story is really about parenting and destiny.

Watching the film now, it is hard to see past the abortion scenes because the right has been (nationally) taken away. The young girls dying because they don't have access to professional health care in 1945 should seem like a barbaric relic of the past instead of a glimpse of our imminent future. Dr. Larch doesn't judge the women who end up on his doorstep. He only helps. The fact that Irving made the decision to have the anti-abortion perspective come from one of the orphans who grew up in Larch's orphanage is pure genius. "Life at any cost?" the doctor asks Homer Wells (Tobey Maguire). What else would an orphan believe? If his mother had chosen abortion, he wouldn't be here. But in the same way, it is ridiculous that Americans let male, eighty-year-old non-medical judges and senators decide what a woman should do with her body, it would be just as slanted to allow an orphan to make the choice of if abortion should be legal or not. Hence, we get to the actual cider house rules.

Irving does not come out and tell why the film is called *The Cider House Rules*. The answer to that question has surely been written by many a college English student on tests over the years. It probably used to be an essay question for high school students, but no way would a high school allow any student to read a John Irving book now. I will forever thank my high school English teacher, Mrs. Whetstone, for having me read *A Prayer for Owen Meaning* and turning me on to my favorite author. The cider house and its rules comes into the film when Homer sees an old piece of paper hanging in the cider house listing the rules for the Black apple pickers who live in the dilapidated structure. The first bit of irony is that none of the apple pickers know how to read. So the rules are totally pointless. When Homer, the orphan, ends up staying there, they ask him to read the rules to them. Each rule is basic common sense (don't smoke in bed) or totally pointless (don't eat your lunch on the roof). It is just a list of rules written by people who have no idea whom they are making the rules for. The point is to control the people and display their power, just like our male-based government does for women. This film allows the viewer to follow the moral journey that Homer takes from pro-life orphan to pro-choice apple picker. As his world gets wider, the people he encounters get more diverse, and his morals are replaced with wisdom and understanding over judgment and righteousness. When you have a movie that is setting out to tackle those topics, you have me.

The direction by Lasse Hallström needs to be studied by current filmmakers. I get that people want to focus on flashy directors like Tarantino, Nolan, Scorsese, but there really is something about a director who channels their energy into telling a story with logical staging and good editing. Just like *The Prince of Tides*, this film doesn't waste a second of dialogue or a moment of film. Every scene is staged to tell the story and every edit is there to move you forward. When you take a novel the size of *The Cider House Rules*, there is no time to waste. Hallström uses a few transitions that are just a delight to watch. Homer and Candy (Charlize Theron) go to a closed drive-in movie theater because Homer has never seen one before. They pretend to watch the movie, and then the screen fades to the orphanage, where they are watching *King Kong*. For a moment, it looks like *Kong* is playing on the drive-in screen, but it is just going to the next scene. Another time, Dr. Larch says Homer is just a field hand at the apple farm. What could possibly hold him there? Hallström jump-cuts to Candy in a car laughing with Homer. The audience knows exactly what can make a boy want to leave his family: a first love. It moves the story along without having to tell us that Homer is falling for Candy.

Hallström also stages the scene where Homer leaves the orphanage with such care. This is a film based on a novel where readers get to know many of the orphans. Even the script introduces quite a few of them for a two-hour movie. We know that it is a big deal that Homer is leaving the orphanage for the first time to start his life as an adult. Hallström achieves this feeling not by having anyone say this explicitly, but by showing the reactions of the characters hurt by Homer leaving. Michael Caine's Larch will not come out to say goodbye to his de facto son. In fact, we only see a glimpse of Caine in the window before he walks away as the emotions get the better of him. When Homer leaves, Hallström cuts to Buster behind a tree, Fuzzy in his tent, and Nurse Edna walking away from Homer quickly as she lightly touches his chin with her hand. Homer is breaking everyone's heart by following his dream and trying to escape a place that no child would or should ever want to stay. They all know that children leave their home, but here is a child who was expected to never leave. Larch assumed Homer would just stay forever and work as a doctor performing abortions and delivering orphans. When a person wants more than they were born into, the world and the loved ones around them will always punish that person. In America, we are told that we can achieve anything, but when we try to stand and jump over the boundaries that society sets up, we will always be singled out and told to sit back down.

With my selections of *Citizen Ruth* and now *The Cider House Rules*, it would be easy to say I am trying to convince you of being pro-choice or pro-life. That is furthest from the truth. Remember, I am Gen X; trying to make you think what I think is never my goal. I am selecting these films because they are *about* something. And even more than that, they are about something for a reason. This truly isn't a film about abortion. It is about following in the footsteps of your parents. This film decimates me when I watch it because the fact that Homer doesn't have a chance to do what he wants to do in life is just so incredibly painful to me. Dr. Larch started teaching Homer how to be an ob-gyn doctor before he had the choice to pick that as his career. Larch knows he is getting old and will be replaced by a doctor who won't allow these women to have a choice, so he has picked Homer to do it for him, ironically taking away Homer's right to choose.

My path in life wasn't exactly chosen for me in the way that Homer's was. My father didn't say, "You can't be a writer," but he was very clear that I would be going to college to major in either business or education. Being an artist was not an option. I went to college, majored in marketing, and then never got a job in that profession. I just couldn't get behind a desk and try to sell things to people that they didn't want or couldn't possibly need. I get the twist ending that I now spend my days trying to sell my books to people who don't want to hear about the art I cover, but what can you do? I grew up in a small town, just like Homer. All I wanted was to get out and try to be more. To interact with artists and be able to create. Homer does leave the orphanage and finds a job as an apple picker, living in a one-room barrack with individual a single cot for a bed. It looks exactly like the orphanage, but he is *free*. He is not a doctor. He is not performing abortions. He is not delivering babies. He is not following the path laid out for him; he is wandering in the woods on his own. The film's display of free will is why it is one of my favorites. In most movies, the main character moves on to somewhere bigger and better. Here, Homer is basically at the same place, doing a worse job, and still taking care of the people around him, but it is his choice. He loves Dr. Larch. He is his father figure, but you can't live your entire life for your parents. You have to be free or you are still a kid. The key to being an adult is making your own choice. Choice is everything. Even when you make the wrong choice. Irving is trying to show how important choice is to each of us. In life. In pregnancy.

Due to circumstances that happen at the apple orchard, Homer comes to realize that while he will never get to make his choice in life, it isn't fair for him to force his decision on every woman. When the truth comes out at the orchard, someone asks him, "What is your business?" He says, "I'm in the doctor business." From that moment on, his destiny is set in stone. Just like women's choices are gone in America, his choice has been made. He will be a doctor. He will perform abortions. He will deliver the Princes of Maine, the Kings of New England. He will not see the world. Dr. Larch's choice becomes Homer's future. He has no option but to replace his father. The circle is complete. When he returns to the orphanage, everyone is happy to see him. The children and the nurses are thrilled. Even the score of the movie is in on it, as it swells with the beautiful theme Rachel Portman wrote for the film. Homer sacrifices his future so that the underclass of Maine doesn't have to. The end of the movie, as he returns home, always makes me cry. I have asked a few people through the years if they think this is a sad ending. They always answer no. It breaks my heart. I did not stay in my small town. I did not follow the path my father set out for me. I was able to make my own choice, and it has made all the difference in my life. Homer doesn't get to. America's women don't get to. As Mr. Rose says about the rules that are posted in the cider house, "Someone who don't live here made those rules." The rules we live under now are written by men who don't live under the rules they make, or in the conditions that their rules cause. The effects of years and years of people making rules that don't help the very people they are created for are felt every day and will continue to abort any chances of the workers to enjoy the apple cider that their daily work creates.

B: *Eyes Wide Shut*

"YOU'VE BEEN WAY OUT OF YOUR DEPTH FOR THE LAST TWENTY-FOUR HOURS."

The very first shot is o Nicole Kidman standing with her back to the camera. She lets her black dress drop to the floor, revealing her naked backside, and steps out of her dress. *Eyes Wide Shut* has begun. The second shot we see is of Tom Cruise fully dressed in a tuxedo. The film gives us two sexual stereotypes in less than ten seconds. A completely naked female movie star and the hottest male movie star of multiple decades fully clothed in a tux. Well, there's your money shot. What are we going to do with the rest of the 158 minutes of this film? The hot fantasy stops pretty quickly, as Tom Cruise asks, "Honey, where's my wallet?" Of course, she knows exactly where it is. He walks into the bathroom, where Nicole Kidman sits on the toilet in a knockout black cocktail dress. She wipes and stands up. This film is a study on marriage, boredom, sex, and love. The audience can try all it wants to look away, but every aspect of marriage will be seen in this film. It will be impossible to look away whether your eyes are wide open or wide shut.

Baby Did a Bad Bad Thing

When this film was released, there was so much drama surrounding the making of the film, the actual picture really never had a chance to stand out. The film was entered in *The Guinness Book of World Records* for its four-hundred-day shoot. The director of the film, Stanley Kubrick, died four days after turning his first cut into the studio. Digital people had to be edited into the final release during some of the sex scenes to ensure that the film didn't get an NC-17 rating, which was considered a death sentence, since some theaters wouldn't screen a film with that rating. Today, the rating just doesn't even exist, because an R rating is practically a death sentence. Rumors started to leak out that the making of the film was destroying real-life married couple and costars Nicole Kidman and Tom Cruise. The couple did get a divorce in 2001. With all that swimming around in the press, did anyone even pay attention to all that Kubrick presented to his audience? That is part of the beauty in returning to this film now. All of these pointless distractions are long faded away on blogs that got eaten alive by Google's algorithms or in dumpster bins across the country full of all the issues of *Entertainment Weekly* that covered the film. The world just wanted a sexual, dirty romp that starred two of the world's hottest movie stars. That was never what the film was about. Despite all the sexual innuendos throughout the picture, neither Kidman nor Cruise ever even have sex with anyone besides their mate.

The film is actually a study of what happens when marriage boredom collides squarely with jealousy. Once Alice (Kidman) proclaims to Dr. Bill (Cruise) that she once had a fantasy that involved having sex with a hot naval officer while the married couple was on vacation, the good doctor just can't handle the idea that his wife even has a thought about having sex with another man. The only reason she confides this fantasy is because she is jealous of her husband seeing, and touching, naked female patients at work. Both Alice and Bill are worried that they are no longer enough for each other, and they want to take a shot at making the other jealous. When he tells her that he is certain she would never cheat on him and he trusts her completely, she laughs at him, hard and strong. Her laughter goes on for so much longer than we expect. It is emasculating. It is a complete take down of his manhood. Just as Alice's fantasy goes from an idea to really just being mean to her husband, he gets called away to a patient who has died. He has to go out into the darkness of New York City in the middle of the night, where anything and everything can happen.

Over the next hour or so, Bill climbs deeper and deeper into a world of sexual deviancy controlled by powerful men. Each choice he makes, from stopping to talk to a sex worker, to going to her apartment, to heading to a jazz club, to a costume shop, and finally to an orgy all is his male reaction from his wife *fantasizing* about another man. The film is not overt. Even the orgy isn't as racy as other erotic films from that time. Yes, there are plenty of naked women, but it is the fear, the slowness, the coldness that Kubrick creates at the mansion that makes the film feel dirtier than it ever is. I wouldn't be surprised if many casual viewers didn't even notice that Cruise doesn't have sex with anyone during his night out. But he does think about his wife having sex with the young naval officer throughout the picture. When he does, Kubrick cuts to black-and-white footage of Nicole Kidman naked, having sex with a hot young naval officer. Why should Bill get so upset? This isn't real; it is just in his imagination. This is where the casting of real-life husband-and-wife actors comes into play. When Tom Cruise imagines the sexy naval officer having sex with his wife, that act might not have occurred in the fictional world of Alice and Bill, but I am sitting there watching a hot attractive young man grinding on a completely naked Nicole Kidman, who is *actually* Tom Cruise's wife. So is Cruise acting? Is it real? Or was it a fantasy? Well, it must be real, because I just saw her act out the fantasy. This blurring and playing with reality is what makes this film so intoxicatingly dreamy. But at the same time, it is what also made critics and ticket buyers not like it. They didn't watch this movie to think. They wanted to get off.

I'm in the Mood for Love

The film constantly puts the couple in conundrums of fidelity. In the first real sequence of the film, Alice and Bill go to a fancy party hosted by Sydney Pollack, who plays one of Bill's rich patients. Alice meets a French man who charms her. He actually sees her as a woman in a way that Bill just doesn't anymore. So if she is getting an emotional need satisfied from a man who is not her husband, is she cheating? Well, guess what Bill is doing while she dances. He gets called to the upstairs, where a completely naked woman is passed out because the host allowed her to do more drugs than was advisable and has had his way with her. Bill uses his skills as a doctor to save the woman but also touches her body, sees her naked, and gives her comfort. Is this cheating? Is Alice cheating by flirting and dancing? Neither of them had sex, but she was charmed and he saw a hot woman naked. Where is the line? What is fidelity? What is monogamy? Is it only the sexual act? Shut those eyes, folks, the movie has so much more to not show you.

The deeper Cruise's character is pulled into the rich, powerful, and sexually open world, the more everything starts to seem like a conspiracy. Bill uses his doctor's ID like it's a police badge. And it works. Each time he flashes it, he gains access or information. We live in a society that loves giving men with credentials access to anything and everything. He spends these twenty-four hours learning that the world isn't as black-and-white as he once thought. When he is told that in order to attend the orgy, he must have a costume, he gets access to a rental shop late at night by, of course, showing his doctor's license. Here he finds that the store owner's very young daughter is having sex with two older men. The father yells and screams; the girl hides behind Cruise, but the father keeps slipping back into salesman duty and happily makes the sale for the costume. Later on, when Bill discovers that this was an act, all part of a plan by the shop owner to fulfill some sexual fantasy for the two other men in the shop, we realize that we really have no idea if that was his daughter. Was this staged for Bill? The other men? The shop owner? Is someone pulling the strings for everything? What do we really know about other people's sexual desires? Nothing.

When Cruise finally gets to the orgy, he enters a room where a dozen women are making a circle around a red-hooded, masked person with incense. The women strip to wearing only a thong, and then kisses each other with their masks on. It is all ritualistic. It is part tribal, part voodoo, part porn, and all one-percenter. Each woman is released to pick a masked man from the crowd and leave with him. One of the women from the circle knows Cruise shouldn't be there and tells him to leave. Then another man takes her away to a large room where all kinds of people are gathered around having sex. It is this room where shadows of people were digitally placed in the film to help the movie not get a NC-17 rating. I like this use of technology in films. Here special effects come around to help allow an artist's vision to come to fruition in a way that most viewers wouldn't even know happened. Did putting these figures in the film hinder anyone from understanding what was going on? Um, no. We know they are hitting it, but even in the nineties sex was considered to be evil. So let the conservatives have their literal digital cockblockers. We can watch a man get his head blown off in *Natural Born Killers*, but we can't see a man thrust into a woman. Whatever.

At the orgy, the attendees know right away Bill is an imposter. How did they find out? This must be a conspiracy. Everything that happens in the film leads us to believe this is either a major conspiracy that involves prostitution, murder, and corruption or it must all be a dream. If this was a David Lynch movie, it would certainly just be a dream. But Kubrick has no interest in letting viewers, characters of the film, or critics off with a cop-out answer like it's all a dream. It's not a conspiracy either. It was just a look into what was brewing in our culture at the time.

Strangers in the Night

Throughout the nineties, money was flowing in like a river of tech ones and zeros. President Bill Clinton oversaw a time of growth for the country that started to create the superrich. The film shows us just how pedestrian Dr. Bill's thoughts are. How small and silly it is to follow any sort of rule of law. That rule is there for only the poor. None of the rich folk actually care what he does or doesn't find out. When Sydney Pollack comes back around for the final act of the film to explain to Bill what has been going on, Bill is certain the girl from the orgy has been murdered because of him. Viewers are right along with him. Because we are just as much of a tourist as Bill. But Pollack rightly tells him and us, "It had nothing to do with you." She was just fine. She OD'd. It was all nothing. It isn't a conspiracy. It isn't a dream. It isn't magic. We live under different rules than the superrich and powerful. They don't care about a doctor's license, a marriage, a sex worker, morals, rules, or norms. In fact, when you think about that orgy again, is anyone really having any fun? No. This is all a reaction to pure decadence and boredom. They have it all, and they just want more. Throughout the eighties and nineties, Congress updated the tax code, deregulated financial markets, and rolled back social safety nets, all in an effort to increase the value of stock options and financial securities for executives and shareholders. The world began to change in the midnineties, and as the decade came to a close, we were on the precipice of the superrich. This film shows how the systems will no longer protect the institutions that we clung to in the prior century. The people in the mansion, at the orgy, at the party at the beginning of the film, they are going to take everything America has to offer. They will not care if their wives fantasize over another man, like poor little Bill has done for the last day. Pollack says to Cruise, "Life goes on. It always does. But you know that, don't you?" No big deal. None of it matters. They can buy their way out or not. No rich white person is going to be prosecuted for anything anymore. We will be distracted by the masks, the nudity, the fake idea of morals, but the true power and money will all be up for the taking. These men were just getting started in 1999; there was so much more take. In the nineties, people were still working one job. Isn't that cute? They weren't renting out their house to strangers for the weekend. They weren't driving strangers to the airport in their cars. They weren't fighting each other because we were on different political sides. The average American, let alone Dr. Bill and Alice, who can hardly be accused of being middle-class, will never have a chance in the new world economy. The men in the mansion aren't hiding a damn thing. All of their consumption will happen in the open. Under the American flag, while the people they steal from cheer them on. There will be no reason for anyone to hide it. The powerful men knew that all of us were standing there watching them take it all with our collective eyes wide shut.

C: Magnolia

"THE BOOK SAYS WE MAY BE THROUGH WITH THE PAST, BUT THE PAST IS NOT THROUGH WITH US."

Who am I to argue with the great Harry Nilsson? He said one is the loneliest number, but I say being an avid fan of *Magnolia* in a room of *Boogie Nights* fans is the loneliest number. I have always been on team *Magnolia*. *Boogie Nights* is a great tune, but *Magnolia* is an opera. It's art that doesn't hide from being art. It knows what other movies do, how others tell stories; it knows what it should be, and it just doesn't care. It's a perfect fit for a girl in need of a tourniquet. It's Kabuki theater during a time of grunge rock. In fact, sometimes during the film you can't even hear the dialogue over the volume of the music. Sometimes the songs are Aimee Mann and sometimes the songs are *Carmen*. I'm sure today people turn on the subtitles to be sure they read every pointless thing John C. Reilly's cop says. But every word isn't important. Every feeling is.

Wise Up

The film is a study on coincidence, chance, and cancer. I suppose I could have saved my opening-six-minute study of a film, that I did for *The Big Lebowski*, and done that with *Magnolia*, but *Magnolia* would never settle for just six minutes. However, just like *Lebowski*, this film sets its tone before anything gets started. It begins with a narrator telling us three different stories from three different eras. All three tales have the feeling of an urban legend where major coincidences collide with eerie occurrences. The stories are too unbelievable to accept, so we immediately believe them. The narrator assures us that these kinds of things happen all the time in real life, but we always discard them when they happen in the movies. I remember the very first time I watched this film, I was immediately pulled in by these stories and figured that for this beginning to be here that meant during the end of the film something unbelievable must happen, and the writer is trying to prepare us from the beginning not to just dismiss it as bad writing. I knew that I would judge this movie on the ending, and the ending more than lived up to the prologue. Speaking of endings, I will be ruining the ending of this picture, so if you have not seen this movie, why did you ever start reading this book in the first place?

Earlier in the book, I covered *Short Cuts*, which told multiple different stories and showed how strangers are all connected. It would be easy to think that writer-director Paul Thomas Anderson (PTA) was building upon what Robert Altman did in *Short Cuts*, but that isn't the case. The two directors would work together on Altman's final picture, *A Prairie Home Companion* (2006), where Anderson was on set to back up Altman in case the elderly director couldn't complete the task; he could. But that is where the similarities end. *Short Cuts* was multiple stories that intersected. *Magnolia* is one story moving forward pushing each character from a starting point of pain, bitterness, and being trapped in their past trauma to a place where they have been set free in a new future where they will let go of the wrongs that were done to them. PTA says, "It's one story. So you are not watching piece, piece, piece. It all has to be one connection." The connections last throughout the film. There are times when each character is waiting (Tom Cruise waits for the interview to end, Julianne Moore waits for her prescription to be filled, Phillip Seymour Hoffman waits to be connected on the phone), each character is broken (The "Wise Up" sequence where each character sings the same Aimee Mann song), and finally at the end, when everyone is free from the past that held them back. Each character is on their own and at the same time is part of everyone else's path. It isn't that Tom Cruise's story has anything to do with William H. Macy's story directly, but the two men are emotionally going through the same thing. Both characters were done wrong by their parents. Macy's parents stole his game show prize money, Cruise's parents stole his childhood. Both are making mistakes in their present day because of the sins committed against them in their separate but similar pasts. They have to fall on their face, literally when Macy falls off a telephone pole, and figuratively when Cruise finally confronts his dying father and falls apart, in order to wise up and just give up on allowing the weight of the past to drown them. The connections are there, but they have nothing to do with each other. We just are on a shared emotional journey of one story told through nine or ten main characters.

There are plenty of online articles that can walk a fan through all the connections of the characters, or of all the recurring uses of the numbers eight and two, and how that connects to Exodus 8:2 from the Bible. It's a fun rabbit hole to go down, but that isn't what I want to focus on. There are a lifetime of lessons and philosophies to be mined from this opera. But I would rather spend some time discussing how this movie became the period on the sentence of the last decade of cinema. Despite I have no proof to back up my claim (like that has ever stopped me before), it really felt to me like PTA took every bit of artistic freedom that was alive in the nineties and shoved it into this film. Of course, no one knew an era was about to end, they might have been worrying that a decade was ending, but artists don't know how history will judge their art in the moment they create it. PTA was just telling a story, using the tools that were available at the time. When he was working on this, movies were personal, they were expected to be original, they were supposed to have an "independent" feel to them (whatever that was). They were to be shot on 35MM film, and directors knew they could supplement their stories with new computer effects to bring to life a magical concept that couldn't have been realistically done just years before. So while I conceded that PTA didn't do it for this reason, it sure as hell feels like when the frogs fall from the sky at the end of the movie, that moment is the end of nineties cinema.

Driving Sideways

Back in 2000, I had rented the DVD from that old, trusty Video Time. As I said earlier, the beginning of the film made me very interested in how it would end. What I didn't mention was that while I was in the middle of watching it for the first time, the DVD I rented stopped playing two hours into the film. I went back to the store, and all the copies of *Magnolia* were rented. So I drove to Sam's Club and bought the DVD and came home and finished it. (Aw, to be young and have discretionary funds.) That was the same DVD I screened for my family in 2023. I didn't have to search for this film on twelve different streaming platforms to see if a corporation would give me permission to watch this piece of art on the exact night I wanted to watch it. I didn't have to wonder. I *owned* the motherfucker. That is just another example of how the film feels like such a period on this long, long sentence of an era. For me, it means everything that I have the ability to watch this film, in nonpixelated quality, whenever I want. Owning a piece of cinematic art is basically a relic of the past. This DVD two-disk special edition was such a great release back when studios put a lot of time and money into making the home video product something that was worth shelling out what you now pay just to buy a movie ticket that you see once and comes with forty-five minutes of commercials. The second disk had a making-of feature called *That Moment*. You don't get bonus features on a stream. (Although at the moment of this writing, *That Moment* is on YouTube, but if New Line gets a new attorney, it could be taken down in a second.) As of now, no one can come into my house and take back the DVD I bought at Sam's club for $17.99. I don't have to pay a monthly fee, it doesn't buffer, and the picture plays wonderfully. *That Moment* might just be the most honest making-of bonus feature I have ever seen, because it isn't a slick studio PR amalgamation of slogans slapped together to try to convince someone to watch a film they already own. It is a dark and honest look at the torture that PTA went through to get this piece of art out of his head.

From the first scene of PTA telling us how he struggled to write a follow-up to *Boogie Nights*, it is evident that he feels pressure to create another hit. *Boogie Nights* was the "it" film of 1997. It might have gotten lost in the undertow of *Titanic*, but it was what everyone was talking about. It resurrected Burt Reynolds' career like *Pulp Fiction* did for John Travolta. But what this documentary really covers well is the flak and just utter crap that PTA had to go through because of the length of what he had written. Many of the references to the length of the script are done with jokes through William H. Macy ribbing his friend about the script, but it can be seen in everyone's eyes how much pressure is on them to deliver this film within budget and for it to be a success. This era of the nineties was just at the end of the time when studios were supporting the independent game. The only reason they were was because that was what ticket buyers were demanding. Despite the fact that *Magnolia* isn't an action film, the story and scope is the kind of movie that can only be made with a large budget. The game show set, the large cast, the constant rain throughout the film, and having a huge star like Tom Cruise will all add up to a cost that makes this film way outside of the independent genre. What is this movie about? It is about death, cancer, parenting, and forgiveness. Those are not what big-budget films are about. They are about car chases, men who can fly, or spaceships that shoot. So why bother to dump all that cash into something that is so small and personal? What could possibly need all that money? Did I hear someone say ribbit?

Save Me

Throughout the making of the film, the production company keeps coming to PTA and asking him about the frogs. The climactic moment in the film is when all of our characters are caught in a frog storm. Just like the plague from the Bible, frogs rain from the sky. This is the moment when our characters forgive the sins that were committed against them and are baptized in holy water and set free. They will not continue to be burdened by their own chains from their own past. They are free. It isn't just a few frogs that drop from the sky, and they aren't small. It is a massive pounding of huge Kermits that causes car crashes, windows to break, and ambulances to flip. The raining of the frogs are done as things were in 1999, with a mixture of practical in-camera tricks and special effects. In the making-of feature, it is fun to see John C. Reilly drag William H. Macy across the pavement as union crew members in hydraulic lifts pelt rubber frogs at them from twenty feet in the air. I was mad at myself that when I watched the film in 2023, I just assumed it was all digital effects, because I am so used to them. But the contraption that someone had to build to put on top of a car just to pelt one frog on the windshield was mind-boggling. I should have known the frogs were mostly practical effects, because the sequence seemed so real. The amount of times that PTA must have had to defend the scope of the frogs is staggering, and heart breaking for this artist. You can feel the weight of this on him throughout the documentary. How many times did he have to hear someone challenge his vision? "Do you need this many frogs? Do they have to be so large? Does every character have to be pelted with them? Couldn't we just have it in one scene? Do we have to see the place littered with frogs at night *and* in the morning?" The answer is yes.

These questions start to build up on PTA. He is also being judged for how slowly he is filming the movie. The shooting schedule was set for seventy-nine days, but it ended up taking ninety. (There's that number again.) Thirty years later, who gives a squashed toad if it took an extra eleven days to work on something this different? Sure, keep Kevin James to a tight schedule on *Mall Cop*. But when someone brings you a script like *Magnolia*, you aren't purchasing a treasury bond; you are donating money to help someone chisel the *Venus de Milo* out of marble. The documentary spends so much time focusing on money, and the cost of printing so many feet of film. You can just hear someone today saying, "Just shoot it on digital and then it will be cheaper and easier to do digital frogs." Throughout the production of the film, producers worry about how much time they have the sets, the kids, or Tom Cruise. None of the discussions are about what the film has to say about losing a parent to cancer. It's all about money. Producer Daniel Lupi is trying to balance the monetary struggle while allowing PTA to achieve his vision.

In one scene, PTA just sees Lupi coming on set and he starts to groan and tries not to be seen. Lupi seems to have a good sense of humor about the situation, but also is clearly feeling pressure from every side. There is an executive over Lupi giving the pressure and one over that executive too. PTA knows he has to make his schedule but also understands he is trying to do something outside of the norm. He is striving for something outside of what any other film has ever tried to say or do, even within the nineties. This film is obviously very personal and close to him. Julianne Moore said, "There aren't very many people who have the desire or the bravery to be that emotional.

It is dealing with issues of death and cancer and all the things he had been going through. It was grand and hugely emotional but really personal." You don't just stumble upon a nine-minute monologue for a man on his deathbed. You have to go to some dark, reflective, and highly honest places to write that speech. At the time, the Jason Roberts's speech was divisive. Director Kevin Smith wrote an entire blog (back when blogs almost, kinda mattered) about how much he hated that speech and the film. Another example of the importance of owning something over letting it just exist in the stream of the net, is that Kevin Smith's blog has been scrubbed from the internet. It doesn't exist anywhere. In fact, all I could find is people arguing over whether he really wrote one or not. Man, isn't that just perfect. So I can't footnote that comment; all I have is the knowledge that it existed because I lived through it. What could be more on point of how useless internet criticism is than the fact that Kevin Smith's decimation of the film is just gone? Only film fans like me remember it and the rest deny it. But the film lives on.

In the end, it doesn't matter what the film cost, what Silent Bob thought, or if *Magnolia* is better or worse than *Boogie Nights*. It matters how this piece of art makes you feel. It makes me feel energized and alive. It makes me want to create, to attempt to try something brave and daring. It makes me remember that what others think of my work is as irrelevant as a blog. Even if we are living in a time when people won't debate the movie, dissect it, and want to own it, I did, and I still do. This was a film that mattered to me and has mattered every time I have popped it into my DVD player. It isn't a film I watch a lot. I like to have at least five years in between screenings because I want it to be fresh and be to a point where I almost forget what happens next. I want to feel the sting of being pelted by rubber frogs by teamsters each and every time I take this journey.

One of the last scenes in *That Moment* has PTA with his then love interest, songwriter Fiona Apple. They are playacting a scene where Fiona Apple is pretending to embody *Magnolia* and PTA is the world. She tap-dances and smiles a wide, pleasing smile. PTA grabs her hard with both hands and says, "When people say that you are too long. You are too long. When your friends say the Jason Roberts's monologue

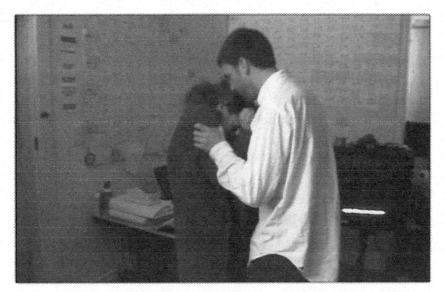

Fiona Apple and PTA act out their feelings about *Magnolia* with some good old fashion performance art. (Photo courtesy of New Line Home Video.)

isn't too long, they are lying." She bows her head in shame and then starts back up again and taps and smiles and tries to snuggle with him. He comes at her again and says, "It's all just too fucking too! You are the only child that is too long. People don't care about her smiling." Referring to the final shot where Melora Walters smiles.

I have made self-deprecating jokes about my work. It is the easiest thing to do when you truly put yourself out there. Their little skit is cute. It is playful, but it is also the act of a writer who is hurt. I can tell you I don't have any bloody idea what *Magnolia*'s legacy is. I don't know if it was a success, if critics loved it in 1999 or hated it. I don't care. I liked its tap dance. I feel rejuvenated by its smile, and it has helped me make it through times when I almost allowed others to judge my art instead of living just for the spoils of creation. This film can save me. It can save others. It just couldn't save cinema. Nothing could.

One

One of the things that I have been lamenting throughout this project is the loss of what happened to the artistic soul of the film industry. The time when movies went from being larger than life to being zombie-viewed on a one-inch cracked screen. In rewatching this film, I decided to show it to my twenty-two-year-old daughter. She watched the film, but the amount of times she had to grab her phone during the film was heartbreaking to this old man. Moments after Melora Walters looked directly into the camera and gave us her first genuine smile of the film (and maybe her life) and the film cut to black, I looked over and both my wife and daughter were already checking their phones. And let's be honest, being away from our texts, notifications, and likes for three hours and eight minutes is longer than any of us ever want to go. I get it, but did they have to reach for the phone the first second after her smile? Couldn't there have even been just a minute of wonder? Just a fleck of reflection? What did it all mean? Why did the frogs fall from the sky? Where did the gun drop from? Why did she look directly into the camera when she smiled instead of at the cop? How were they all connected? Whom have I hurt in this life? Who hurt me? Will Tom Cruise drop-kick the dogs on his way to the hospital? A film like *Magnolia* isn't meant to be watched *while* you are doing anything. It is one of the films that I remember setting aside an entire evening to watch. I would invite my cousin Lisa over. We would have already planned out all the snacks and drinks. We would clear our entire evening. She would spend the night because we knew, we *knew*, we were gonna talk all night about pain, grief, trauma, and we were gonna say "That ain't mine" at least a dozen times. In 2023, it was evident there was no place for this film. From *Goodfellas* to *Before Sunrise* to *Magnolia* and everything in between lead to Melora Walter's smile, and now there is no one left to see it. No matter how directly she looked into that 35mm lens that was about to be pink-slipped.

Magnolia began filming in January 1999, and it debuted in December 1999. Its very creation occurred in what I am calling the last year of cinema in the last decade of cinema. And what others have called the greatest year of movies. So much of the film is about coincidence and chance. Is it just by chance that a film would be so brazen as to tell ten stories as if they were one? Could it be filled with independent actors like John C. Reilly, William H. Macy, and Luis Guzmán right alongside big stars like Julianne Moore, Jason Robards, and Tom Cruise? Could it be as long as it needed to be? Could it have practical effects and special effects to create its climatic ending? Everything is there. When the frogs fall from the sky, the curse has been cast. According to the story in so many people's Bible, Moses told the Egyptian pharaoh, "If you refuse to let them go, I will plague your whole country with frogs." He was talking about the Israelite slaves. I suggest that he might just as well have been talking about the movie audience. That if the studios do not release the audience from what is about to come, mainly digital nonsense like 1999's *Star Wars: The Phantom Menace,* he will plague the industry with IP, franchises, and schlock. He will plague audiences with Jar Jar Binks—a descendant of frogs if I ever saw one. The choice would be ours. What would we choose? Art or our phones? And so it is in the opinion of this writer that the choice was universally made. The frogs fell from the sky. The curse began. The world became a slave to movies that risked nothing, and the monetary rewards were plentiful for the already rich. And *this* book says we may be through with the past, but the past is not through with us.

D: Star Wars: The Phantom Menace

"No, no, mesa stay. Mesa culled Jar Jar Binks. Mesa your humble servant."

The defense rests.

Chapter 12
Fear Concurs Art

As the last decade of cinema came to an end, it sure felt like the great directors of the era tried one last shot at art. Terrence Malick meditated on war in *The Thin Red Line*. Stanley Kubrick tackled sex in *Eyes Wide Shut*. Paul Thomas Anderson focused on death in *Magnolia*. Each film clocked in at around three hours a pop. No one was in a hurry; time was up anyway. After deep dives into sex, war, and death, what else was there to talk about? Digital was on its way in, and 35mm on its way out. Americans always seem to believe whatever they are told by the establishment, no matter how many times they have been lied to in the past. They were told digital was better, so they believed it. Never mind that it was cheaper for studios to make and easier for the theaters to project, so digital was film's destiny no matter what anyone wanted. I suppose it is easier to take as an outcome if we just all line up and believe the sales pitch. Maybe that is what humans are best at, happily accepting their fate without a fight? I guess what we all suspected is true. I'm just not human.

It's not like when *Next Friday* was released in January 2000 movies suddenly had no story, simple characters and were all special effects. I am quite sure that throughout that year, no one even noticed that the decade ended. I mean, we were all just breathing a sigh of relief that we lived through Y2K, but also we never really were afraid of it. CDs were still selling, DVDs were still renting; everything was the same. The change in the film industry was closer to the warning Albert Brooks gives Holly Hunter in *Broadcast News* about what will happen when we allow people with no integrity, like the one William Hurt portrays in the film, to take over. "He just bit by little bit lowers our standards where they are important. Just a tiny little bit. Just coaxes along; flash over substance." That was what started happening in the midnineties as big studios like Disney bought small ones like Miramax. Each major studio created a boutique division to create "independent films" that were actually just big films disguised as small. It is business-impossible for the same company to have a division where one film makes a billion dollars and the other one just breaks even. No CEO can justify that to the board of directors. The change was in the cards throughout the end of the nineties, when the studios started sneaking into the art game. Remember when I began this book, I mentioned how *Goodfellas* and *Pretty Woman* had a lot of the eighties in them? The same is true for the year of film in 2000; *Wonder Boys*, *Almost Famous*, and *High Fidelity* totally have a nineties sensibility to them. If life had just gone on as it was supposed to, I am sure that Albert Brooks would have been correct. It would have been a bit-by-tiny-bit slide into our current situation, but the new millennium had something in store for us that no one saw coming. I remember making jokes about Y2K; everyone did. That was how Americans handled any national crisis, with wit and common sense. It is so weird to look back and realize that Y2K was the last man-made fake-worry event that level-headed Americans would take with a grain of salt. Everything, including movies, were about to get hijacked.

The true end of cinema occurred when we all let fear be our main emotion. To be sure no Albert Brooks movie line gets left on the table, he created an entire movie around fear in 1991 called *Defending Your Life*. His advocate in the film, played by Rip Torn, warns him, "Everybody on Earth deals with fear, that's what little brains do." Well, little brains lost their minds on September 11, 2001. Fear came in and took a hold of our politics, our xenophobia, our news cycle, and eventually our film industry. No one was going to make waves anymore. The culture became you are "with us or against us." Those were the options. Yes, it happened to be a Republican president at the time, but Democrats were eagerly pleased to align with their pretend counter side to allow fear to take over. Movies were no longer a place to take a hard look at what we were doing, thinking, or considering. Movies became a place to reflect one idea: EVERYTHING IS FINE. KEEP BUYING SHIT YOU DON'T NEED.

It wasn't like I just gave up my cinephile ID card at the end of the nineties. I happily bought a ticket and was in the opening audience on May 3, 2002, when one of my favorite actors, Tobey Maguire (*The Ice Storm, The Cider House Rules, Pleasantville,* and *Wonder Boys*), suited up as Spider-Man. I loved the movie. Tobey was great in it, and it really had a ton of good action. I mean, how did they make him fly from building to building and spin that web right out of his wrists? Sure, I was excited to see Stan Lee in his cameo. "Hey, that's the guy from *Mallrats!*" I remember getting choked up at the end shot of the film. Do you remember what it was? Tobey Maguire walks away from a graveyard and says, "With great power comes great responsibility." He calls it his curse. His gift. Then he flips and flops all over the buildings of his great city and goes all the way up to the top of a building where, by golly, there was the American flag waving in the wind. Spiderman, Marvel comics, Sony pictures, and George W. Bush were all banding together to tell us there was no reason for us to think anymore in this safe space. It was all fine. Heroes would save us. You just grab another tub of popcorn and chow down what corporations have to serve. I didn't know that Tobey Maguire would only make one more film that I would ever watch: 2003's *Seabiscuit,* directed by 1998's *Pleasantville* director Gary Ross. I didn't know Spider-Man wasn't joking about having great power. Why would anyone bother to *Magnolia* when you could *Ironman*? Why get into the controversy of *Eyes Wide Shut* when you could just *Fast and Furious*? Why risk it? Why risk anything?

Amy Heckerling worked so hard to create a new world where teenagers had their own lingo. Tyger Williams stressed and tears poured down his face when he wrote about Caine going to visit Pernell in jail in *Menace II Society.* Why? For what? Just bring back R2-D2 again and again and again. Just watch another version of *The*

Little Mermaid and shut the fuck up. Why try to develop something and risk getting boycotted by armies of people who are beyond certain that they are right and you are wrong? Once risk was removed from film, it was over. If a drug-addicted criminal in a movie can't talk in the way that criminals talk, why have one in your film? If a writer can't write a comedy that allows a specific religious character to behave judgmentally without audiences saying that means the writer feels that *every* religious person is judgmental, how can any writer create any character? Why can't a director explore the sexual escapades of how a young couple might engage in degenerate sexual situations regardless of their sexual orientation without it casting a shadow on everyone's sexual desires? No one had these sweeping thoughts about how artists would be held accountable for fiction in the nineties. Geena Davis's *Thelma and Louise* character was not seen as describing every woman in the world. Movies were a place to explore lives that we would never take part in.

So why can't writers write these complex films and just get them made? Because no studio wants to risk the investment. For every successful attempt by a writer to create a movie as beautiful as *The Shawshank Redemption*, there are going to be twelve other prison movies that truly suck. Remember that I started this book by saying there were over ten thousand movies released in the nineties? I only took a look at over 160 of them. Even in the glorious nineties, most of the movies that were made sucked, because most final products are just not spectacular. It's hard to hit a home run every chance at bat. You should taste the dinner I made last night. It was horrible, but that doesn't mean I want to eat at McDonald's for the rest of my life, where every meal will be exactly the same quality. I want to take a shot at making a few gourmet meals every once in a while to avoid a life of Big Macs.

So while I truly believe that when the frogs fell from the sky in *Magnolia*, that was metaphorically the end of the most creative time in filmmaking, it can't be discounted how much September 11th influenced the end. One day in 2001, we voluntarily gave up our personal thoughts and freedoms to the government and the media. Once the culture bought into the idea that art and the act of wondering was the exact same crime as actions, the spirit of independent cinema had no chance but to cease to exist. Yes, nineties directors like Tarantino, Lee, PTA, Campion, Lynch, and Payne went on to still attempt to make films that required an element of audience thought, but it would become virtually impossible for a new artist to rise to the top with truly inventive, thought-provoking, nongenre, popular work in a time when money and power had a stranglehold on the wide release to the masses. Even more upsetting is that all the major studios now own all the streaming platforms that young artists watch films on. So they can control which films are remembered. What streaming service is going to promote *Citizen Ruth*? None. With physical media fading away, where can anyone watch these films at home if they don't stream? If a film doesn't stream in the woods, can anyone hear it? As leaving the house becomes more dangerous and phones become more important, where and how will *Swingers, Before Sunrise,* and *The Prince of Tides* have a chance to compete against *Guardians of the Sorcerer's Superhero*?

After my interview with Helen Childress, she asked to read my introduction to this book. Her email back to me was so incredibly thoughtful and the best email I ever received. She described the idea of this book as a tribute to and a eulogy for, films from the nineties. I hadn't intended to do either. I mostly just wanted to explain why I just couldn't stand to watch any more pointless movies. As I am getting older, my time becomes more precious to me. I suppose this book, which has gotten so long that I'm now talking about people's reaction to it, is in fact a eulogy, because that era is dead. I so enjoyed watching all these films and pretending that I am still living in a time when provocative thoughts mattered. I have not wanted to stop writing about this time period, because it was all so magical. In fact, keep reading, because there is an epilogue to the book where I cover thirty more movies. I swear my affection for these films has nothing to do with my least favorite word: nostalgia. I did not start this book, nor have I wanted to stay covering these films, because I am experiencing nostalgia for my twenties. The nineties were not the best decade of my life. Right now is the best time of my life. The nineties was just the decade when complex movies were the norm. That is my attraction, not a sentimental look back at my stupid youth. The person I was back then could never have written this book. It is the art that I miss, not the era. The fact that popular cinema had a moment where reflective, complicated, meaningful art actually dominated the box office, even for a decade, probably should have never happened in a capitalistic society. It kind of is and was unnatural to how business works.

I am not hopeful that this kind of art will be resurrected, because young artists are inspired by the work they see when they are growing up. So many of the artists of the nineties were just reacting to the work they saw in the seventies. I don't have a lot of faith that any young, potential writers will look backwards thirty years and be inspired to create similar work ten years from now. It isn't with sadness that I write that. I think this new generation is more concerned with social justice than consuming long-form art. They are already Tik Toking about global warming. They are accepting of people with disabilities. They welcome all sexual choices and genders. They are letting go of racism. All those things are much more monumental than the importance that my generation overly put on movies. Movies were just little stories strangers told us. Today, my children get their stories from podcasts, Tik Tok, Instagram, and Snapchat. I am not here to say that is better or worse. Gen X put too much importance on film, music, and television. I know I allowed it to totally shape me. I know today's generation is not getting inspired in the same way by current films because no film ever lasts for more than today, an opening weekend. They come and go. Insert Skip Credits or Next Episode button here. Don't think about it. Consume it. Forget it. They view films like we viewed what strangers had for lunch, unimportant and of no interest. I never took a picture of my lunch on my Kodak disc camera. I am part of a past where movies were seen as very important. I am so thankful to every writer and director who crafted any film mentioned in this book. To each person who grabbed a pen or a camera to widen my mind, make me uncomfortable, upset the easy path of my thoughts, made me see a point of view that wasn't mine, angered me, challenged me, satisfied me, made me laugh, caused me to cry, and made me feel so very, very much alive in the real world through a world that was make believe. I will forever remember the work that the artists in this book created. I am forever changed because of characters like Andy Dufresne, Tom Wingo, Alabama Whitman, Lelaina Pierce, O-Dog, Armand Goldman, Vincent Vega, and The Dude. My life has been enriched by the words of Quentin Tarantino, John Irving, Pat Conroy, Helen Childress, Elaine May, and James L. Brooks. The most important moments of my life—sadly or happily, depending upon your generation—were when art made me feel more alive than real life ever could. Sondheim wrote about art in *Sunday in the Park with George*, "All it has to be is good."

The nineties were good.

The End

Epilogue:
Thirty More for the Road

Wait! Don't stop reading. I know you are mad at me because I didn't pick your favorite movie from the nineties. I know, I know, I really do suck. But let's see if we can part as friends before you give me a three-star review and then go on to say how much you loved the book. (People seem to do this to me all the time: they give three stars but praise my books. You either give a five-star review or you don't review at all. Those are the new rules in a Yelp-driven society.) So to maybe bump up that review, I am tossing in thirty films that almost made the list. These are movies that I rewatched and truly considered writing about but, for one reason or another, didn't believe they could sustain an entire essay. To be honest, the majority of the films on this list are among my favorite films. I truly was cutthroat when picking the twenty-four films I wrote about. Here are a few more that I think deserve mention. Also, this was a great way for me to sneak in my interview with actress Patricia Arquette.

1990

Mo' Better Blues has so much color in it. Spike Lee uses red, blue, yellow, orange, any color he can get his hands on to light a scene. The leap forward in his directing between *Do the Right Thing* and this movie is remarkable. It's not that he was bad before, he just is so much more confident in this film. Also, his continual use of score, which doesn't always work in his films, works perfectly in a film about jazz. The film is a piece of jazz right down to the fact that the ending goes on just a bit longer than you would want it to. Denzel Washington is pitch perfect as a trumpet player who plays better than he manages his career. Spike Lee was on fire in the nineties and while there is no doubt that *Malcolm X* is his masterpiece, I found this film to be smaller and more delightful than any of his other nineties films. There isn't any overt anger in this film, and it is kind of refreshing. (I know I had singled him out earlier because he is so good at pushing our buttons, but this film was a nice break from that.) There is no such thing as best, but that being said, I really think this is the most confident directing of his career. Every shot is just beautiful. Was there a ton of story here? No, but have you ever heard jazz before? Plot isn't where it is at. It isn't a pop song. It's jazz.

Postcards from the Edge got knocked out of the main book because of my rule that I could pick only one movie per director. *The Birdcage* won, but this is one of my all-time favorite films. This is the rare example of the movie being better than the book. Carrie Fisher was trying to adapt the book, and it was Mike Nichols who told her to focus on the mom-and-daughter relationship. The scenes between Meryl Streep and Shirley MacLaine are divine. The dialogue is as crisp and snarky as you can get. As you know, I am always on the search for a grown-up movie; this is such a grown-up movie. The relationships are real. You so easily see the line of parenting from the grandmother to Shirley MacLaine to Meryl Streep. This film includes one of my favorite movie quotes, delivered by the grandfather (played by Conrad Bains, Mr. Drummond from *Diff'rent Strokes*): "Get off my back, woman. Yap. Yap. Yap. That's all you do all the livelong day." Without anyone pointing it out, it is evident that there is a long line of bad parenting and withholding of love that has been drilled down into Meryl Streep, and we truly understand her addiction. But we also know her mother loves her. Most films want to turn the mother and daughter into a villainous relationship. There is nothing but love in the film.

I can watch the scene where MacLaine sings "I'm Still Here" and Streep sings "You Don't Know Me" over and over. Do yourself a favor and watch this to learn how to direct a party scene. Nichols knows when to cut to the crowd, when to cut to the singer, when to cut to the family member watching them sing. It is a lesson in directing. Also, this is a great time for me to complain about how many wonderful, life-changing songs from the nineties have been lost to the world. These two tracks were never put on the soundtrack, and I can hear in the piano part that there is an edit in MacLaine's "I'm Still Here," that means somewhere out there is a longer version with an extra verse. Sondheim rewrote this song for MacLaine, and I have read the entire lyrics, but I want to hear them.

Pump Up the Volume. It is true that *Heathers* made Christian Slater a star, but *Pump Up the Volume* made him an icon to me. I believe Allan Moyle's script is the best teenage-movie screenplay out there. This 1990 film didn't make a splash and didn't start the barrage of teenage films that *Clueless* did later in the decade, but it made an impact on every angsty teenager who didn't know how to fit in. Slater plays a kid who is too shy to talk when schools didn't accommodate the emotional needs of students, and everyone was expected to be like everyone else. The only place he can express himself is on a pirate radio station that broadcasts just around his small town. He vents about how hard it is to be different back in the eighties, when everyone was supposed to be as happy as the Cosby kids. Samantha Mathis and Cheryl Pollak do such a great job crafting their female characters, one a rebel with the mind of a scholar and the other the opposite. I showed this to my millennial kids when they were teenagers. "What's a pirate radio?" they asked. I said, "It's like a podcast." They came back with, "Why doesn't the gay kid just report the bullies to the school?" I ended up turning off the movie and watching it by myself later. Times have changed and in many ways for the better. The boxes that different kids were shoved into have all been cracked open. Kids don't feel angst any more—that is what pills are for—but man, did this movie mean a lot to me when it came out.

1991

Defending Your Life is written and directed by Albert Brooks. Everyone always talks about *Modern Romance* or one of his eighties movies as his best work, but this is his masterpiece. If this book had been a collection of pieces about my favorite nineties movies, this would have been a main essay. Yeah, I get that the Bible has a lot more fans, but I think this movie offers the most believable assessment of the afterlife that anyone has come up with. The film begins with Brooks driving his brand-new car into a bus while listening to Barbra Streisand sing Sondheim's "Something's Coming." The movie had me right there. I literally can't think of a better way to leave this hellscape. He then goes to a purgatory-type afterlife that looks like a cheap hotel and strip malls in southern Los Angeles, where he has to prove that he has learned to conquer his pedestrian human fears. Meryl Streep and Rip Torn are picture-perfect as Brooks's love interest and defense attorney. The idea that we are all held back by our fears and are destined to keep returning to Earth until we learn to get past them is a really provocative concept that I have never stopped thinking about since I watched this movie. The prosecutor shows clips from his life when he either succeeded or failed at being a better person—not a good or bad person, but someone equal to their ability. I often wonder which of my days I will be judged on. When I first saw this movie, I was paralyzed by fear. I was in college earning a business degree because I was too scared to tell anyone I wanted to be a writer. Those would be some harsh times to have to relive; hopefully they will see how much I have moved forward and I can run away with Meryl Streep to the next dimension

My Own Private Idaho. George Griffith, Em Marinelli, and Sharon Parks are all friends of mine who are honestly mad at me for not covering this film in the main section of the book. I get it. I really do. But my focus was on movies that rocked mainstream culture. This film, while making a huge impact on queer and independent cinema, was not making the same waves as *Terminator 2* in mainstream America. That doesn't mean it wasn't one of the best films of the decade and certainly influential. I also had a rule about not picking two films from the same director, and I had much more to say about Gus Van Sant's *To Die For. Idaho* could only have come into being in a decade when people wanted something out of the ordinary from their movies. Is this an actual story? An analogy? A tribute to Shakespeare? A dream? I don't know, and neither do you. But here is the main point: it doesn't matter. It is a journey, and it is most certainly something you have never seen before and have not seen since. It will probably go down in history as the film most responsible for eliminating the stigma for straight actors who played gay characters. Of course, now having straight actors playing gay characters is considered anti-gay, but at the time, having a huge star like Keanu Reeves saying that it was okay to play a gay character was a big deal. It brought people to this film who otherwise never would have seen it. Here is my hot take on the plot: I personally think Reeves doesn't exist. I think he is the alter ego for River Phoenix's character. It is almost a pre-*Fight Club* idea. Next time you watch it, notice that it really could make sense that Rivers becomes a brave gay man (Reeves) who doesn't mind putting himself out in the world whenever he gets nervous or has a bout of narcolepsy. I am sure I'm wrong, but it is fun to think about.

JFK is the best edited movie ever. It is always great when a film comes around that lets a person who is spectacular at their craft rise to the top. Joe Hutshing and Pietro Scalia edit this three-hour masterpiece. One could make the argument that at that length, maybe the film needed more editing. Nonsense. They give you five hours of information in that three-hour window. Director Oliver Stone has a simple plan with *JFK*: he wants to manipulate every viewer in the same way that he believes the government manipulated the populace with the Warren Report. He had a lot of information to disperse, and he does it by allowing moments of the film to rest on-screen just for a second, so your brain can barely keep up and keeps you lost in the conspiracy. He does the same thing with the script. Next time you watch this film (might I suggest next fourth of July?), notice how he will have one character use a phrase like "cross triangulation" and then another character who would never be connected to the first character use "cross triangulation" again, making viewers think, "Wow, they both said it. It has to be true." But don't forget, both lines were written by Oliver Stone. He is making the connection, not history. But none of that matters. I don't watch *JFK* to learn about history. It's a movie, and a damn good one, mostly because of what Hutshing and Scalia accomplish. They move this film along with confidence and skill. The movie is a mental beating, but it might have been a complete disaster if not for such skilled editors.

1992

Singles is the ying to *Reality Bites's* yang. Just like *Magnolia* and *Boogie Nights*, *Singles* and *Reality Bites* fans usually make us pick sides. My choices are pretty clear, seeing how two of the films made the main portion of the book and the other two are here. But let's be clear: *Singles* is a damn fine movie. The problem is that Cameron Crowe went on to make *Jerry Maguire* and *Almost Famous*, which are better movies. But *Singles* has a ton of heart and is actually a really, really believable love story. Kyra Sedgwick and Campbell Scott's scene after their first lunch when he is asking her out again and she is saying no and they just talk over each other and stammer and stutter just makes you fall in love with them. The film is full of happy scenes that make you smile. On the flip side, we have Bridget Fonda's obsession with Matt Dillon. Her feelings are so relatable, because we all have fallen for a person who is just horrible for us, yet we are helpless not to pursue them. This is certainly one of Crowe's strong points as a writer. He knows that pain. Fonda's comment that she has to do something bizarre soon because "somewhere around twenty-five, bizarre becomes immature" resonated so much with me at twenty-two, when I first saw the film. What I, and Fonda, didn't know is that bizarre never goes out of style. You just learn to care less about what others think, but in *Singles*, they all care, and it makes us love these characters.

Reservoir Dogs has to be the best directorial debut anyone ever had, right? Don't answer that question, because I don't care what anyone else thinks. It just is. There is no way to deny that *Pulp Fiction* will always be the heart of the nineties, but it was this film that lit the match for nineties filmmakers. Could this movie even be made today? I think the fact that there are no women in it would have halted Tarantino before he even got started. But if you look a bit closer, you will see there is a female character, and it is Mr. White (Harvey Keitel). Maybe Tarantino was ahead of the curve when it came to busting gender stereotypes. Mr. White is clearly the matron of the crew. He protects Mr. Orange (Tim Roth) from the beginning to the end. He stands up to Mr. Blonde (Michael Madsen) and runs that warehouse like he is the head schoolmarm. This movie may seem tame when it comes to gore and length compared with what Tarantino has created since, but in 1992 this blew a hole in everyone's brain. The scene in which Roth memorizes a fake story about a run-in with some cops, then tells the story and we see the story as a flashback (remember, it didn't happen) is one of the trippiest moments ever shown on-screen, and I bet most people don't even realize how meta that scene is. Speaking of gore, at the time, everyone was up in arms over the scene in which Mr. Blonde cuts off the cop's ear. So many people said that scene was too much. I would ask them, "Did you close your eyes?" They all said yes. Well, you can open your eyes; Tarantino never actually shows the ear being cut off, but so many people are so afraid of seeing it, they close their eyes and don't realize that the camera drifts over to the wall while it happens. Now that is violence that it is hard for the do-gooders of the world to stop: violence that you don't actually see but swear you do. Only a master filmmaker can pull that off.

Glengarry Glen Ross is such a marvel of bringing a stage play to the big screen. Sometimes you have to let a thing be what it is. And *Glengarry* is a play about salesmen. The film doesn't try to be more. If you have ever had to sell anything in life, this is the film for you. Every actor in the film gets a chance to swing at a perfectly thrown pitch, and each one hits a home run. I am always amazed just by the dialogue that David Mamet, who adapted his own play for the screen, gives these acting legends. First-time viewers can enjoy the mystery and repeat viewers can enjoy the characters. Who broke into the store and stole the new leads? It isn't the point of the film, and the revelation kind of comes as a surprise because it wouldn't have been shocking if the film didn't tell you whodunit, but we already know the answer: America did it. This is a look at how obsessing over the bottom line will forever prevent us from reaching the top. This film is a last look at a time when viewers could still be shocked at the Mitches and Murrays of the world who would offer you a car, a steak knife, or a pink slip. Now we don't even know who Mitch and Murray are, because they are an EIN numbers filed with the state, and you just get fired.

Scent of a Woman makes everyone want to just yell out an Al Pacino "hoo-ah." This is a simple film about a young man who is having trouble at school and an old man who is having trouble adjusting to retirement and blindness. Viewers take such a delightful journey with these two characters, one innocent and one whose innocence is long gone. Here is a pointless description of what I think of when I think about this film: it is a movie. *Scent of a Woman* is a movie, and if my point hasn't been hammered home enough, they just don't make these movies anymore. The film focuses on honor and duty and doing the hard thing, which is always the right thing. The lessons this film teaches us are the same lessons studios are trying to con us into thinking superhero movies are covering. The relationship between Pacino and Chris O'Donnell is magical. You can kind of believe these two will never see each other again after the events of the film, and on the other hand you can believe they remain a part of each other's lives, but it doesn't matter. It was this weekend that got them both through a moment. The underbelly of the story at the school is so damn important. A silly prank that upsets the headmaster turns into an investigation in which one poor kid and a few rich kids are suspects. Pacino's wise retired soldier knows who is gonna take the brunt of that investigation. The film looks at how kids in the nineties handled bullies, how the rich increasingly managed to manipulate society so that they were considered beyond reproach, and how the concepts of leadership and honor were being diminished or ignored in education. Pacino cements his "louder is better" acting approach with this film, and while it won't always work for him in future films, here Martin Brest (who directed my beloved *Midnight Run*) manages to keep it under control.

1993

Schindler's List is such a force to be reckoned with that I feel weird writing about it at all. Steven Spielberg, who pretty much dominated every decade from the seventies to the aughts, doesn't need much help from me to secure his legacy. It is easy to just expect him to do great work. In the nineties, he made *Schindler, Jurassic Park,* and *Saving Private Ryan.* That is stellar work. I don't think any other director in the decade can even touch that output. He is a great example of the brilliance of nineties filmmaking, because while he had started the whole summer-blockbuster movement with *Jaws* in 1975, it is this film, which is far more meaningful and far more powerful, that has to be singled out. It is remarkable that one of the most commercially successful directors of all time would choose to make a movie that highlights humanity's ugliest impulses through Nazi Germany's treatment of the Jews during World War II. Screenwriter Steven Zaillian wrote a film that is emotionally devastating and so hard to watch. I remember wondering at the time if we really needed to be reminded of these atrocities because, I thought, they were so well-known. I had no idea that not only would some of us need this reminder, but that others of us would deny it ever happened. Thankfully, Spielberg leveraged his fame to get this movie made, documenting how easily we humans can turn our hatred and fear on a group of "others" just to feel safe ourselves. I so wish this film didn't need to be made, didn't need to be remembered, but it is even more important today than it was in 1993.

Falling Down is the film that was closest to earning an essay in this book, but just not quite good enough. Still, as an artifact of its time, it needs to be watched. This film is racist, sexist, and filled with one-dimensional characters who make you realize just how horrible cop movies can be. So why am I including it on a list of thirty movies that I think shouldn't be forgotten? Because this movie captures the truth of what was just being born in 1993. We are living in a very strange time. We all know racists live and work all around us. They don't wear white sheets anymore. They don't always wear a black hat to let us know. Most times they wear a white button-down shirt and have real jobs, nice houses, and families. If *Falling Down* were made today, the world would call Michael Douglas a racist because of the things his character says and does. His character, referred to as D-Fens, has no idea he is wrong. He, and all of America, also had no idea this movie was foreshadowing the MAGA movement. These were not evil people. They were lost, taken advantage of, small-minded, and duped into believing that immigrants and people of different color skin or different sexual orientation were the enemy. D-Fens is the enemy. He is the bad guy in the movie, but he doesn't find out till the last act. The film, which again is really, really poorly written and directed, sends out a warning that goes unheard. It is fascinating to watch now and realize that we all probably should have listened a little more closely to what this film was saying, but who the hell would have guessed that Joel Schumacher was going to be the one to warn us about the future?

Six Degrees of Separation is such a Scott movie. It has that Alan Alda feel to it, which I always love. It's a movie whose title is more famous than the film. The idea that we are all separated by no more than six strangers became famous once some joker decided that each actor was separated from Kevin Bacon by six films. The story is told with such glee. The editing is so much fun for rewatchers. Director Fred Schepisi is constantly cutting to other parts of the story, which a first-time watcher might find confusing, but it all connects. This is loosely based on the true story of a young con artist who scammed rich people into letting him bunk for free in their upperclass apartments by telling them he was Sidney Poitier's son. While no real crime is ever committed, the couples whom he cons can't stop talking about their experience with this "criminal." Stockard Channing's end monologue about how we turn the heartbreaking and heart-skipping moments of our lives into safe, watered-down stories to tell at dinner parties truly shaped my storytelling life. Should we take the moments that matter the most to us and share them with others or should we keep them inside? This has always been a major struggle for me, but I think Instagram probably answered the question for most of our society. Share the story. Get the likes.

True Romance is one of the most rewatchable movies there is. The love affair between Alabama (Patricia Arquette) and Clarence (Christian Slater) is the best movie romance ever. This is technically Tarantino's first script, despite the fact that *Reservoir Dogs* came out first. Director

Tony Scott made the film more linear than Tarantino had written it, and in doing so made it a better movie. This love story didn't need any of the intrigue that can be found in *Pulp Fiction* or *Reservoir Dogs* by having the audience not know what happens before the action begins. I would never pick my favorite script by Tarantino, because that changes every day, but come on, it's *True Romance*. It is funny, sad, loving, action based, and thought-provoking. I interviewed Arquette for my previous book, about a Lynch film, *Lost Highway*. During that interview, I had to ask her a few *True Romance* questions.

Ryan: What was it like to film the fight scene with James Gandolfini in *True Romance*?

Arquette: The *True Romance* scene we shot for days on end. I worked with my acting teacher at the time, Roy London. The concept behind that scene, which we worked out, was that Alabama was kind of stalling. And it was there in the material. She was waiting for her boyfriend to come save her, and trying to charm him, and to use all these survival mechanisms she had to bide time for her boyfriend to come back. At a certain point, she realized he wasn't going to come back in time. Something in her rose up. At the beginning of the scene, he says, "The first time I killed someone I threw up." You change after you kill someone. By the end of the scene, she has killed someone, and she is no longer the same.

Ryan: What is your strongest memory of making that film?

Arquette: I loved director Tony Scott so much. I can't tell you how much he gave to me. I grew up unaware, but as a girl in the world, I would try to appease people and make sure they were okay. I'd try to have my mind, choices, and thoughts but also appease others too because they didn't always like that or agree with me. So how could I get them to see my point of view? It was a lot of work. When I showed up on *True Romance*, it was like Tony was this idealist dad for a girl. Every idea I had he said, "Great idea. 'Bama's got an idea. Let's do this." I never had someone say, "Yes, yes, yes, yes." All the way down the line. I had done *True Romance* before I had done *Lost Highway*. So he really kind of taught me to listen to my instincts, and they weren't bad. It wasn't always going to be scary for someone to hear your ideas; maybe they were really good. There was only one time that he said "I don't know about that idea." I said, "Okay, that is cool. Let's do it your way." Then he said, "I think 'Bama's right; let's do it her way." Meanwhile, every idea that Christian Slater came up with Tony would say, "That is a terrible idea." Christian was like "What the fuck, man?" That changed my life. The relationship a director can have with an actor can really change everything forever for you. For good or for bad.

Ryan: I can't watch *True Romance* without watching David Lynch's *Wild at Heart*. They go together so perfectly. Do you see a connection between the films?

Arquette: Sure. I mean there is a lot of the same kind of costumey thing. There is a lot of crossover between Nic Cage and Christian's character visually—even Laura Dern's character and mine. There is a poppiness, kind of a bubblegum coolness thing going on. There are also two lovers on the road. Sure, I can see that. It's funny, because for so long the stories were about buddy movies, and they were about two guys. These couples aren't buddies; they are lovers. But it was a couple. There weren't a lot of those before these films.

Ryan: I just think when you think of romantic couples, you feel that Alabama loves Clarence so much, the same way that Lula loves Sailor so much. It's because they do these crazy things together. I think *True Romance* is one of the best love stories ever told. It is up there with *The Way We Were*.

Arquette: The thing about it is that in a lot of relationships they don't give someone else the benefit of the doubt, and we don't even think of it as the way relationships work. But 'Bama supports Clarence except for when he gets the stuff from the pimp. They are pretty much supporting each other—in who they are and how they see the world and the choices each other is making—and that is what doesn't happen in a lot of relationships. They don't give them the benefit of the doubt, and they don't have good will toward each other.

Ryan: Like when she is crying after he kills the pimp, and then she says she is crying because it was the sweetest thing anyone ever did for her.

Arquette: That was actually one of the hardest scenes for me, because I was like "Shit man, she is saying all this to a dude who just killed somebody?" Yes, the pimp was a bad guy but, like, whoa. My acting teacher helped with this. This isn't something you are going to see in the movie, but he said, "But how scary must this be to be in a room with someone who just killed someone, who is capable of killing someone? What are you gonna say, 'What the fuck did you do?' What if he kills you?" Of course it is a survival mechanism. I, as the actress, had a hard time, and the audience doesn't know that, Clarence doesn't know that, and 'Bama may not even know that, but that is part of what is playing underneath the scene. "Okay, you are a murderer, wow, okay. How do I survive this moment?"

1994

The Professional is the best action-adventure film you have never seen. It is also the cutest father-daughter comedy hidden inside an action-adventure film. In fact, why have you never seen this film? This is one of the rare movies you can show your sons and daughters and everyone will be happy. Here is the tricky part: there are two versions of this movie. There is the original, French version, *Léon: the Professional*, and there is the American edit, *The Professional*. I strongly suggest the American version, which I know sounds crazy for someone who has been saying he is are a cinephile and here I am picking the version that a corporation cut down. But the edits make it a tighter, purer film. The French version murks up the relationship between Léon (Jean Reno) and Mathilda (played by a delightful Natalie Portman), and it adds just a bit of ick when there is no need for it. Léon is a child in a grown man's body, and his bond with Mathilda isn't sexual at all. The few additional scenes try to take away some of the innocence, and it just doesn't work for me. The most amazing part of this film, besides watching Gary Oldman scream "EVERYONE," is how brilliantly the action scenes are staged. Once *Die Hard* made all that money in 1988, every studio tried to outdo all the others with its next candidate for summer blockbuster of the year by adding another explosion. Here, director Luc Besson wins the award for the best opening action sequence of any film of the decade. Then he stages a hallway shootout that makes *Heat's* machine gun-blasting scene in the streets of LA feel like the work of a student filmmaker. These two action set pieces bookend a delightful story of two childlike characters who have misplaced their affections on others and finally find someone to truly care for. If you can watch the celebrity charades scene and not smile ear to ear, call a doctor because you are dead.

1995

How to Make an American Quilt is an all-but-forgotten film. This was Winona Ryder's follow-up to *Reality Bites* and *Little Women,* and she was at the height of her reign as a Gen X goddess. The film has Ryder deciding whether to marry her longtime boyfriend. She spends the summer with her grandma and aunt and gets to know the members of their quilting club. Ryder learns the story of each of the women's lives through the quilt they are making. It is such a fun way to tell a bunch of stories in one film. This is a nice character piece for viewers of any age—a love story that can be watched with your grandma, mom, and daughter. Telling stories of love and loss from a female perspective was not as rare back then as it is now. Hollywood was actually still making movies older folks could go see at a matinee. The story is woven together tighter than the quilts my wife sews, but it is the acting of Ellen Burstyn, Anne Bancroft, Winona Ryder, and Samantha Mathis, among others, that makes this film land. I miss movies like *Fried Green Tomatoes, Steel Magnolias,* and *Quilt* where you just got a nice story. I am glad there are male-cejtric movies like *Swingers* and *Reservoir Dogs,* but it is so awesome that there were movies made especially for females too. There was no need or reason for films to become everything to everyone. I am quite certain my father would have rather hid under a quilt than suffer through *How to Make an American Quilt*, but isn't it nice that there were options for everyone? I have no idea how you are going to find this film to watch. I, of course, own it and have for years, but if you want a nice story of love and family—one that shows us how to pass on the best parts of our lives to the people who matter most to us—check out this forgotten film.

Empire Records is so much freaking fun to watch. This movie captures how life altering it was to have a customer service job in your teens and early twenties. The families I created working at Arby's and Video Time were so important to me. There was no Facebook or cell phones, so I am in contact with none of those people, but I love them with all my little heart. I am quite certain that Gina (Renée Zellweger) and Corey (Liv Tyler) do not follow each other on Instagram today, because they totally lost contact with each other, but they would hug forever if they bumped into each other at a Rex Manning concert. The film has multiple scenes that display how much joy music brought to Gen X. Just having a subplot in which each worker at the record store gets one free pass on skipping listening to a CD during the workday shows that for us, music wasn't just something that played while we did other things. Music was always the main dish, not the side dish, for my generation. Allan Moyle's best film is *Pump Up the Volume*, but both films illustrate how music keeps us, and our friendships, alive and how important it is to share what we love with the people we love. The reason this movie doesn't rise to the *Reality Bites* or *Singles* level is purely because the main love story between Corey and A. J. (Johnny Whitworth) just isn't deep enough. It feels forced, and we really have no reason to believe in their love beyond them telling us that we should. The film might actually have worked better if Moyle had skipped the rom-com component and let it be what it truly is: a snapshot of what record stores were like before Spotify ruined it for all of us.

The Usual Suspects was the film of 1995. It's a great example of how a flashy director can turn an average movie into something worth watching. Bryan Singer, who would go on to be a superhero director, set up some nice shots in this Tarantino-wannabe script, featuring a tricky ending. I hadn't seen this film in twenty years, and while I had certainly remembered the ending, I was impressed that it was adequately supported by everything that had preceded it. The film is masterfully staged. A really nice "reveal" shot early in the movie shows four characters talking in a jail cell for a while before we find out there is a fifth person in the shot as well. Singer does it again later when we first see a cop at the scene of the crime and then, as the camera pulls up over the actor and a building, we discover the huge ship is on fire. This movie has all the elements of *Reservoir Dogs*, but just doesn't have enough character development or story to be a truly great film. Still, there is no doubt that it has enough originality to be a fun watch. Some films you can watch a million times and some films are made to be watched once and then, like that . . . woosh . . . are gone.

Welcome to the Dollhouse is the movie that actually captures what it was like to go to middle school when you weren't as hot as Alicia Silverstone. Shocker: I wasn't. It is amazing that a couple of times in the nineties the same movie was made by two very different artists and the results are incredible (See *The Thin Red Line*/*Saving Private Ryan* for another example). *Clueless* and *Dollhouse* came out the same year, but they don't even exist in the same universe. This movie captures what it was like to be bullied back in my day, when bullying wasn't a text concept but rather an actual one, with people grabbing hold of you and saying horrible things to you in person. There was no one to protect you; in fact, if you were bullied, you were much more apt to get in trouble than the bully. Dawn Wiener (man, they even gave her a dick last name) is bullied by everyone. There were no safe spaces for her. Not at home. Not at school. I don't know if writer/director Todd Solondz followed me around as a kid, but he sure captured my fear of school and other students. No "as if" here. This is exactly as school was for me.

Home for the Holidays is what I am watching when you are watching *It's a Wonderful Life*, *Die Hard*, or *Planes, Trains and Automobiles*. I watch this movie every Thanksgiving. Jodie Foster directed this magnificent look at family and what brings us together and what keeps us apart. The movie drops you in the middle of the story. Character names are mentioned as if you are expected to know who they are, and you will figure it all out. (Who is this Jack they keep talking about?) It is a pretty intricate script for a holiday movie. There is a backstory with Robert Downey Jr. that is told in such a delightful, authentic way. The family knows what went on with him, so no one really explains it to the viewer, but you catch up. Downey is so wonderful in this film. He is the reason I have watched this movie twenty-five times. He is alive in every scene. He is dangerous, improvising, and yes, he is most likely high as a kite. I'm sure he drove Jodie Foster and the cast crazy, but it was all worth it. There is a ton of comedy in the movie, but it is the end monologue by the late, great Charles Durning about one day on an airplane runway with his family that brings tears to my L-tryptophan-riddled body. The movie ends with Nat King Cole's "The Very Thought of You," which is now considered a holiday song in my house. Next year, give up Old Man Potter and join the Larson family; just make sure you wear a bib when they carve the turkey.

1996

That Thing You Do! is a perfect example of how movies don't have to punish you for caring about their characters. I get so sick of third acts in which every character must pay the ultimate price for their dreams just to create a phony sense of drama. This film is joy upon joy, and each and every plot point comes from character not the writer's hand. That invisible writer's hand just happens to belong to Tom Hanks. I wish he was better known in the nineties for writing and directing this film than his other projects from the decade, *Forrest Gump* and *Philadelphia*, which can't hold a candle to this film. I dare even the most grumpy human out there to watch the scene where the Wonders hear their song on the radio for the first time and not smile a smile wider than Liv Tyler's. This is a feel-good film that can warm a viewer's heart even though it doesn't really have a happy ending. It has an expected and deserved ending, which is exactly what a well-written film should have. Also, in a decade of great soundtracks (I'm looking at you *Reality Bites*, *Lost Highway*, and *Pulp Fiction*), this soundtrack should always be in the discussion for one of the best of the nineties.

Beautiful Girls is the movie I most wanted to cover in the main section of this book but didn't. I have a love for this movie that is so deep. Timothy Hutton is a struggling piano man who comes back home for his high school reunion. Unsurprisingly for a coming-home film, he feels compelled to assess the trajectory of his life, especially as it compares to the lives of his friends from back in the day. The movie centers on men's attraction to, and desire for, beautiful girls. This simple, small film, directed to perfection by the late Ted Demme and written by Scott Rosenberg, comes alive in the debates and discussions that you can only have with people you have a history with. Natalie Portman is just about as adorable as a teenager is legally (and almost illegally) allowed to be in this film. There is no doubt that today's culture cops would be upset by her relationship with Timothy Hutton, but it is all innocent, and it shows how men just long to be around a beautiful woman, even if she is just thirteen. Matt Dillon, Michael Rapaport, and Uma Thurman all give wonderfully nuanced performances in a movie that should be watched at least once a year. My guess is this one slipped past you; rectify that mistake today.

1997

Boogie Nights was the film that made Paul Thomas Anderson one of the premier directors of his generation. I already have spoken about how I like *Magnolia* more, but that doesn't mean that *Nights* isn't one of the best nineties films. The opening shot alone makes it all worth it. I remember seeing this film in the theater. I had been bombarded by loud previews for movies I would never, ever watch. Every trailer was begging for your money despite having no plan for compounding your time investment wisely. When the previews finished and *Nights* started, PTA did something that I had never seen before. He gives you a moment. After we see "New Line Cinema Presents," the screen goes black as we hear quiet organ music. It stays black for *twenty-five* seconds. That is a lifetime in a movie. I remember just looking around to see if something went wrong with the picture when BAM! Disco lights and music bring us into the world of dance, drinking, and porn. We can feel PTA's confidence as a director throughout the film. The characters are so strong and well-developed, especially the supporting characters. Don Cheadle's character doesn't even really have a B story, but you can't help but feel for him as he tries to latch on to every fad, and even more so when he tries to secure a loan to start a legitimate business but is turned down because he previously worked in adult films. Yes, this was a movie that covered the porn industry as it transitioned from film to video, but it was never about anything dirty. It was about family, friendship, and what happens to artists when they don't adapt to changes in technology. Though I doubt this was PTA's intention, but the film sure is a nice farewell tribute to creating art, any art, with care and what happens when art is replaced with something that is cheaper and its only purpose is for the rich to make more money off it. (See digital replaces 35mm.)

As Good as It Gets is one of those movies that make me wonder if people who didn't see it in the nineties would be able to handle it in today's judgmental culture. Melvin Udall (Jack Nicholson) is described as an "absolute horror of a human being." Let's think about what that means. If Melvin is a horror of a human, do you think he says nice things about people? Will he be open to people who aren't exactly like him? Would a horror of a human being be empathetic toward homosexuals, Jews, or single moms? No. Melvin says some things that are basically played for laughs but he just couldn't get away with today. That is why this movie is so damn good. James L. Brooks crafts real characters in his films, not social media lesson plans. At the beginning of the film, Melvin is a misanthropic best-selling romance novelist, who got rich through other white men, whose life is populated with straight white people like himself. As he slowly opens the door to Blacks, homosexuals, and a single mom, he learns that they are not so different from him. The only way we can grow and change is by welcoming people who are outside our bubble in. This film takes viewers on that journey. It is done through humor, some of which is inappropriate. But watching a work of art that makes you feel so uncomfortable that you are willing to reexamine your values and grow as a person is just about as good as any film gets. Don't cancel this movie just yet; give it one more spin and enjoy three complex characters who make you feel, care, and make you "wanna be a better man." (Oh, wait, a better person.)

1998

Out of Sight is the sexiest movie of the nineties. So many erotic thrillers were created during the decade, before nudity was at everyone's fingertips on their phones. In the nineties, you mostly had to watch really crappy movies to satisfy your nonporn prurient interests. Most of these movies, from *Showgirls* to *Bound* to *Color of Night*, were just bad movies with sex in them. *Out of Sight* doesn't even have any nudity in it. What it does have is Jennifer Lopez and George Clooney locked in a trunk together for six straight minutes, lit only by the red light from the car's tail lights. Put your clothes back on, Sharon Stone, we have a winner. The film has that *Get Shorty* feel, mostly because both are based on Elmore Leonard stories, but director Steven Soderbergh balances the sexual tension, the comedy, and the action so skillfully. Every actor who is in this picture, and just about every actor IS in this picture, nails their character. A fun aside is that Michael Keaton plays the same character here whom he plays in Tarantino's *Jackie Brown*, also based on a Leonard novel. So I always watch these films back-to-back. In earlier essays, I complained about directors who didn't know when to tell a story out of order; *Out of Sight* follows the trajectory of its characters out of order for a reason. But really, who am I kidding? This movie works because JLo and Clooney are just so damn hot.

The Thin Red Line is a film I had never seen until 2023. But when I finally did see it, I saw it in the most nineties way possible. I was visiting LA for a book signing and I got to check off a longtime item on my bucket list. I went to the theater that Quentin Tarantino owns, the New Beverly Cinema, and saw Terrence Malick's film in glorious 35mm. Technically a war movie, the film felt more like a *National Geographic* documentary and was so beautiful to watch in a movie theater. It was a Thursday night in June, and the screening was sold out. Not one seat was empty. There was a line outside the theater just to get in. I felt like I was in line to see *Batman* in 1989. Someone from management delivered a wonderful speech before the film, stating unequivocally that if you checked your phone or even let it light up for a second, you would be asked to leave and would be banned from the theater for life. If you talked, you would be banned for life. If your Apple watch lit up, you would be banned for life. It made me think that maybe this book would be appreciated after all. Maybe there truly is a group of people who want to see movies from the nineties in 35mm under optimal circumstances. I sure wish there was a theater that treated film like a religion close to my house.

The Thin Red Line is another long piece of art that spends no time explaining where you are or what you are watching. It is set during World War II and takes viewers through two or three battles, but it is mostly unconcerned with things getting blown up or armies defeating other armies. It is a study rather of what we see and feel when we think we are about to die. The soldiers who are about to die see a leaf, a bug, a bat, or a ray of sunlight, and whatever their vision is, it seems to slow everything down for them. The film is amazingly beautiful on a big screen. There are stunning shots of animals in their natural habitat including one at the beginning of the film of an alligator submerging itself in water. But what about humans? Well, they are in their natural habitat too, senselessly killing individuals, who never did a thing to them personally, over dirt. Nick Nolte is fantastic as a military leader who is in over his head and doesn't care how many of his men die if it means winning the battle. A leader who sacrifices his subordinates? Sounds like humans in their natural habitat to me. The film stuck with me for days. I can't quite say I *enjoyed* it, but it sure reinforced how stupid war is.

1999

Election. As I have already stated many times, 1999 just had too many great films. This film really deserves a major essay in this book, but I couldn't break my rule of only one essay per director. Alexander Payne had already been chosen for *Citizen Ruth. Election*, starring Reese Witherspoon and Matthew Broderick, covers the high-stakes drama of running for president . . . of the student government. The genius of this comedy, as in all of Payne's films, is that it finds its drama in the mundane. The seriousness with which this film handles the student presidential election, which truly doesn't help anyone but the student who wins, is why you laugh. We all went to school with that overachiever, and this film shows us how those students can drive a teacher crazy. But Tracy Flick (Witherspoon) is not just a villain. She is a fully developed character whom we actually feel sorry for once we get a glimpse of her home life and the pressure she is under to get into college. Also, there is no overt mention of the double standard for smart males versus smart females, but it is all there in the subtext.

The casting of the teachers and students is spot-on. No one in this film looks like they are from Hollywood. They all look like they are from Middle America. The debates over morals versus ethics, Coke versus Pepsi, and apples versus oranges will all have a totally different meaning for you after you watch this film. So many teenage films were released in 1999 (*Cruel Intentions, 10 Things I Hate About You, Jawbreaker, She's All That*), but none captures the feeling of high school through real characters better than this one. Just like in *Citizen Ruth*, not one character's motivation can be questioned. The trick ending comes just like a twist should, as a total surprise that had been foreshadowed right at the beginning of the film, but that we had somehow forgot.

Being John Malkovich was my first foray into the sparkling mind of Charlie Kaufman. I am so glad his first movie was born in the nineties. It is true that his best movies were made in the next decade, but *Being John Malkovich* has that big, crazy concept, but combined with a very small, independent-film idea: would we trick someone into loving us by pretending to be someone other than who we really are? The plot is too convoluted to summarize, but all the extras come together to create a world that unique, refreshing, and ingenious: the business office that is stuck between two floors, the puppets, the scene in which the only people and dialogue spoken is all Malkovich, the surprise ending, the dark, dirty look of the film. Director Spike Jonze took Kaufman's world off the printed page and brought it to glorious life.

Mystery, Alaska is a sports movie that's actually strong on character development. The film is about a small town in Alaska with a local hockey team that plays against each other every weekend. Now the New York Rangers come into town for an exhibition game, bringing the modern world along with them to Mystery, Alaska. Written by my favorite television writer, David E. Kelley, this film evokes *Ally McBeal*, *Picket Fences*, and *The Practice,* all Kelley-created TV shows, through its humor and character development. It also features a strong B plot about a Walmart-type chain store coming to Mystery and ruining the small town atmosphere. Burt Reynolds plays the local judge with just a bit too much gravity, but because the characters around him are so lively, the film still works. Most sports movies are all about winning, but this film is more concerned with creating a beguiling cast of small-town characters as everyone anticipates the big game. Sadly, the film came and went quickly, which isn't surprising given that this type of small movie was starting to fade away at the end of the decade. If it is one you have never seen, I suggest you take a look. It is even better the third or fourth time you watch it because you start to really care for the characters.

Dogma ends our list. So for all you nineties fans who were angsting where Silent Bob was, fear no more. Kevin Smith made *Clerks* (a critical fav), *Mallrats* (my personal favorite of his), *Chasing Amy* (his best script), and *Dogma* (the fulfillment of all the films) in the nineties. Any of them, and all of them, should be in this book. Kevin Smith is the Stephen Spielberg of the nineties, just without all the hits and money. He became a pop culture star and the only director I know who toured to sellout crowds and still does. *Dogma* takes religion on in a funny, spiritual way. Only a Catholic like Smith could take Catholicisms own rules to show how silly religion is yet how important it is to those who believe. Yes, I did have a Buddy Christ dashboard Jesus in my car in 1999. Any film that portrays God as a nonspeaking Alanis Morissette has to win for nineties movie of the decade. The film follows a descendant of Christ, Catholic dogma, and how both might just end the world. It also had Ben and Matt, at their height of popularity, as fallen angels. It sometimes seems like every film in 1999 was taking swings at high concepts and just didn't care how long it took to get that concept out, but it sure does feel like all those films succeeded. Yes, I am sure I should have picked *Fight Club*, but it just feels like the first rule of this book is that no one remembers to talk about *Dogma*. Everyone seems to remember *Clerks*, which certainly was a revolutionary film, but *Dogma* displays a mature, thoughtful Kevin Smith, while still having all the dick jokes that we expect from Jay. Heaven helps us, we made it through all fifty-five films. Now go eat a Mooby-burger and find out when the next superhero movie opens.

Are you upset that your favorite nineties movie wasn't even on my extra list of thirty films? Of course you are; that is my point. There were a ton of quality films in that decade. Keep them alive. Get them screened in 35mm at your local theater, and let's not allow this art form to die. They took our VHS tapes from us and we said nothing. They took our DVDs and we said nothing. Let's not let them take our 35mm films too.

The End, for real this time.

Appendix 1:
The List of Movies

Here is the list of movies that I started my research with. While working on the book, I watched most, but not all, of these films.

1990
Dances with Wolves
Mo' Better Blues
Goodfellas
Postcards from the Edge
Fisher King
Pretty Woman
Wild At Heart
Misery
Awakenings
Mermaids
Pump up the Volume
Hunt for Red October
Ghost
The Godfather Part 3

1991
Boyz n the Hood
Prince of Tides
Defending Your Life
Little Man Tate
Thelma and Louise
My Own Private
Idaho
Fried Green Tomatoes
JFK
City Slickers
Father of the Bride
Silence of the Lambs
Terminate 2:
Judgment Day
Cape Fear
Batman Returns

1992
Bob Roberts
Unforgiven
The Crying Game
Singles
The Last of the
Mohicans
Reservoir Dogs
Malcolm X
Glengarry Glen Ross
A Few Good Men
A League of Their Own
Scent of a Woman
The Cutting Edge
Basic Instinct
The Player
Buffy the Vampire
Slayer
Sister Act

1993
So I Married an Axe
Murderer
Dazed and Confused
Menace II Society
Short Cuts
True Romance
Jurassic Park
Falling Down
A Perfect World
Six Degrees of
Separation
Dave

Sleepless in Seattle
Indecent Purposal
The Age of Innocence
Boxing Helena
Schindler's List
Groundhog Day
The Firm
The Fugitive
Philadelphia
Grumpy Old Men
The Piano

1994
Four Weddings and a
Funeral
Muriel's Wedding
Pulp Fiction
The Shawshank
Redemption
Reality Bites
Leon: The Professional
A River Runs Through It
The Ref
Clerks
Nobody's Fool
The Paper
Disclosure
Speed
The Mask
Natural Born Killers
Forrest Gump
Little Women

1995
The Usual Suspects
To Die For
How To Make An
American Quilt
Devil in a Blue Dress
Empire Records
Casino
Before Sunrise
Apollo 13
Sense and Sensibility
Clueless
Bridges of Madison
County
Welcome to the
Dollhouse
Dangerous Minds
Billy Madison
Friday
Heat
Seven
Home for the
Holidays
Tommy Boy
Crimson Tide
Something to Talk
About
The American
President
Boys on the Side
Mr Holland's Opus
Forget Paris
Show Girls

1996
Citizen Ruth
The Birdcage
Romeo & Juliet
Swingers
Trainspotting
Jerry Maguire
That Thing You Do!
Courage Under Fire
Fargo
Happy Gilmore

Beautiful Girls
Scream
Sling Blade
Twister
Independence Day
Striptease

1997
Boogie Nights
Two Girls and A Guy
Good Will Hunting
The Ice Storm
Lost Highway
My Best Friend's
Wedding
Jackie Brown
As Good As it Gets
Wag The Dog
In & Out
LA Confidential
The Opposite of Sex

1998
Titanic
Saving Private Ryan
He Got Game
The Wedding Singer
Buffalo 66
Shakespeare in Love
Truman Show
Big Lebowski
Sliding Doors
Out of Sight
Chasing Amy
Pleasantville
The Thin Red Line
Meet Joe Black
Hope Floats
You've Got Mail
Armageddon

1999
Election
The Cider House
Rules

The Matrix
Being John Malkovich
Magnolia
Flight Club
Mystery, Alaska
The Straight Story
The Sixth Sense
Office Space
Happy Texas
Cruel Intentions
Dogma
Eyes Wide Shut
10 Things I Hate
About You
American Beauty
Star Wars: The
Phantom Menace

Appendix 2:
Ten Movies Made Before And After

Because I know people are going to ask me the question: Do you like any movies made after the nineties? I decided I would answer that question with two lists of ten movies in no particular order that I like before and after the nineties.

Ten Movies Before
Skin Deep
When Harry Met Sally
Tootsie
Midnight Run
The Best Little Whorehouse in Texas
Broadcast News
Tucker: The Man and His Dreams
Dangerous Liaisons
Fabulous Baker Boys
Parenthood

Ten Movies After
Three Billboards Outside Ebbing, Missouri
Eternal Sunshine of the Spotless Mind/Adaptation
Wonder Boys
Almost Famous
Boyhood
A Cool Dry Place
Dan In Real Life
Good Night and Good Luck
High Fidelity
500 Days of Summer

Special Thanks

Helen Childress is truly one of my heroes and getting to talk to her was unthinkable. My entire life I have chased interviews with Sheryl Lee and Helen Childress, and now I have conducted both. I will forever be grateful to what she gave our generation. I could tell throughout the interview that she just doesn't realize how much *Reality Bites* means to so many. Box office tallies truly mean nothing. It is how art lands. Her art is marble, granite, bronze—durable. Helen called us comrades, and that was my favorite moment of this entire project.

Natasha Gregson Wagner gave me such a sweet and cute interview about *Two Girls and a Guy*. I have loved her character for thirty years, so it was scary to actually meet her, but of course she was even sweeter in real life. She read my last book, about *Lost Highway*, and sent me a really nice note. Most people don't do that.

Alexander Payne makes such human pictures. His characters are always right out of everyone's family. So it seemed just about right when on the day of our interview, he took time out of his family life to speak with me. It was his mom's hundredth birthday. I am no Willard Scott, but I wished her a happy day.

Patricia Arquette spoke to me for my *Lost Highway* book, but I had to ask her about *True Romance*, so I used some of that interview in this book. She really is an amazing actress and was very kind to me. I want to get her a copy of both books. So will someone make that happen?

Tyger Williams was the first person to say yes to an interview for this book. That sure helped in getting other interviews, when you have a screenwriter who wrote one of the best movies from the decade. He had so much knowledge to share. I am hoping it will inspire other writers to write from the heart and create more great movies.

George Griffith sent me a list of his favorite nineties films and it helped me to round out this book with more of the art house moments of the decade. He also was an avid first reader of this book. We had a wonderful conversation where he said the best sentence: "I felt like I had to find a landline to call Scott Ryan." Now that is someone who gets this book. Check out his film *From the Head*. It isn't a nineties film, but it sure feels like one.

Joe Dougherty was the first person I discussed this book with. He thought it was a crackerjack of an idea and was a supporter of this concept even though he was darn sure I was totally wrong.

Spencer and *Sharon Parks* are movie buffs whom I met at a Lynch filmfest. They were very supportive of this project. Sharon, you can now thankfully stop suggesting movies for this book. It's done. It's printed. Leave me alone.

Daniel Knox is the smartest cinephile I know. His help on this book was incredible. He reminded me to be sure to cover the 35mm aspect, and I would have been so mad at myself if I forgot that part. He also puts on a hell of a film fest.

Josh Minton is always talking about Ghat CPT. He loves AI so much that I asked it to write his thanks. It came back with this: Fuck you.

Matt Howe is the Barbra Streisand expert, which he has nothing to be guilty of, so it was very kind of him to give me a quote about one of the meanest interviewers ever.

Mindy Morrow watched the movies I wrote about as I wrote them, which made it fun for me to have someone to talk to about them. Sorry I told everyone we held hands when we were fifteen.

Hannah Fortune created a wonderful cover for this book. Her art is always worth looking at. Follow her at: hannahfortuneart.

David Bushman always hates having to edit my writing. In my other books, it was mostly interviews, so imagine how much of a pain it had to be for him to read my longest book yet. He is a great business partner, and there's no one else I would rather run this company with.

Quentin Tarantino will never read this book and never know about it, so why put him in here? Because he changed my life, inspired me to believe that movies could do anything, thrilled me for years, and is one of my heroes.

Melanie Mullen only buys some of my books, so how do I know when to thank her and when not to? She is a big film buff, so she should buy this one, but she hates everything I do, so why would she? Assuming she won't ever see this, I'll admit that I love her.

Courtenay Stallings and *Bob Canode* both supported this project and gave me lots of great feedback. Bob helped me with the *Phantom Menace* parts, but he's probably sorry he did now. George Lucas should know the opinions about *Star Wars* are not Bob's, only mine.

AM Starr is such a sweet, kind, wonderful person. I am honored that we met at a screening of *Fire Walk With Me* and have been great friends ever since.

Anita Rehn, Gobi Randall, HoBro, Diana Guild, and *Becca Moore* are all great friends of mine who always supported this project and me.

Lisa Hession and I watched almost every movie in this book. I am not sure what my life would have been if she didn't become my best friend in 1997 and still is today. Love you, Lisa-Lou.

Michelle Kling was my manager at Video Time and is probably the person whom I talked movies with the most in the actual nineties. I haven't seen her in twenty years, but I know we are still friends because that is just how shitty it was to work there.

Ronda Racha Penrice gave me a wonderful quote for my *Menace* chapter. She put the film in context so perfectly to *Boyz n the Hood*. She also wrote a wonderful book about *The Wire*; check it out.

Mel Reynolds will one day be a writer/director whom everyone who loves film will know, but for now, I know her and love her. Mel is so much fun to talk film with and a wonderful artist.

Rose Thorne and her life mate, *Ben Louche*, if that is your name, which it isn't, are such supportive friends; they will never even know I thanked them in this book. Twingo, bitches.

Em Marinelli hates this book. Em wanted me to write a sneaky memoir about me and these films, but I'm not that interesting. Check out Em's book about movies called *Comfort Sequels*. I am Tao to Em's Elle, so I won't share Em with you, just Em's book. Em also voiced Helen Childress and Natasha Gregson Wagner in the audio book and did a wonderful job.

Joyce Ryan watched *Pretty Woman* all the time, so finally her son wrote about something she knows about. Thanks for all the support throughout the years, Mom.

Alex Ryan has to listen to whatever books I am working on but then, even worse, has to do the paperwork on the sales. I am sure he would quit if he wasn't my son. I am lucky to have a kid who is smarter and all around better than I will ever be.

Jen Ryan and I didn't know each other in the nineties, but we sure did enjoy watching all those movies from the nineties. I love her and couldn't do any of this without her support.

Before you go, I want to pitch you my religion. It's called kindness. The fact that any of you would be so kind to buy and read my book is crazy to me. I have been talking about kindness for years since I've been publishing, and the world has only gotten more unkind. Guess what that means? Besides that obviously not enough people are buying my books. It means that we need to double down. Smile more, let people slide a bit, don't be angry at every little thing that doesn't go your way. These are simple things to do. Help someone at the grocery store, let someone in front of you in traffic, and say please and thank you. Have a great day, everyone. If you have kind words to say about this book, I'd love to hear from you. Email me at superted455@gmail.com

End Notes

1. Tarantino, Q, *Cinema Speculation*. Harper. November 1, 2022. Page 8.

2. Huffstutter, P.J., *Los Angeles Times*, Dec 2002. Page 15.

3. Morris, Rebecca. Lilyvolt.com. "Banned books in 2022? Uh – Generation X would like a word." 2022. Page 18.

4. All quotes in this essay from the crew are taken from the *Goodfellas* DVD commentary. Warner Brothers Pictures. 1990. Page 28

5. Rosenbaum, Michael. *Inside of You*. "Jason Alexander," November 16, 2021. Page 38

6. Erbland, Kate. *Vanity Fair*. "The True Story of *Pretty Woman*'s Original Dark Ending." March 23, 2015. Page 38-40

7. Arquette, Patricia. *Vanity Fair Actors on Actors*. YouTube. 2019. Page 40.

8. De Klerk, Amy. *Harper's Bazaar*. "Hunza G is relaunching the iconic *Pretty Woman* dress." June 2, 2021. Page 42

9. All quotes from actors and crew in this essay come from the DVD bonus features. Tri-Star Pictures. 1991. Page 54

10. Nancy Griffin, "SHOT BY SHOT" *Premiere Magazine*. Dec. 1991 Page 59, 61, 64.

11. All quotes from Eastwood are from Lipton, James. *Inside the Actor's Studio*. Interview. 2003. Pages 71-74

12. Ebert, Roger. "The Moment of Truth Arrives for *Malcolm*". Interview. November 1992. Page 76.

13. Ray, Amy. "Didn't Know a Damn Thing," *Holler*. 2018. Page 77.

14. Rose, Charlie. *The Charlie Rose Show*. Interview. 1992. Page 78, 81.

15. _____ *Entertainment Tonight*. Retro. 1992. Page 80.

16. All quotes from this essay are from the DVD bonus features. New Line Cinema. 1993. Page 93-98.

17. Tarantino, Q. *Cinema Speculation*. Harper. November 2022. Pages 123-125.

18. J. and P. Epstein, H. Koch, *Casablanca*. 1942. Page 170.

19. Kinowetter Interview. "Julie Delpy." Youtube.com. 2021. Page 170, 174.

20. Discussion with Kent Jones. "Ethan Hawke." Youtube.com. Page 170.

21. Wilson Hunt, Stacey. "*To Die For* at 25." IndieWire. July 16, 2020. Page 177, 180.

22. Gunther, Marc. "The Transformation of Network News." Nieman Reports. June 15, 1999. Page 178.

23. Rose, Charlie. *The Charlie Rose Show*. Interview. 1996. Pages 192-193.

24. Pascal, Joe. Hudson Union. Interview. 2016. Page 193.

25. Jacobs, Matthew. "Laura Dern Answers." Vulture. Dec 2, 2021. Page 202.

26. Banfield, Ashleigh. "Hank Azaria says he would not play Agador Spartacus again." *News Nation*. 2022. Page 217.

27. Sondheim, Stephen. *Look, I made a Hat*. Alfred A. Knopf. 2011. Page 219.

28. ____. *The Herald Times*. "Toback: Film mines Downey's character," April 1998. Page 223

29. _____. *Land of Promise*, pages 350, 381-382, 439. Page 272.

30. Mann, Aimee. "Save Me." 1999. Page 274.

31. Rance, M. *That Moment*. New Line Home Video, inc. 2000. Page 275.

MORE TO READ FROM SCOTT RYAN

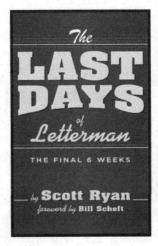

ORDER AT TUCKERDSPRESS.COM

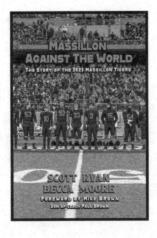